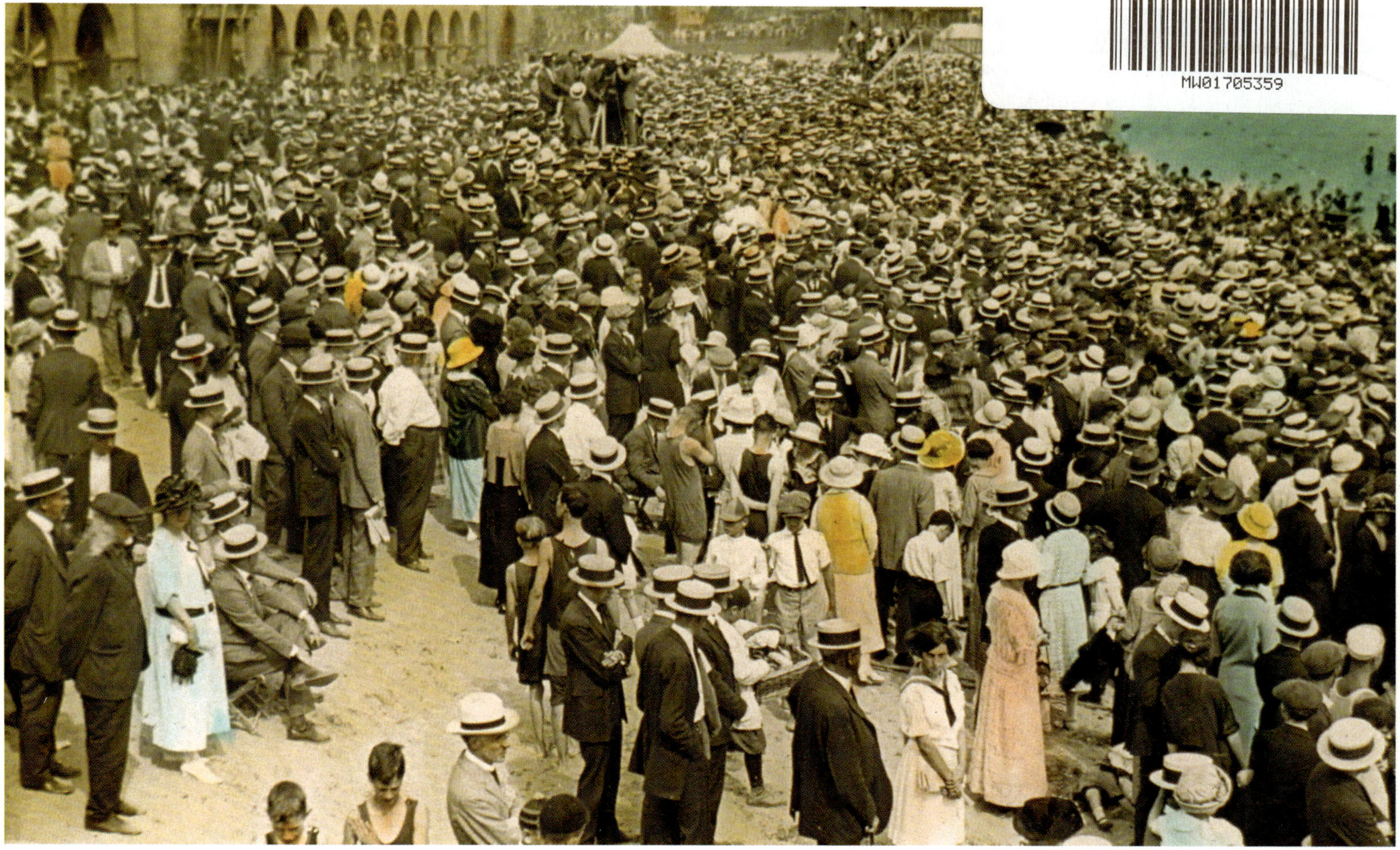

William James' Toronto Views

Lantern Slides from 1906 to 1939

Introduction by Christopher Hume

JAMES LORIMER & COMPANY LTD., PUBLISHERS

TORONTO

James Lorimer & Company Limited acknowledges the support of the Ontario Arts Council. We acknowledge the financial support of the Government of Canada through the Book Publishing IndustryDevelopment Program (BPIDP) for our publishing activities. We acknowledge the support of the Canada Council for the Arts for our publishing program.

Canadian Cataloguing in Publication Data
James, William, 1866–1948
William James' Toronto Views: Lantern Slides from 1906 to 1939

ISBN 1-55028-678-1
1. James, William, 1866–1948. 2. Lantern slides – Ontario – Toronto.
3. Toronto (Ont.) – History – Pictorial works. I. Title.
FC3097.37.J28 1999 779'.9971354103'092 C99-931821-7
F1059.5.T6843J35 1999

James Lorimer & Company Ltd., Publishers
Egerton Ryerson Memorial Building
35 Britain Street, 3rd Floor
Toronto, Ontario
M5A 1R7

Printed and bound in Canada.

All of the images in this book have been drawn from the lantern slides in the William James Collection at the City of Toronto Archives (CTA). The series number for the James Collection is SC (Special Collections) 244.

T = Top; L = Left; R = Right; P = Page

Cover: 244–19.16; P4: 244–15.43; P6: 244–19.27; P7: 244–24.16; P8: 244–91.45; P9: 244–49.41, P10: 244–15.41; P12: 244–2.18; P14: 244–3.1; P15: 244–21.3; P16: 244–36.15; P17: 244–63.2; P18: 244–4.35; P19: 244–21.6; P20: 244–14.43; P21: 244–2.10; P22T: 244–47.8; P22R: 244–85.9; P23: 244–87.45; P24: 244–27.9; P25: 244–24.12; P26T: 244–16.8; P26R: 43.12; P27: 244–29.25; P28: 244–47.3; P29: 244–15.46; P30: 244–8.18; P31: 244–57.11; P32: 244–4.30; P33T: 244–73.43; P33R: 244–52.36; P34: 244–33.4; P35: 244–33.1; P36T: 244–31.27; P36R: 95.16; P37: 244–43.14; P38: 244–25.1; P39L: 244–5.30; P39T: 244–106.10; P40L: 244–24.10; P40T: 244–14.41; P41: 244–2.24; P43: 244–21.1; P44: 244–1.3; P45T: 244–4.13; P46: 244–36.3; P47: 244–82.3; P48: 244–12.4; P50: 244–26.13; P51T: 244–30.16; P51L: 244–1.35; P52: 244–35.32; P53: 244–22.25; P54: 244–24.16; P55: 244–3.42; P56: 244–83.2; P57: 244–52.17; P58: 244–6.40; P59: 244–52.24; P60: 244–42.2; P61: 244–22.5; P62: 244–2.28; P63: 244–55.22; P64: 244–64.2; P65: 244–19.28; P66: 244–23.6; P67: 244–34.33; P68: 244–23.44; P70: 244–45.11; P71: 244–16.18; P72T: 244–5.17; P72R: 244–57.36; P73: 244–39.24; P74: 244–39.17; P75: 244–73.49; P76: 244–47.11; P77: 244–21.4; P78: 244–10.1; P79: 244–10.41; P80: 244–42.34; P82: 244–19.23; P83: 244–19.16; P84: 244–19.17; P85: 244–36.32; P86: 244–19.33; P87: 244–19.22; P88: 244–79.48; P89: 244–21.34; P90: 244–53.15; P91: 244–48.6; P92: 244–106.6; P93: 244–25.35; P94: 244–19.26; P95: 244–23.45; P96: 244–34.39; P97: 244–4.5; P98: 244–51.32; P99: 244–2.5; P100: 244–33.36; P101: 244–59.36; P102: 244–33.33; P103: 244–28.29; P104: 244–5.20; P105: 244–30.47; P106: 244–18.3; P107: 244–41.29; P108: 244–36.16; P109: 244–14.40; P110: 244–21.35; P113: 244–14.35; P114: 244–87.25; P115: 244–23.40; P116: 244–24.2; P117: 244–24.3; P118: 244–24.19; P119: 244–24.20; P120: 244–37.17

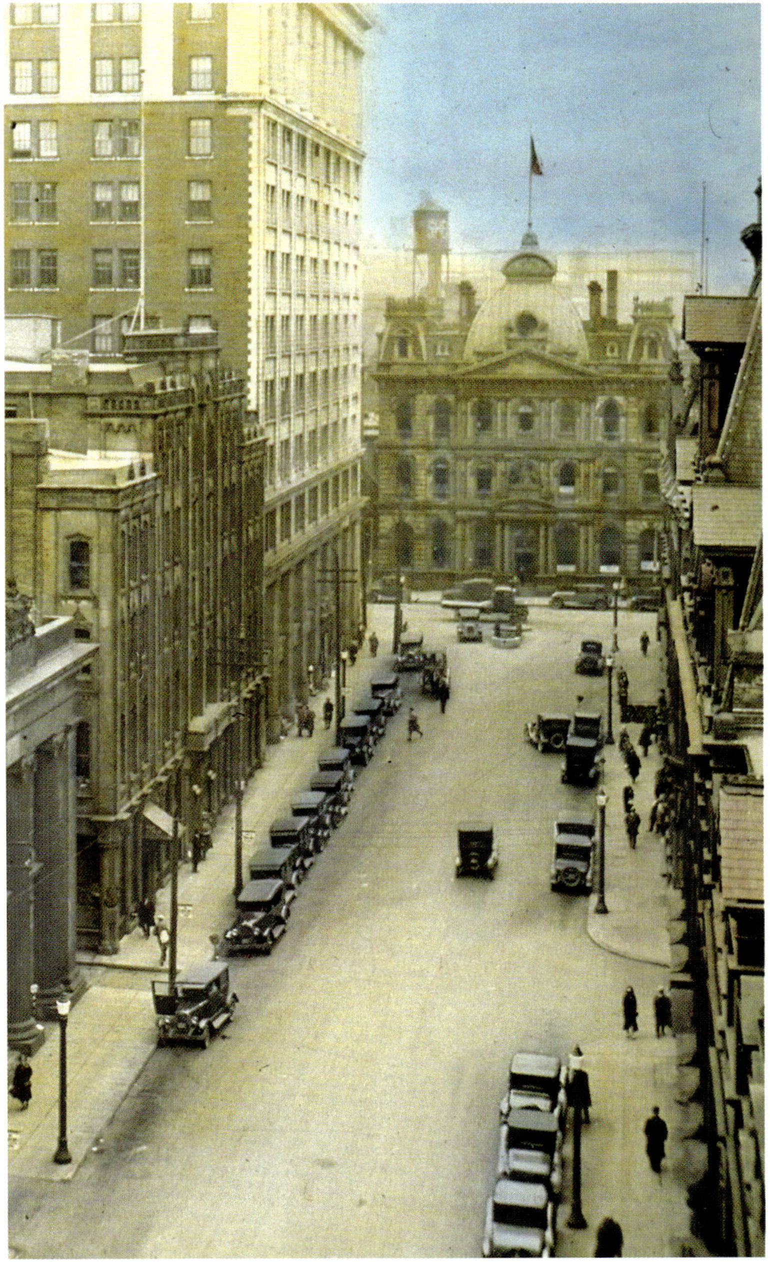

Contents

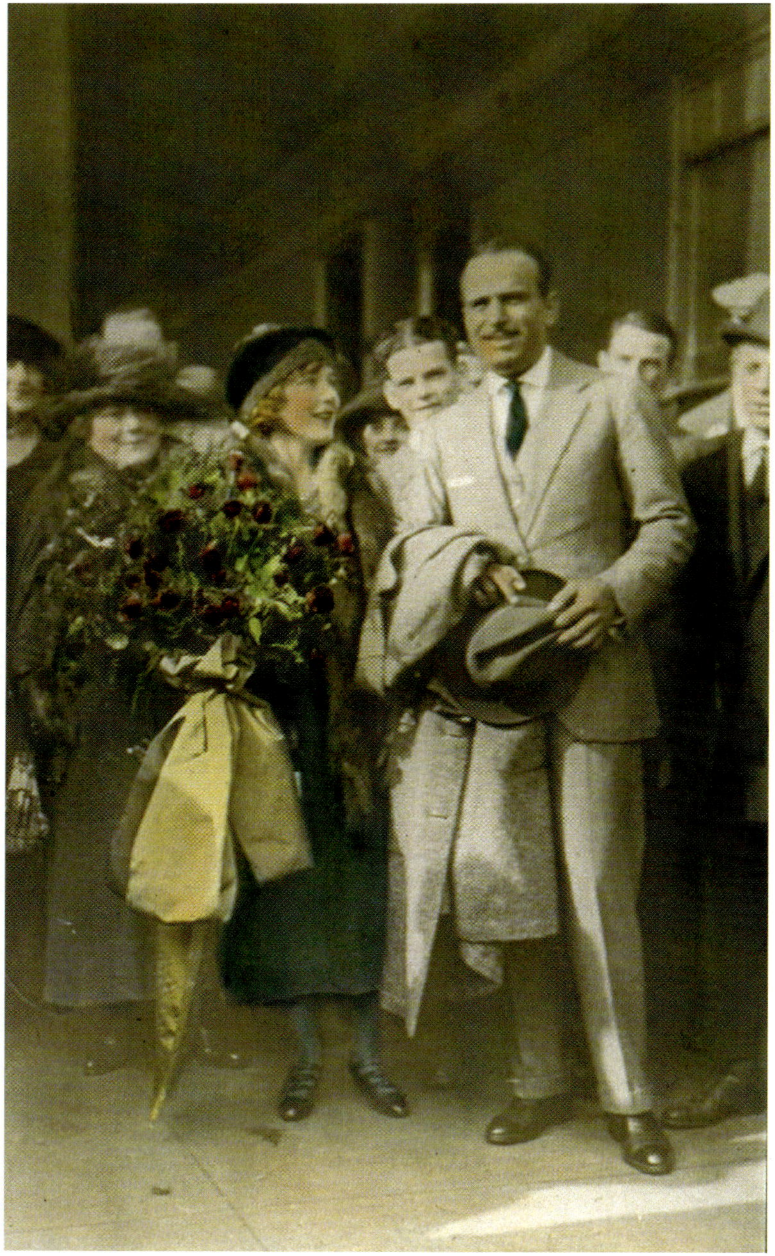

Acknowledgements

The author and the publisher would like to thank Steve MacKinnon and Sally Gibson of the City of Toronto Archives and Mary-Lou Griffin, William James' granddaughter, for their invaluable assistance in the preparation of this book.

Mary Pickford and Douglas Fairbanks, 1922.

Introduction

Christopher Hume

William James (1866–1948) was a prolific photographer who spent more than three decades taking pictures of Toronto and its inhabitants. Yet it would be wrong to think of him simply as a man who made his living with a camera.

More than half a century after his death, it's clear that James was that rarest of creatures, a natural-born chronicler. Though he didn't discover his calling until relatively late in life — he was 40 when he became a full-time photographer — he would soon make up for lost time. When he died, he left behind an archive of more than 10,000 pictures. A surprising number of them are still published regularly and have become icons of early Toronto.

There's no doubt the enduring appeal of his city photographs would have pleased James immensely. Above all, Toronto was his chosen subject, perhaps even the reason he took up photography as a profession.

James arrived here in 1906, the year he and his family immigrated to Canada from England aboard the *Empress of Britain*. They had little in the way of prospects, but were full of hope. Like James himself at this point, Toronto had expectations of a better future. Its glory years lay ahead and so did the photographer's. As the city grew and matured, James kept pace. The start of what was then a new century was greeted with enormous optimism, nowhere more so than in the Dominion; this, after all, was to be Canada's century.

Toronto was already in the midst of a boom, both economic and social. By the first decade of the twentieth century, the city had become a powerful financial, as well as commercial and industrial, centre. Immigration from Europe, especially the United Kingdom, and the influx of rural Ontarians was also transforming the city into a more livable and lively place.

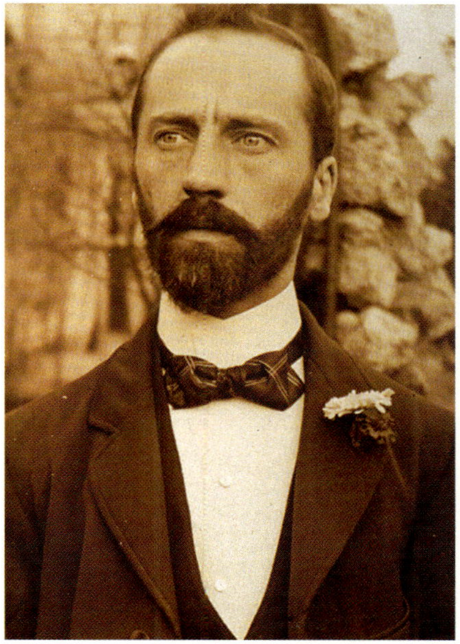

William James, circa 1900.

For James, born in 1866 in Walsall, a tiny English farming village in Staffordshire, the possibilities must have seemed as exciting as they were challenging. His childhood had been passed in a society that had remained essentially unchanged for generations. James' father and grandfather before him were born in Walsall; it was where the family's roots lay.

But for a young man like James, it wasn't enough. After attending local schools, he became an apprentice in a leather-working shop in Walsall. He spent seven years there, which must have seemed interminable to someone as restlessly ambitious as he was. Eventually, he left Walsall and moved to London where he found employment with an insurance company, Prudential of England. That wasn't to his liking and by the late 1880s, he had sailed for the United States. He

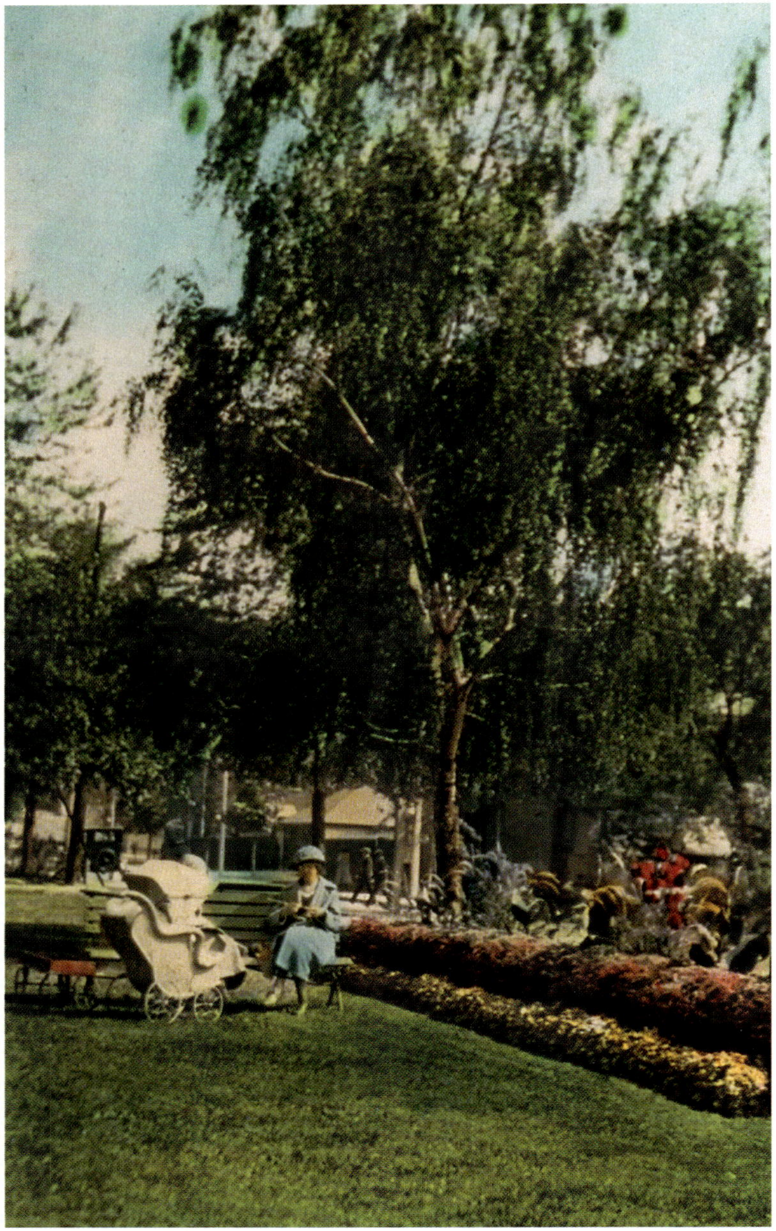

Barton Avenue Park, 1922.

stayed there for three years, mostly in New Jersey and New England, then returned to England — and Walsall. There, in 1889, he married Clara Woolaston.

When the couple landed in Quebec City on November 9, 1906, they had five children and no place to go. The family travelled to Toronto by train and checked into a room on King Street West, where they lived for several uncomfortable days. According to James' granddaughter, Mary-Lou Griffin of Richmond Hill, James had exactly seven dollars in his pocket. Once again, he ended up working for an insurance company, this time Metropolitan Life.

James finally turned to photography in 1908, though he didn't quit his day job immediately. He had mastered the technical skills, which were considerable in those very hands-on days, as a hobbyist in England. His enthusiasm apparently knew no bounds; everywhere he lived he installed a darkroom. That was an absolute necessity for photographers in that pre-one-hour-photo-mart era. Like many men and women of the 19th century, James was fascinated by the still novel science of photography.

Invented simultaneously in France and Britain in the early 19th century, the camera had already left its mark on Europe and North America. The device enabled the user to freeze the moment and in a sense, kill time. Thus, it altered the way people viewed the world around them and, by extension, their relationship with it. James was fully aware of the camera's ability to fix an image and reveal its secrets.

The first photograph is generally accepted to have been one taken by a Frenchman, Joseph Nicéphore Niépce, in 1826, four decades before James was born. The picture, "A view from nature," was registered on a coated pewter plate exposed to direct sunlight. Shortly afterward, another Frenchman, Louis Daguerre, perfected the process and began documenting the attractions of Paris. His pictures enjoyed huge popularity and so did photography.

James' first brush with success occurred soon after the move to Toronto. He came across a notice advertising a photographic competition, decided to enter and won the twenty-five dollar top prize, a substantial sum in those days, especially for a family still struggling to find its feet.

But what enticed James to turn professional was the then-fashionable medium of the stereoscope. It was a viewing device into which was mounted a card that had two photographs of the same scene taken from slightly different angles. Seen through its lens, the two images merged into one three-dimensional picture. The effect was magical, and a large market for stereoscopic prints sprang up.

James soon tired of them, however, and graduated to news and commercial photography. By 1910, he had established himself as one of the first photographers in Toronto to make a living shooting for newspapers. The going rate was two dollars a picture. Without competition from television, radio and computers, the papers set the public agenda. In Toronto alone there were as many as eight dailies.

James' mornings were devoted to taking pictures around the city. Afternoons were spent at various editorial offices selling them. His subjects ranged from society gatherings to scenes of urban poverty. In time, the *Toronto Daily Star* became his best customer. James seems to have established a personal as well as professional bond with Harry Hindmarsh, then publisher of the *Star*. His pictures appeared regularly in that paper, and in 1933 James' third son, Norm, became the first full-time photographer hired by the *Star*.

It is Norm James' daughter and only child, Mary-Lou Griffin, who has assumed the title of keeper of the family records. A small, elfin woman, she remembers James senior as "a tiny man with a fiery temper." According to her, he was very English, very proper and very set in his ways.

"He never swore or drank," Griffin recalls. "If any of his sons came home with beer on their breath, he would get angry. But eventually he mellowed and started to brew his own beer in his basement. He was very opinionated and very proud. He wouldn't accept menial jobs so he spent a lot of time unemployed before he came to Canada. He saw no future for his kids in England so they came here.

"He was a good father, but strict. He hated darkroom work so he tried to pass it on to his sons to do. My dad did about ninety per cent of the darkroom stuff."

James was happiest shooting pictures. Not surprisingly, it was what he did best. Griffin tells of her grandfather's habit of taking a

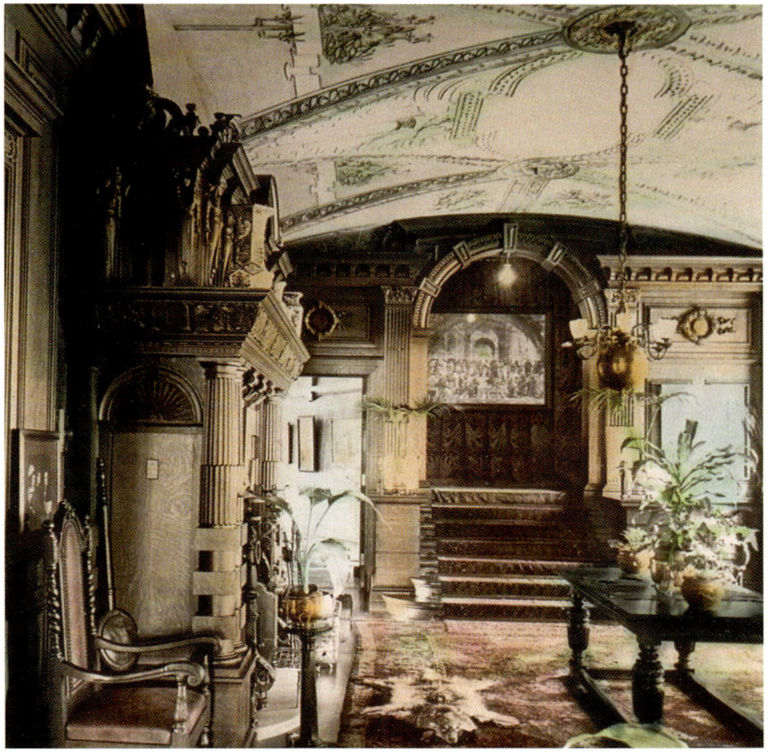

Flavelle House, circa 1920.

step-ladder with him wherever he went. Because he was so short, he needed the extra height to get the photograph he wanted.

"At first, he used to get around on a bicycle," Griffin explains. "Then one of his sons bought a motorcycle with a sidecar attached and the two of them used to drive around in that. My grandfather would ride in the sidecar clutching onto his ladder; they must have been quite a sight. That's how he got his pictures."

But James was also a serious walker who thought nothing of hiking to Hamilton and back to take a few shots. Trudging tirelessly with tripod, camera and bags of equipment in tow, he covered the distances effortlessly.

It may sound rather idyllic, yet times were tough. Various junior Jameses — there were four sons, two daughters — were sent out to

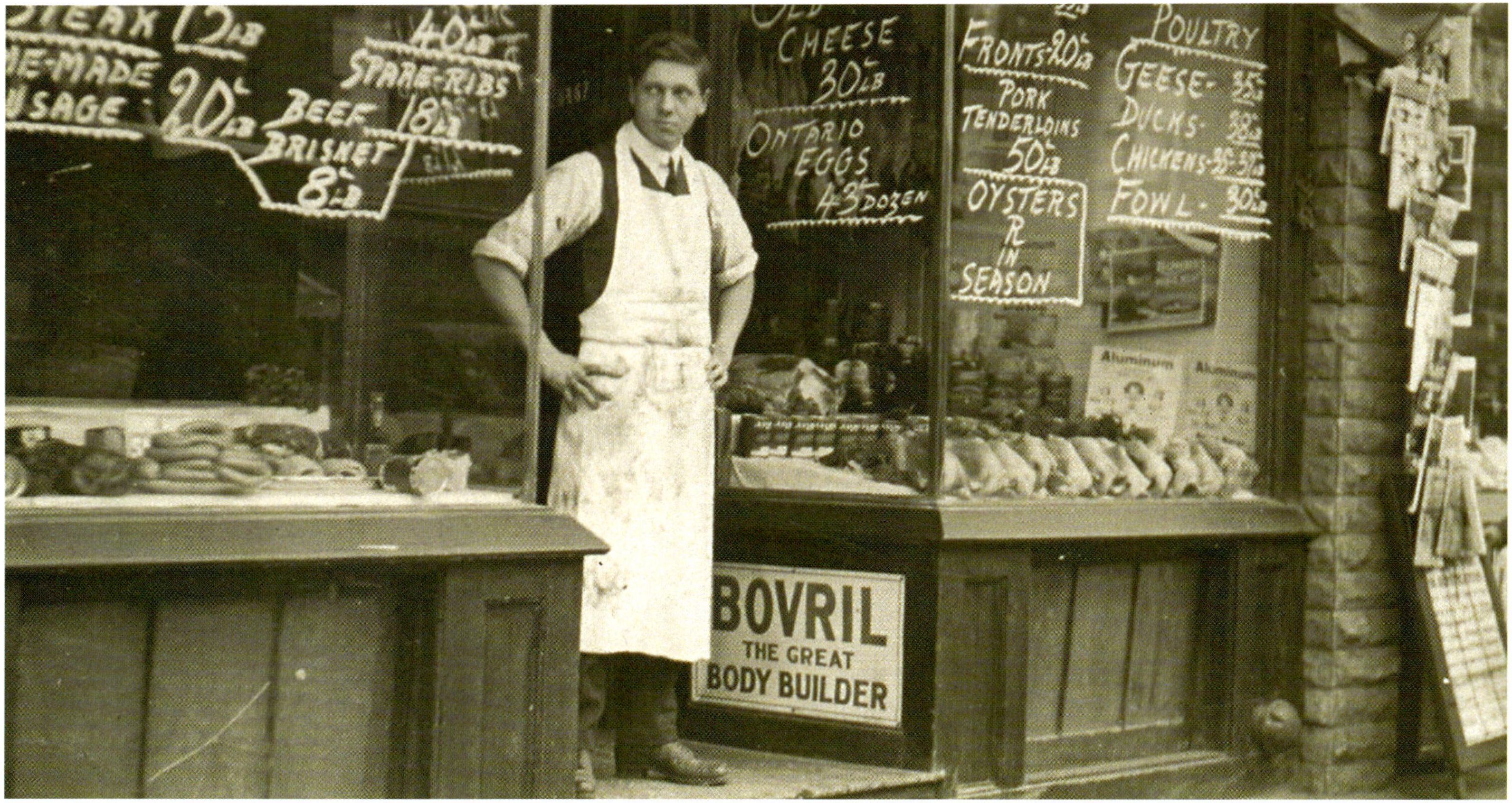

Frank James on Brunswick Avenue, 1922.

work when old enough. The sons weren't pleased with the arrangement, especially since they were expected to hand over their earnings in exchange for an allowance.

When James' eldest son, William, returned to Toronto after World War I, his father took both him and his younger brother, Joseph, into the photographic business. The firm was known as James & Sons, but the partnership didn't last long. It ended when the two brothers left to start their own photographic company, in competition with their father. James Sr. continued on his own until 1928, when his youngest son, Norm, joined him. Norm quit five years later to go to the *Star*.

James didn't retire until 1939, using the occasion of the royal visit of King George and Queen Elizabeth to take his last hurrah. The occasion must have been the final confirmation of James' faith in Toronto and himself. He had left England, it's true, but he was adamant that he "wanted to remain under the British flag." His loyalty to his homeland was such that he refused to use cameras or film that weren't made in Britain.

On the other hand, when it came to cars, he bought only

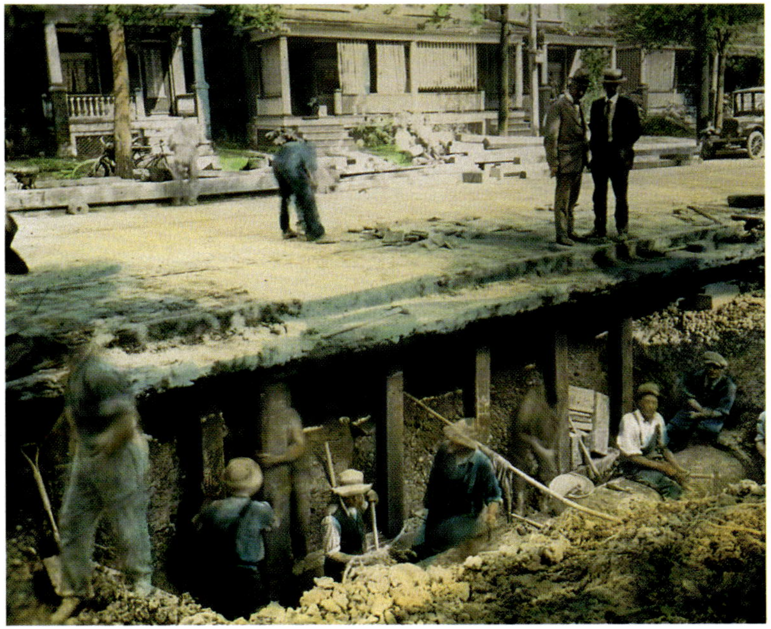

Bathurst Street, 1922.

American, including Ford Model Ts. According to Griffin, James quickly grasped the advantage of owning a vehicle, but not the skills needed to drive it.

"When he tried to learn to drive," she says, "he wasn't the least bit interested in knowing how to stop. On several occasions, my grandfather went around the block half a dozen times until his eldest son, my Uncle Bill, jumped on the running board and managed to stop the car."

James' infatuation with aviation is further proof of his belief in the Brave New World of technology. He was on hand, camera in tow, when the first flights took place in Toronto in 1910. His pictures of the city taken from an open cockpit of a wooden biplane convey an almost breathless sense of delight. To modern eyes, Toronto looks small, rather grimy and drab, but James' excitement makes these aerial views memorable.

Back on earth, he was just as likely to be at Woodbine Racetrack shooting portraits of the smart set as he was to be wandering the mean streets of Toronto's most notorious slum, the Ward, photographing the faces of poverty. He also recognized that even in Toronto the Good, the city of churches, play was as much a part of the human experience as work. His pictures of children and adults swimming, sledding and playing hockey formed a big part of his documentary enterprise. One of his most celebrated images — of a row of bare-bottomed boys sitting on the bank of the Don River — sums up the prevailing attitudes about the virtue of physical activity.

There is an equally systematic presentation of the city at work in James' photographs. He recorded the significant public works projects of the day — laying down new streetcar tracks on Yonge Street in 1921, for example — as well as the workers. There are shots of telephone operators, butchers and builders.

To contemporary viewers, these portraits verge on the naive, not because they glorify labour, but because they come out of James' urge to categorize and classify workers as participants in a great civic endeavour. His subjects are depicted as players in the ongoing drama of the city. A butcher (in fact, James' son, Frank) stands outside his shop, like an actor dressed in a costume. This was a time when clothing, even for labourers, was much more formal than today. In one picture of a road crew tending a broken water main, the men wear jackets and ties. In another shot, a member of a demolition crew wrestling with a steel girder several storeys high sports a straw hat.

Such formality illustrates the strongly hierarchical nature of society at the time. Toronto was no exception to this and, if anything, was probably more rigid than many other communities. Griffin remembers seeing her grandfather maybe twice without a jacket and tie. The occasions were family picnics.

The lines that separated the social classes were distinct, though James was clearly comfortable on both sides. He photographed the rich and prominent as well as the nameless and destitute. Yet his mission never became a cause. His passion was for the city, not the eradication of evil. What characterizes his picture-making was his desire to chronicle the city in all its complexity and contradictions.

To that end, he visited "gypsy camps" and the mansions of the hunting and fishing set at the north end of Toronto. The city was their only common denominator. It was what brought them — and James — together. It was also what kept them apart. When Toronto-born movie queen Mary Pickford and her husband Douglas Fairbanks came to town, James was there to document the occasion. He photographed Canadian prime ministers Wilfred Laurier and Mackenzie King, but he also took disturbing pictures of whole families sleeping on the streets of Toronto. A group of little rich girls in fur coats giggle as they pose for James, while a pair of young boys struggles to haul a wagon through ankle-deep mud, oblivious to his camera. He also made portraits of local aristocrats such as Norman Gooderham of Gooderham and Worts and national heroes, like Viscount Byng of Vimy, who led Canadian troops at Vimy Ridge, the 1917 battle that helped forge Canadian identity.

According to the obituary that appeared in the *Toronto Star* after his death in November 1948, James "delighted in taking photos that he felt would have historic interest." His role was that of observer, of one bearing witness to the changes that would leave the world a different place. His success lay in his ability to meet the immediate demands of daily journalism and the needs of the future viewers who would see the past through his pictures. Thus we are James' heirs as well as his intended audience. In many respects, he took his pictures for us.

"From the beginning," reads his biographical sketch in the City of Toronto Archives, "James' energy, dedication (readiness to climb fences, ladders, trees and skyscrapers to get the photograph), his eye for the decisive (whether at fashionable garden parties or in the Ward), and keen sense of composition marked his work."

"Dad always tried to get a figure in pic," son Norm scribbled on the back of one of his father's prints. Though accurate, the comment belies James' love of the architecture of the city. But often, he combined the two. What may be his first Toronto picture is a 1906 shot of him inspecting the smoking ruins of the grandstand at the Canadian National Exhibition. He would return many times to document the buildings at the C.N.E., then in its heyday. He also visited the splendid

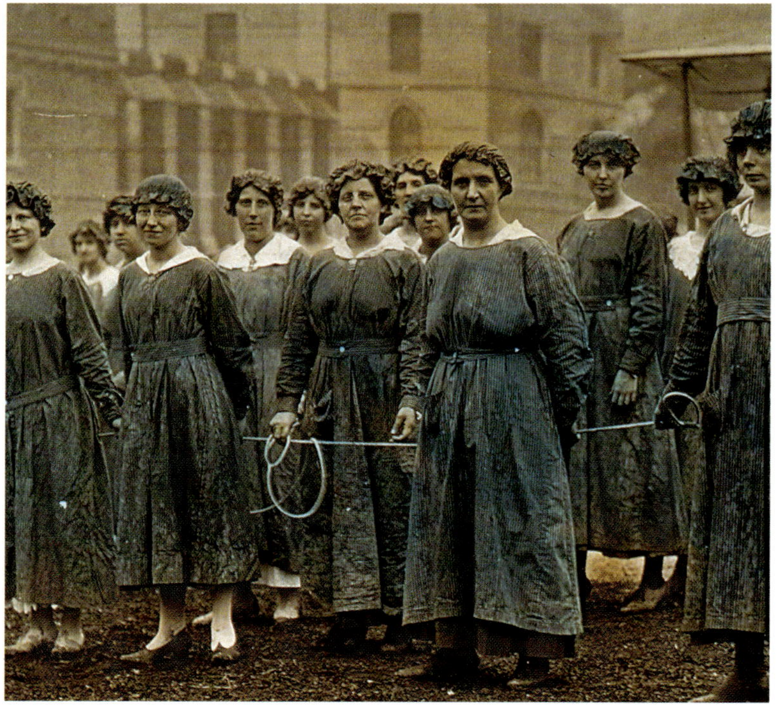

Munitions workers, 1917.

campus of the University of Toronto to take pictures. Hart House, a gift to the university from the Masseys, Canada's only family of architectural patrons, had been completed in 1919. It reflected Toronto's Gothic heritage but translated it into something more ruggedly North American.

Suddenly, the city felt it might have a legitimate claim to architectural greatness. James was keenly aware of this and made a point of photographing Toronto landmarks from Chorley Park, a magnificent government building that is now demolished, to the still-standing Whitney Block at Bay and Wellesley Streets. Along the way, he visited Sir Henry Pellatt's fantasy fortress Casa Loma (designed by E.J. Lennox, architect of Toronto's marvellous city hall, completed in 1899) and the mansions that had started to pop up on Bayview Avenue. One of James' most charming pictures shows the Moore Park train station, long since vanished from the North Toronto landscape.

These photographs form a record of what has been lost and gained. Before the advent of the mass media and a car in every garage, people amused themselves more communally than now. Places such as Balmy Beach, Sunnyside and Hanlan's Point attracted huge crowds during the summer months. Lake Ontario played a role in the life of the city that we can hardly imagine. Long-distance swimmers, male and female, tackled its chilly waters in the hopes of becoming local heroes. James was there, snapping away as they greased down and kidded around nervously. In winter, the action moved to the Olympic-size toboggan runs and ice-skating rinks installed in parks from Riverdale to Christie Pits.

Despite his growing success, James would have to endure one last encounter with disaster. It came during World War I when he was experimenting with moving pictures. After constructing his own movie camera, he shot footage of military training and civilian preparations for the Government of Ontario and the Pathescope Company of Toronto. Though much of his film still exists, James was never paid for it.

"He was fleeced out of any compensation," says Griffin, still angry. "The only cheque he ever received for designing equipment, cameras and tanks for making movies was returned NSF."

James' abiding interest in the mechanics of photography is entirely understandable; the medium was still young, awkward and developing quickly. When he began his career, large coated plates were used; taking pictures was a slow and cumbersome process. By the time he retired, however, film came in rolls. A photographer of James' generation would have worked with flash powder or depended on long exposure times. The pressure to get it right first time around was intense. Indeed, there were no second chances.

Another format that intrigued James was the glass lantern slide. James' lantern slides rank among his most compelling pictures and form the basis of what appears in this book. This obsolete technology was created to project an image onto a screen. The Toronto Archives lists 5,800 such slides, the vast majority depicting the city. Many of these slides have been hand tinted. By painting parts of the print, even tiny sections, James could bring a startling degree of realism to a picture. The results vary but at their best these scenes possess a subtle beauty that has survived undimmed.

Griffin says there is no record that James used his slides to give illustrated lectures, but that was their usual purpose. A network of speakers — idealists, missionaries, travellers — packed auditoriums and church basements with people hungry to see things for themselves. Perhaps James intended his slides to be seen by the thousands of immigrants he helped as a long-serving volunteer with the British Welcome League. Certainly, the photos paint a very pretty picture of a city bustling with opportunities both for work and play. For James, however, the two were one and the same. He was one of those lucky individuals who genuinely loved what he did.

Like all successful photographers, especially portrait photographers, James could strike up an instant rapport, whether photographing heads of state or beggars. Still, Norm James remembered his father as a "severe and stubborn man who didn't have many close friends, but who knew all the other photographers ..." Perhaps the truth about James is more complex. The photographs in the City Archives of James clowning for the camera seem to challenge any simple view of him.

It was Norm James and Mary-Lou Griffin who organized the mass of material left by James and arranged for it to be acquired by the archives. "It was stuffed in boxes, bags and envelopes," says Griffin. "It sat in my parents' basement for years and years. Some of the negatives were stuck together and were in bad shape. During the mid-1960s, I spent nearly three years going through this stuff. People used to call my dad all the time to see if he had a picture of this or that. So that's why we numbered each print, each one."

In 1976, the material was handed over to the archives. A good many images had appeared first in publications as diverse as *Chatelaine*, *Toronto World*, *Mayfair*, *Hunt in Canada* and *Canadian Horseman*. In 1981–82, The Market Gallery on Front Street in Toronto assembled an exhibition of James' pictures. Its title, William James: Pioneer Press Photographer, put him in his proper historical context. The show also helped put James in front of a new generation of Torontonians. With luck, this book will serve the same purpose.

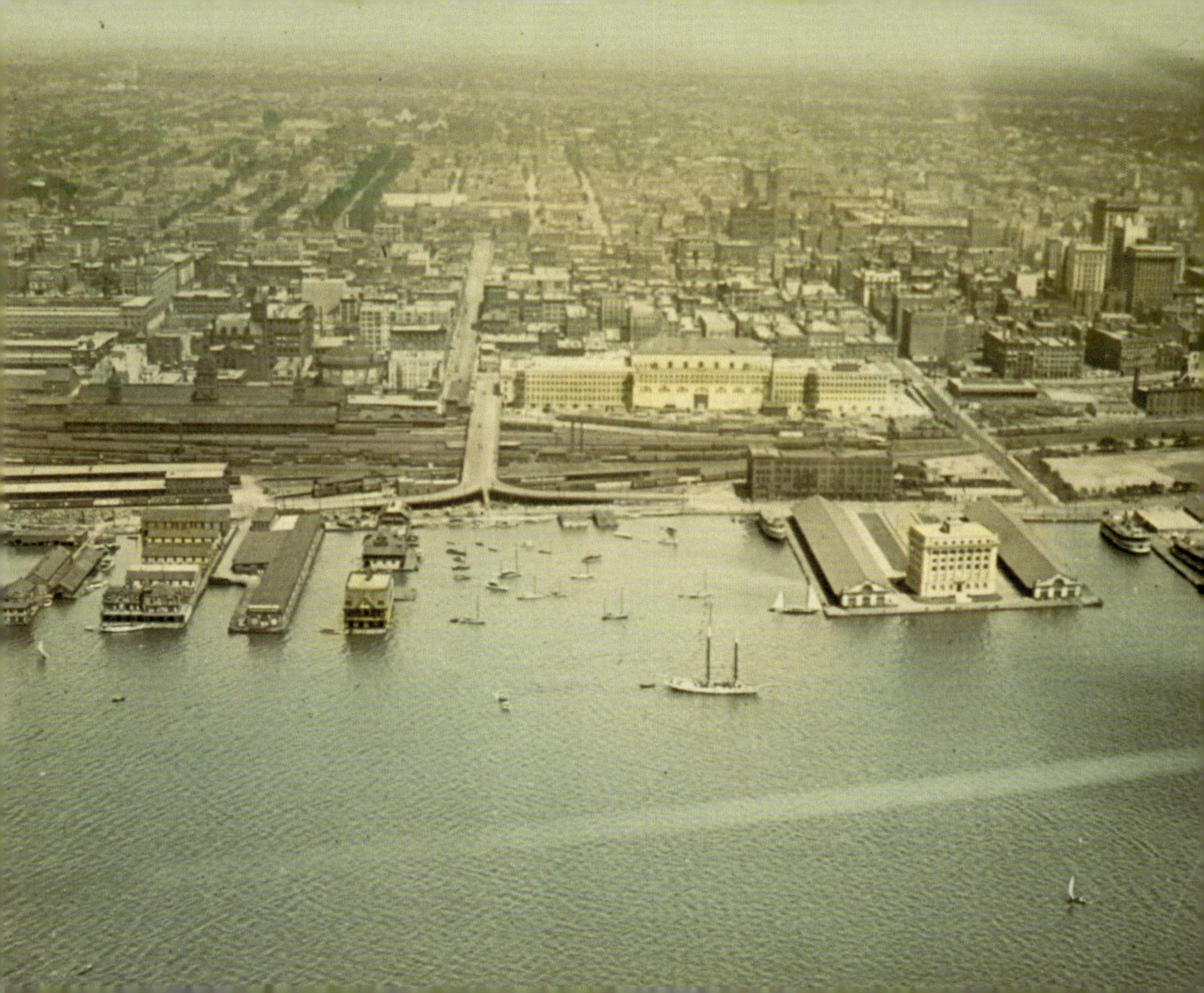

THE CITY

Left: *Toronto's waterfront, 1918. Both the old and the new Union Stations are visible, as well as the new Harbour Commissioners building, which at that time was at the water's edge.*

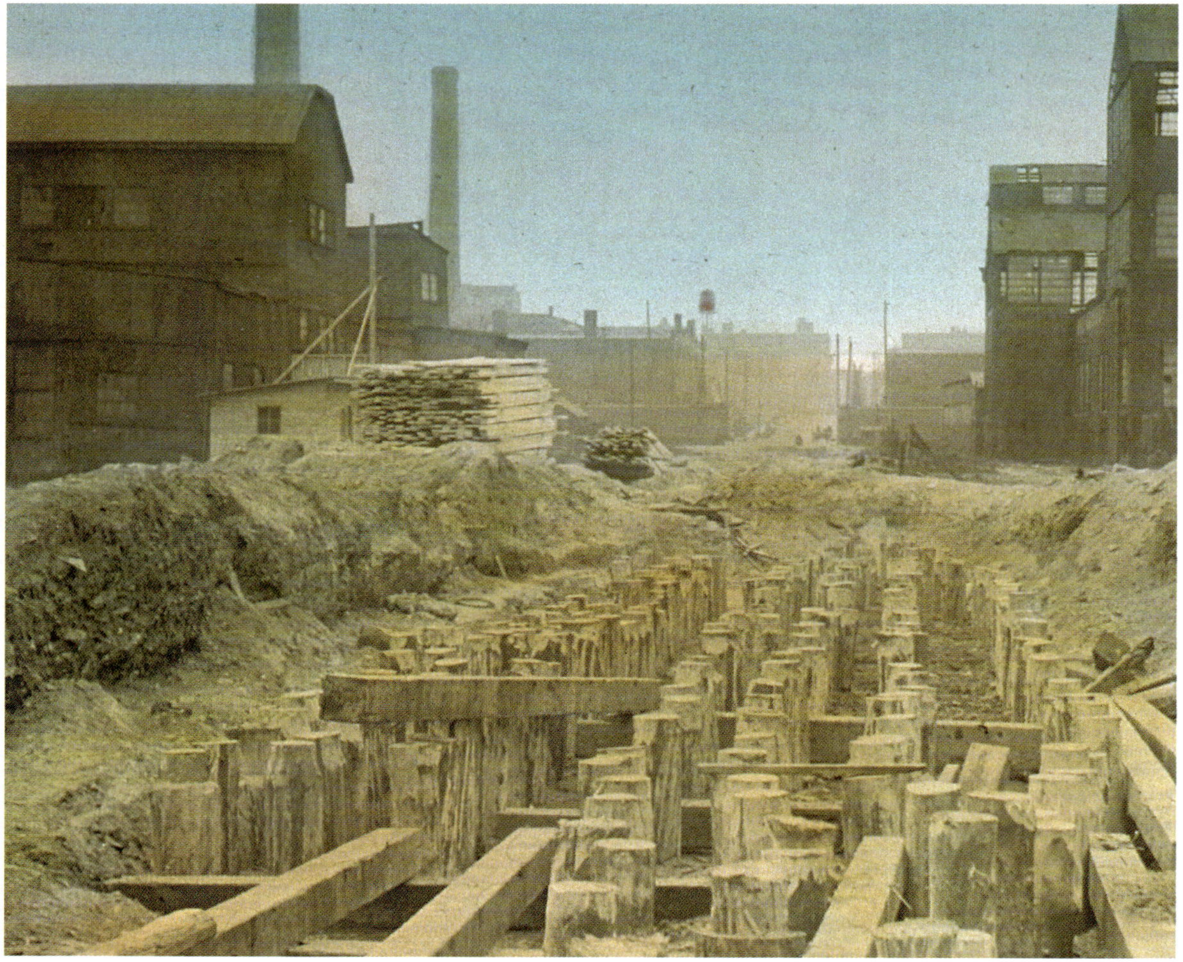

Left: *Preparations for viaduct bridge, Polson's Wharf, 1927. The Polson Iron Works Company was founded in 1886 and launched ships from the foot of Sherbourne Street until 1919.* Right: *Foot of York Street, 1926. Construction workers drive piles for the Terminal Warehouse, now the Queen's Quay Terminal at Harbourfront.*

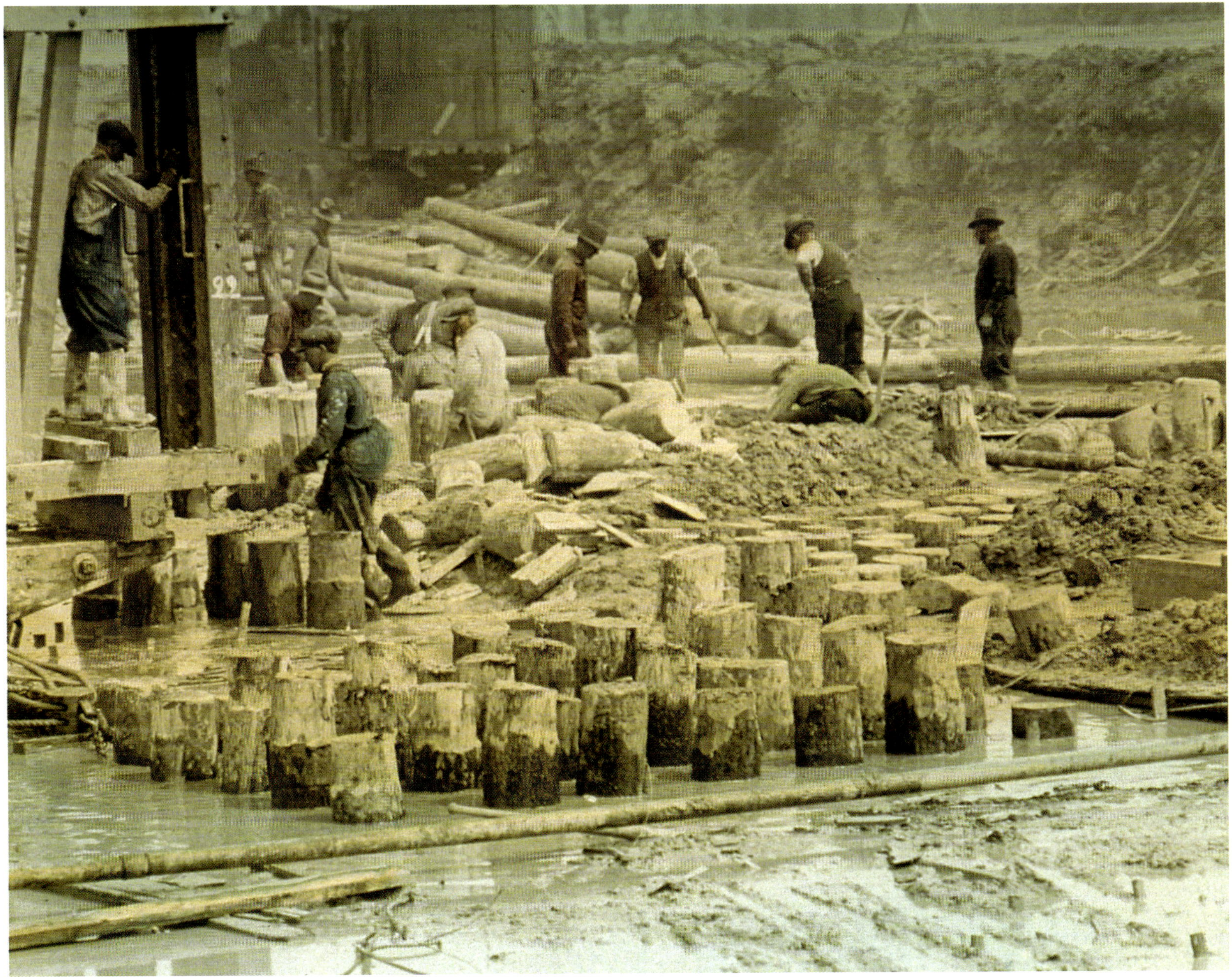

Downtown

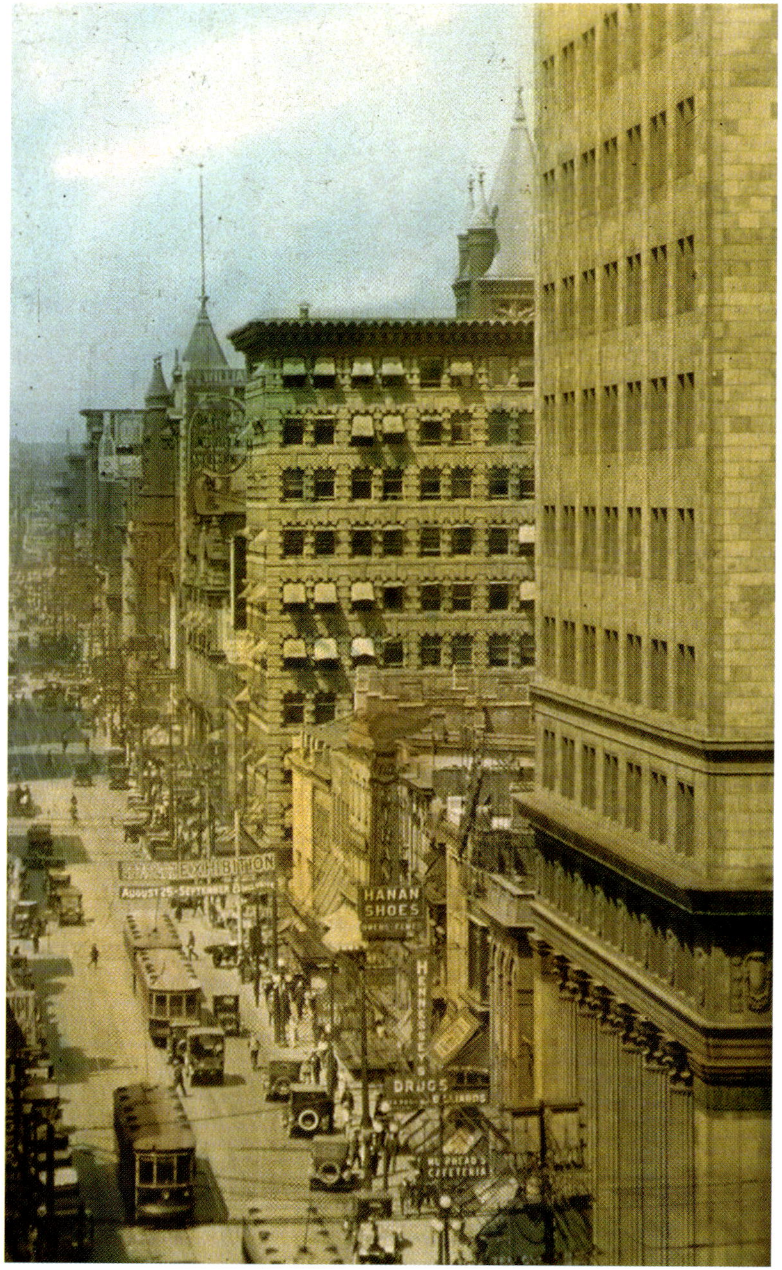

Right: *Yonge Street, north of King, 1927. The Traders Bank, Toronto's first skyscraper at fifteen stories (erected in 1905), is at right.* Far right: *Toronto Street, 1927. The magnificent General Post Office still commands the vista. Its demolition in 1958 marked what William Dendy calls "the beginning of the destruction of Victorian Toronto."*

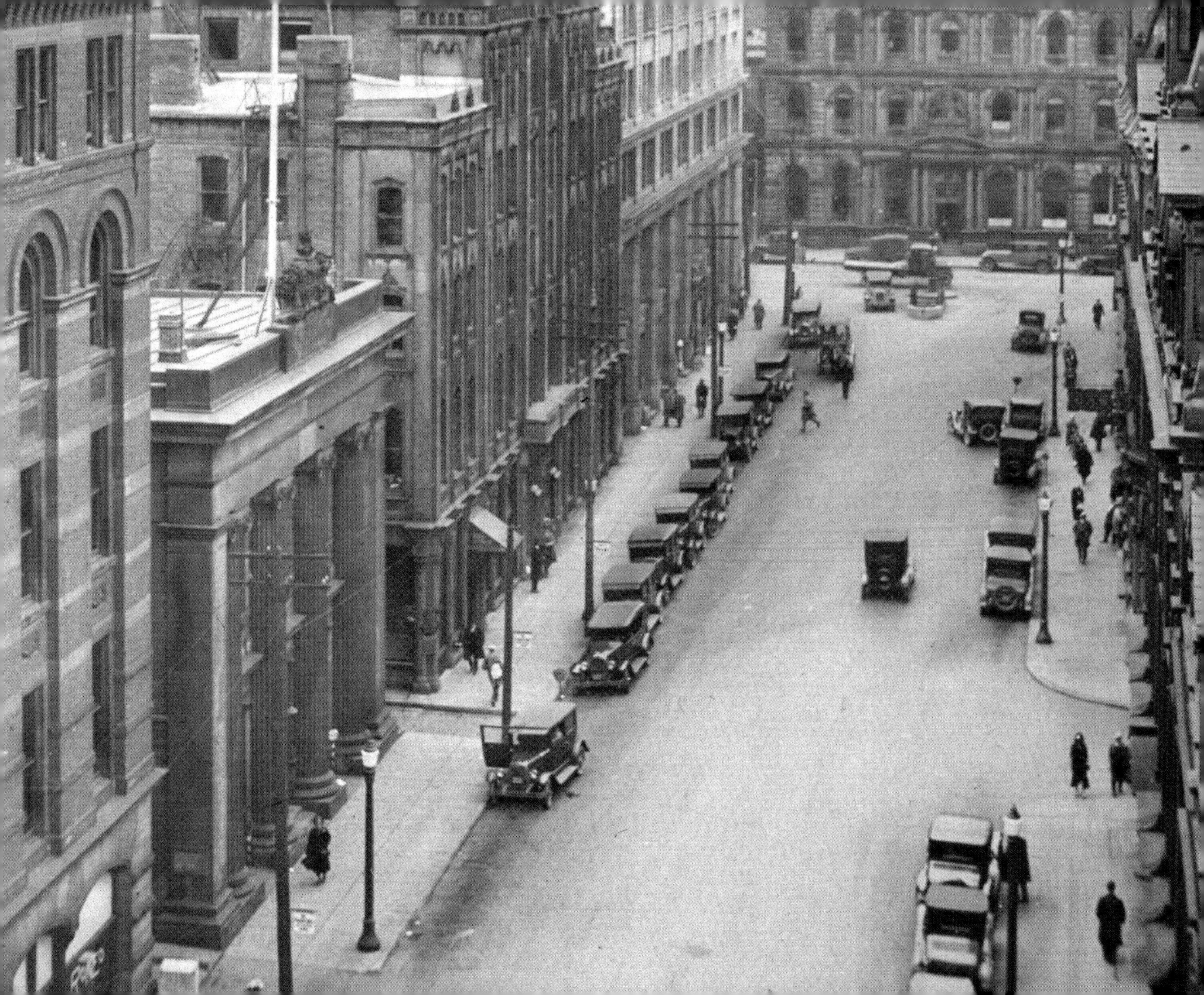

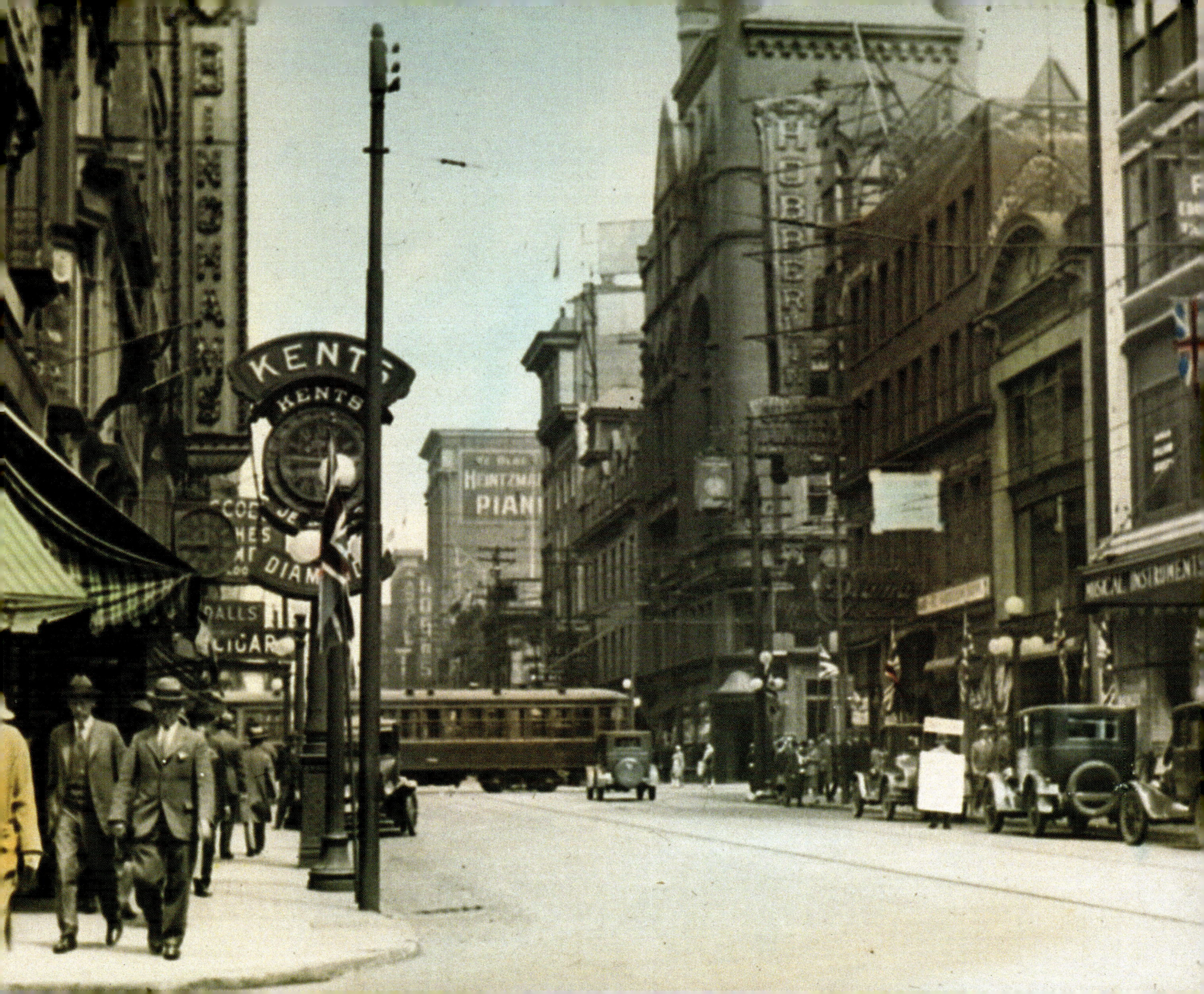
KENTS
KENTS
CIGAR
MUSICAL INSTRUMENTS

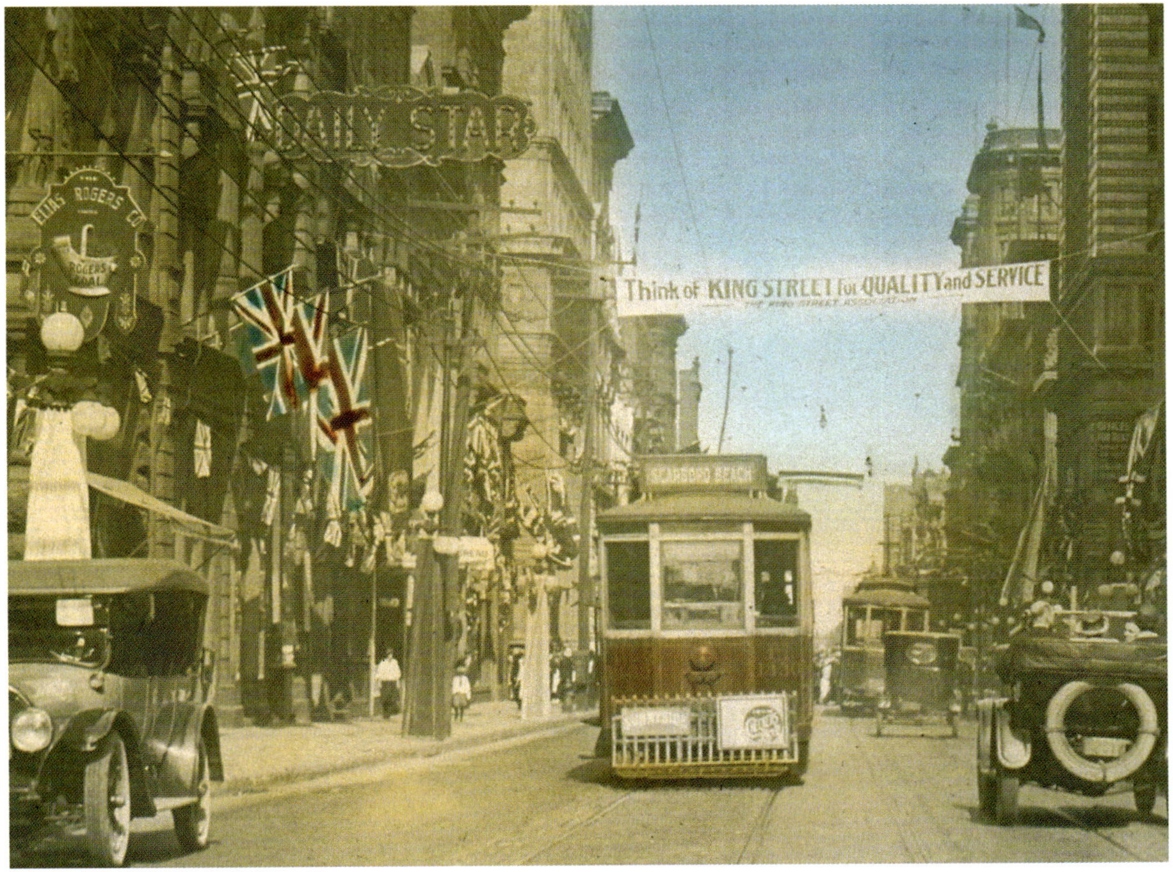

Far left: *Yonge Street at Temperance, 1927. This view shows the Confederation Life Building (built in 1892) dominating the scene. Its Richardsonian Romanesque detailing still graces the lower reaches of Yonge.* Left: *King Street, circa 1920. A streetcar headed for Scarborough beach makes its way along King Street. Notice the overarching banner: Streets, not malls, drew the crowds in James' time.*

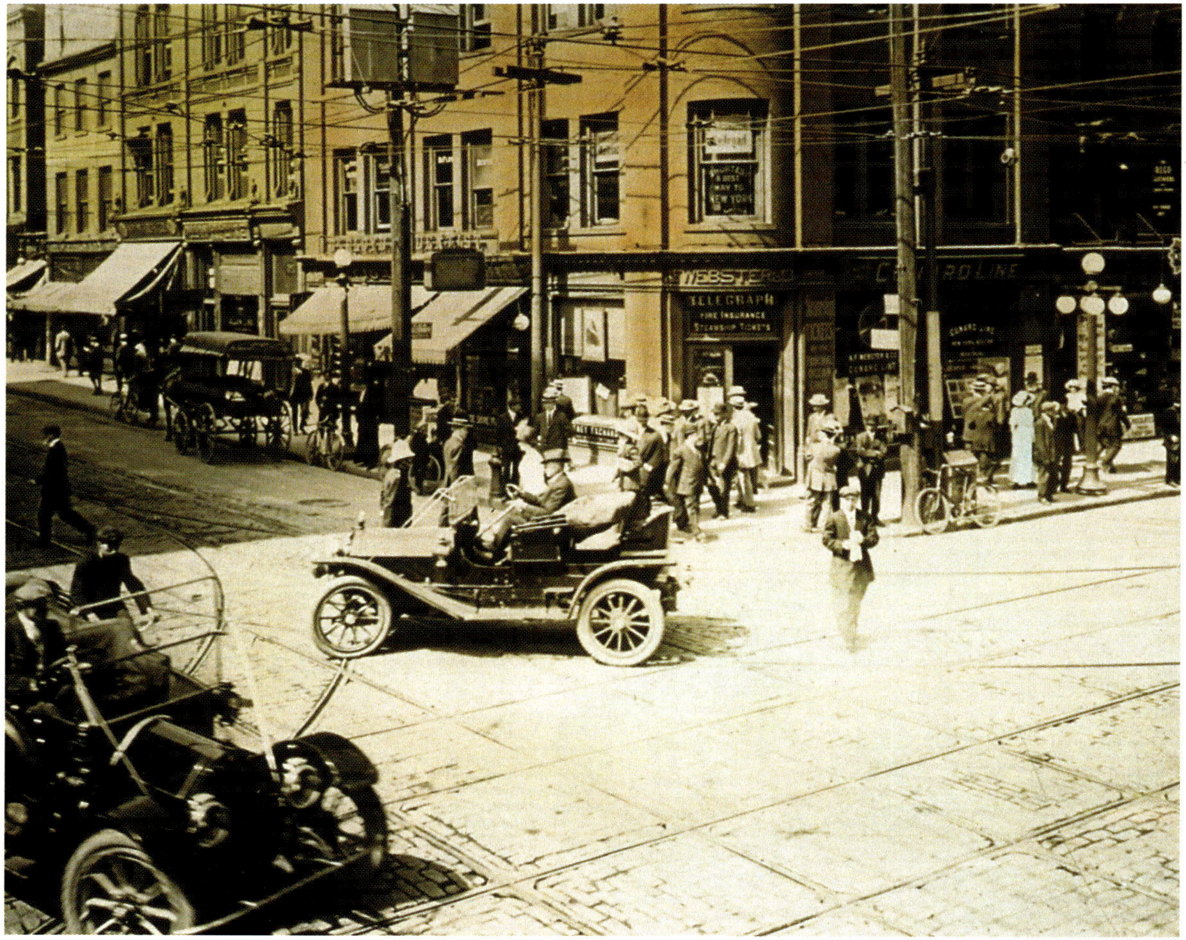

Left: *Yonge and King Streets, 1909.* Far right: *Looking south on Yonge at College Street, 1926. Evidence of Toronto's 1920s skyscraper boom rises in the distance.*

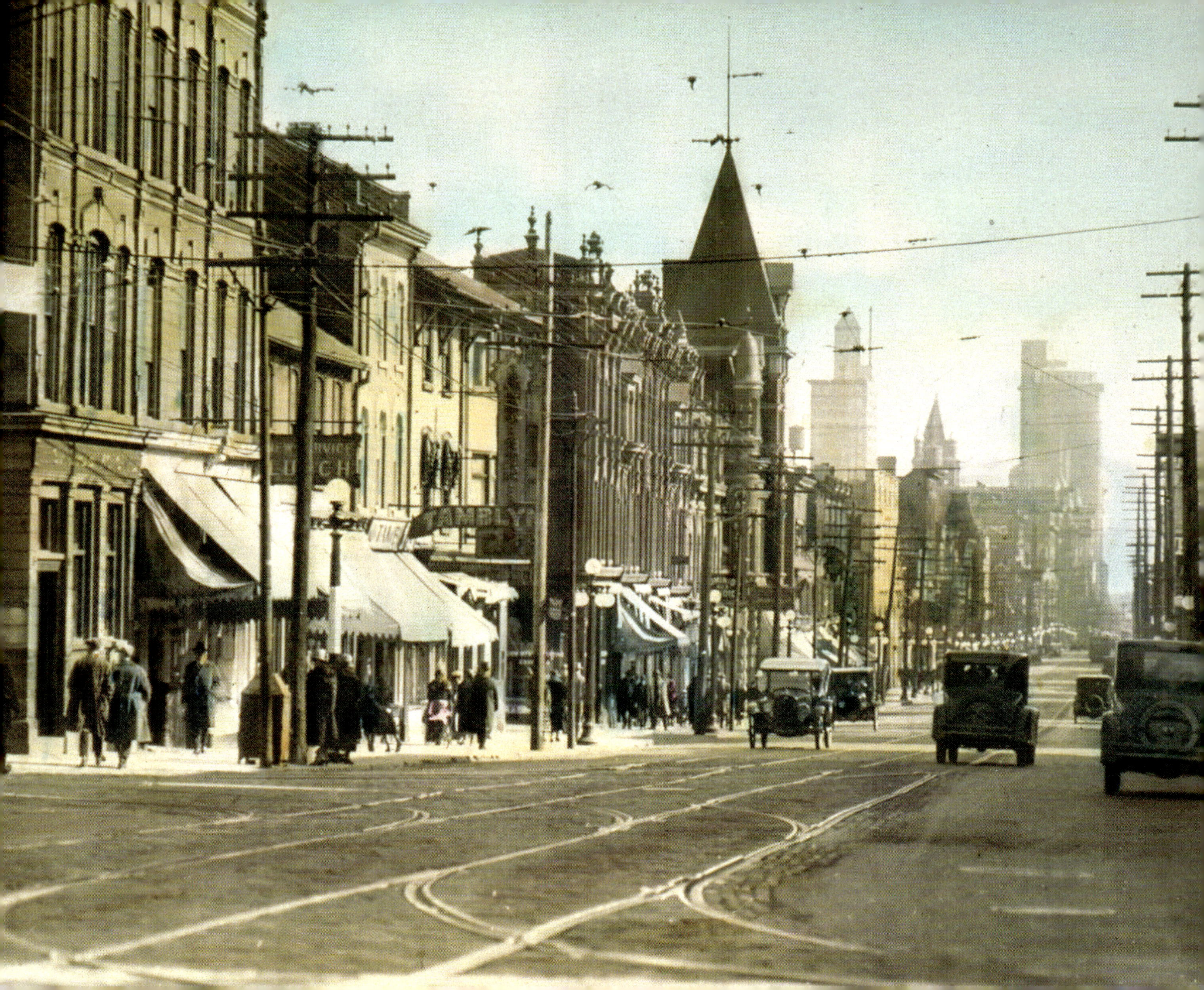

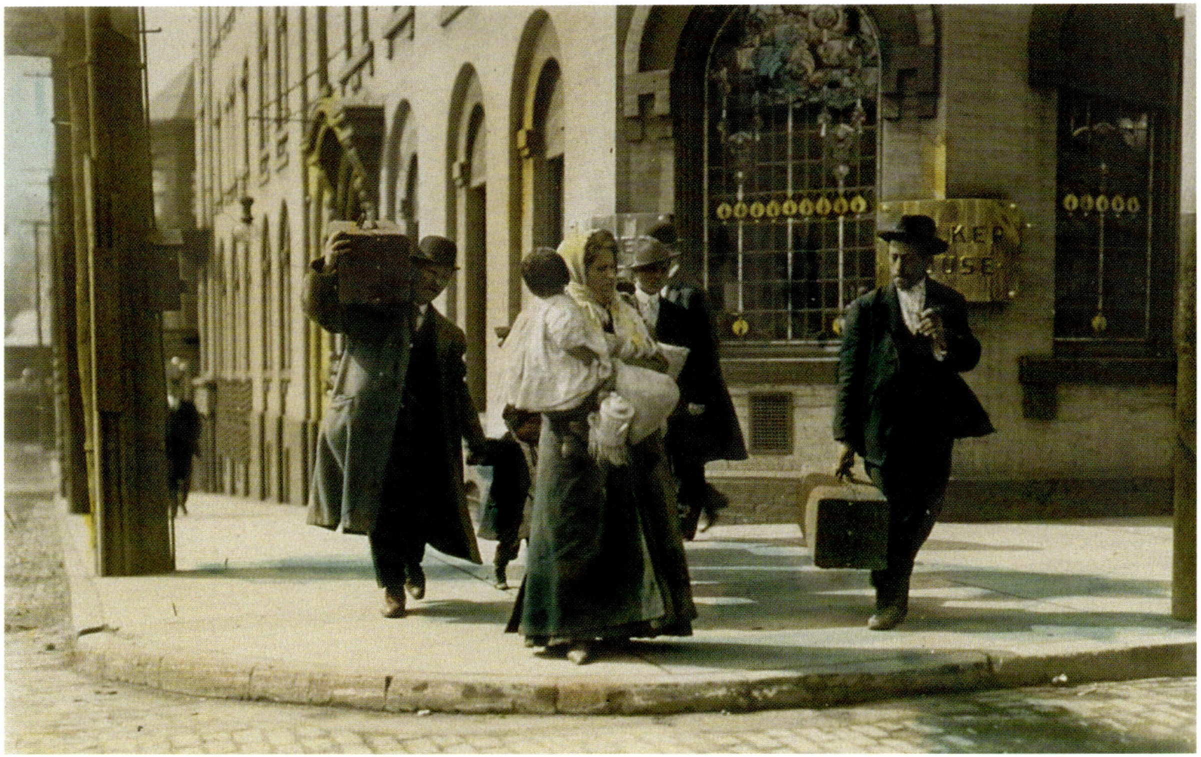

Above: *An immigrant family arrives in the city, circa 1910. James himself arrived in 1906, part of a resurgent wave of immigration that more than doubled the population of the city from just over 200,000 in 1901 to well over 500,000 persons by 1921.* Right: *A recruiting party, 1914. Toronto's response to the First World War was overwhelming. 70,000 of its men went into the armed forces; one in seven did not return. This recuiting party, rolling along "To Berlin," is having no difficulty packing its streetcar.* Far right: *Adelaide and Bay, circa 1910. George Geary, whose election signs grace this building-cum-billboard, was elected mayor in 1910 and served until 1912.*

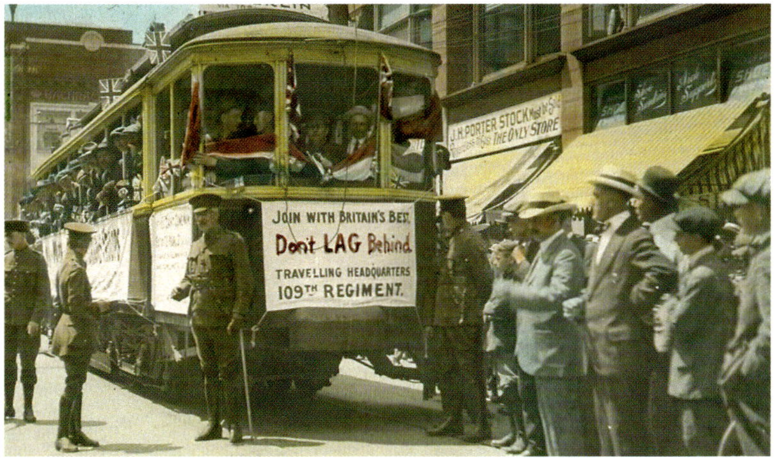

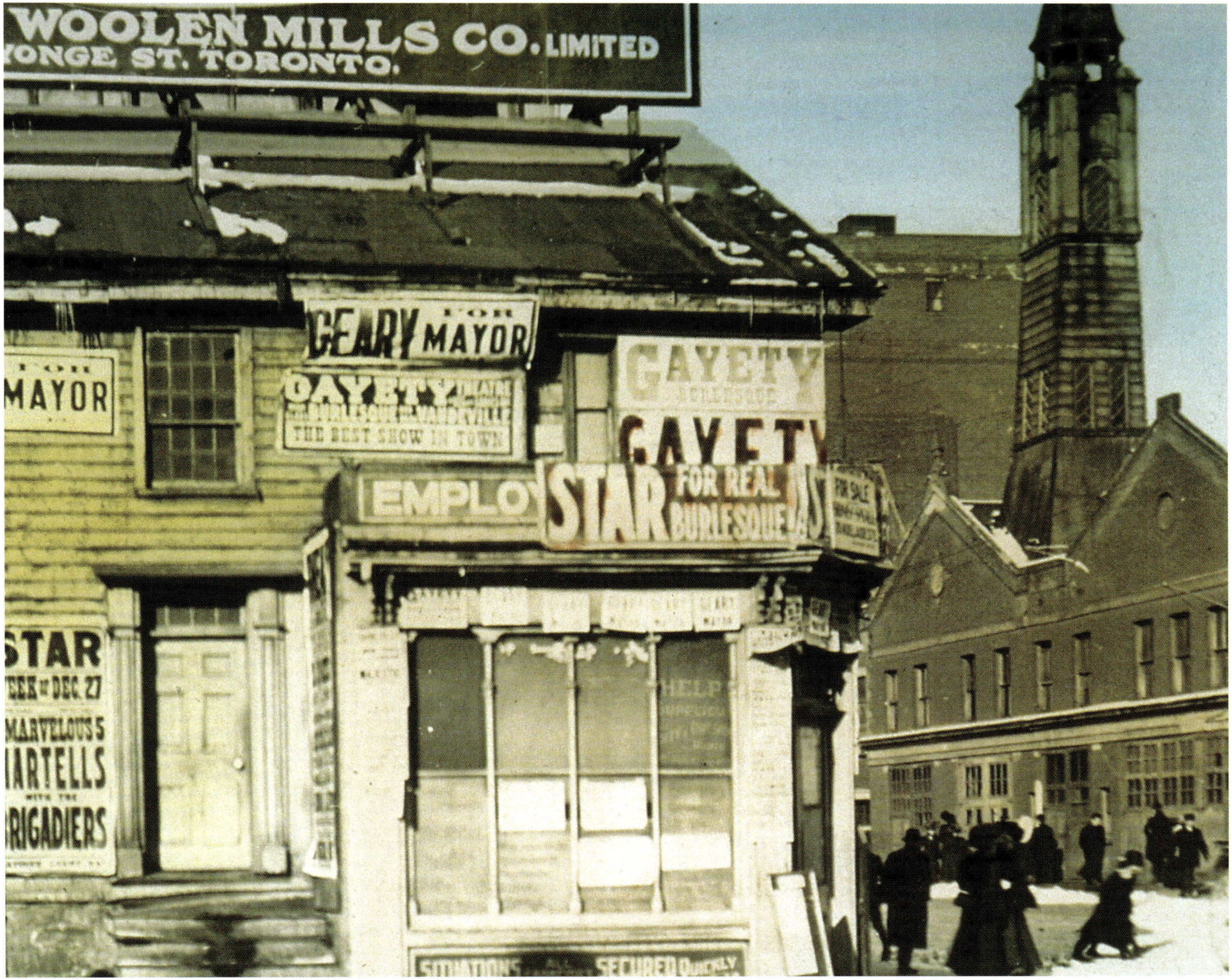
WOOLEN MILLS CO. LIMITED
YONGE ST. TORONTO.
GEARY FOR MAYOR
FOR MAYOR
GAYETY
THE BEST SHOW IN TOWN
GAYETY
GAYETY
EMPLOY
STAR FOR REAL BURLESQUE
FOR SALE
STAR
WEEK OF DEC. 27
MARVELOUS 5
MARTELLS
BRIGADIERS
SITUATIONS SECURED QUICKLY

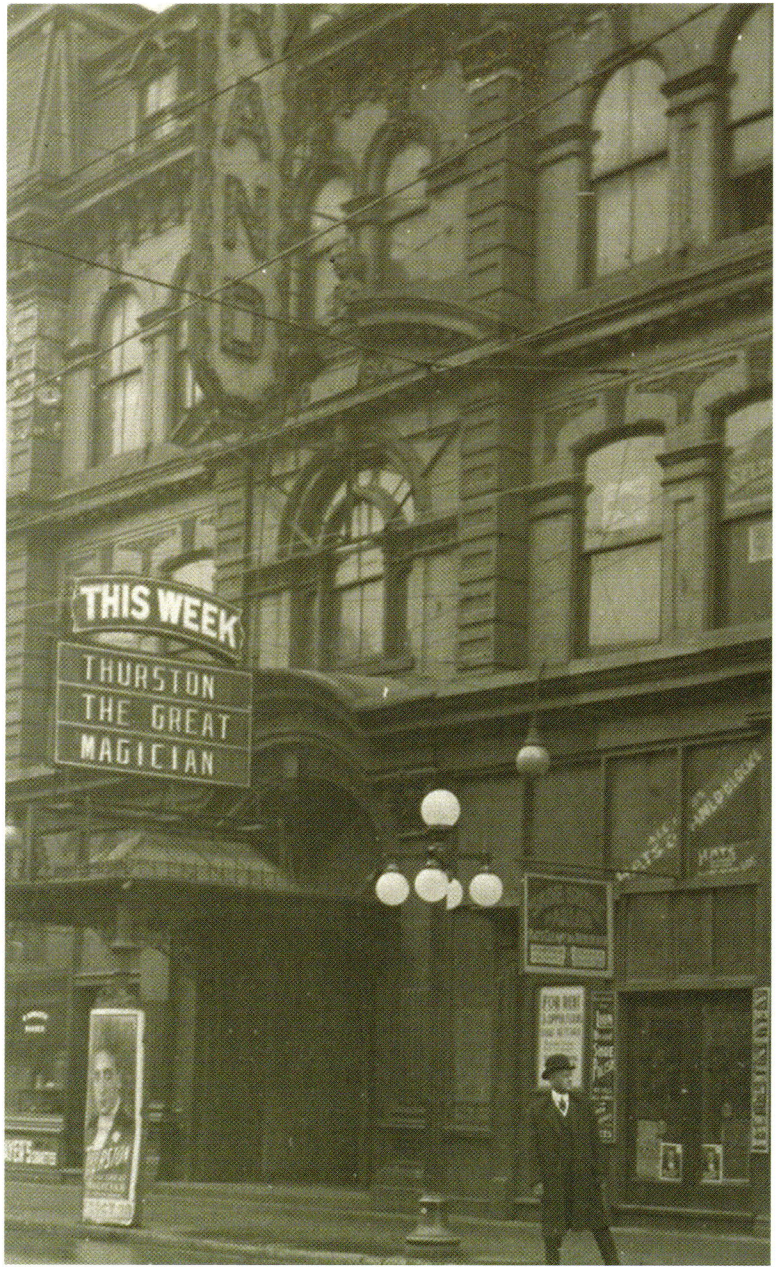

Right: *The Grand Opera House, Adelaide Street West, 1922. A bust of Shakespeare stares out from the frontispiece of the building. Opened in 1874, the Grand flourished until the early part of the 20th century. It was torn down in 1927.* Far right: *The Whitney Block, Queen's Park and Wellesley, 1928. This Ontario government building still stands. It is named after James P. Whitney, elected premier of Ontario in 1905.*

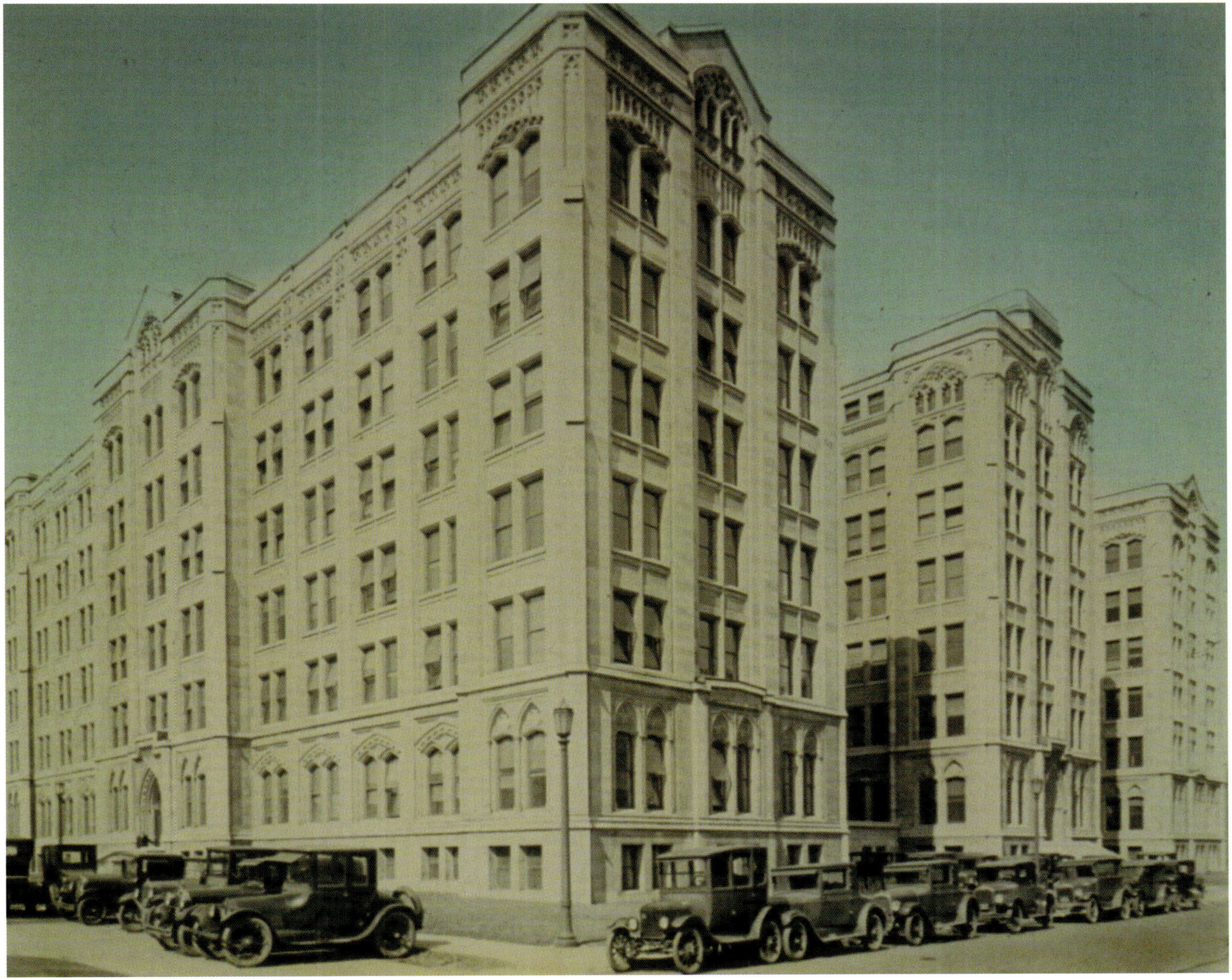

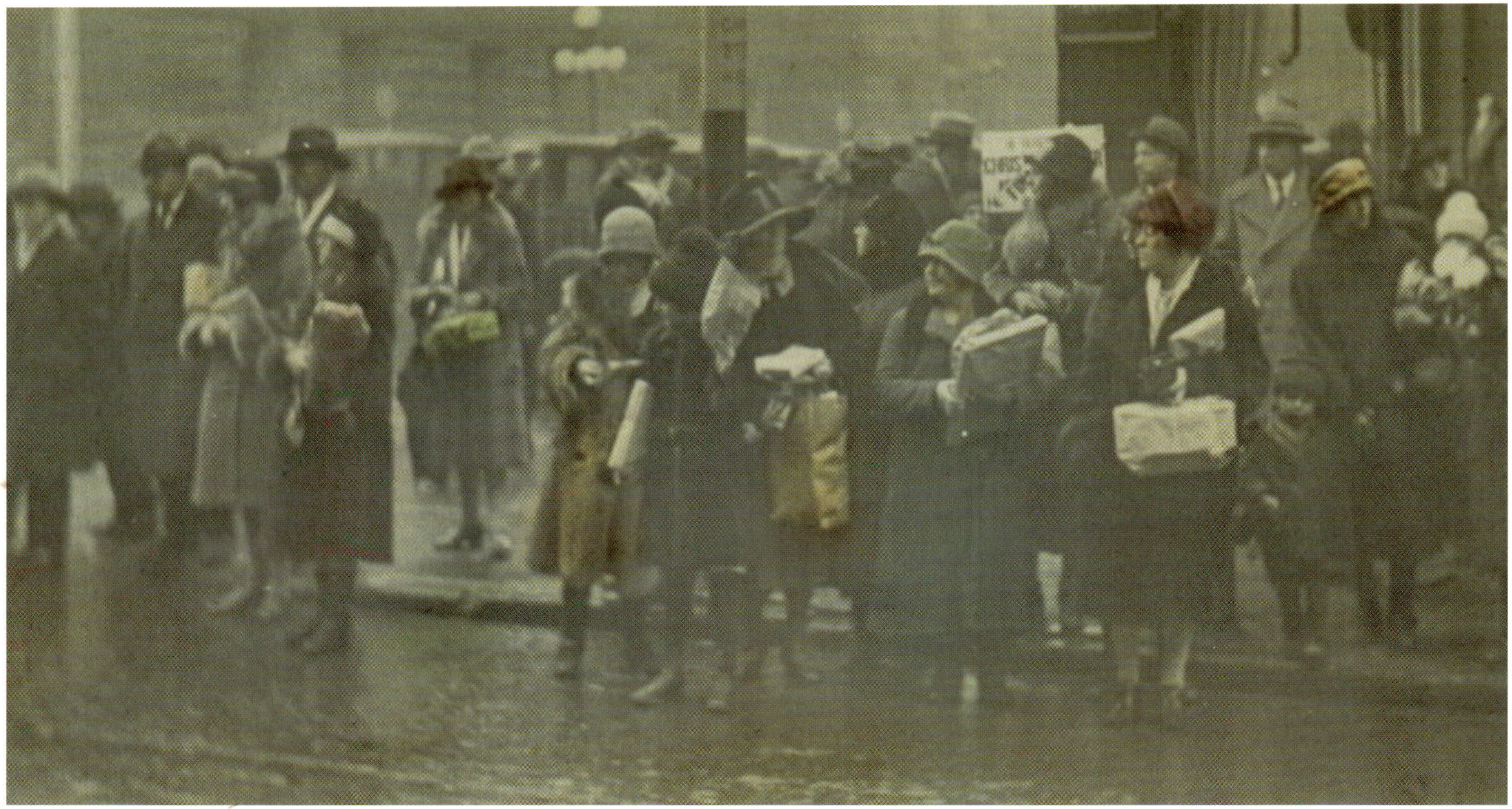

Above: *Christmas Eve, 1927. These shoppers are heading home, most likely from either Simpson's or Eaton's.* Right: *Laying track on Yonge Street, 1921. This was the year the Toronto Transporation Commission (TTC) took over from the Toronto Railway Company (TRC). Spending over $50 million on new rails in the first two years of its existence, the TTC presided over 230 miles of track by 1923.* Far right: *Workers demolishing a building, circa 1910. The exposed cast iron pillars were common in the façades and frames of Toronto buildings from the 1850s on. As several downtown conflagrations made all too plain, however, cast iron pillars also disintegrate in fire. The cross girders shown here date the building to the turn of the 20th century.*

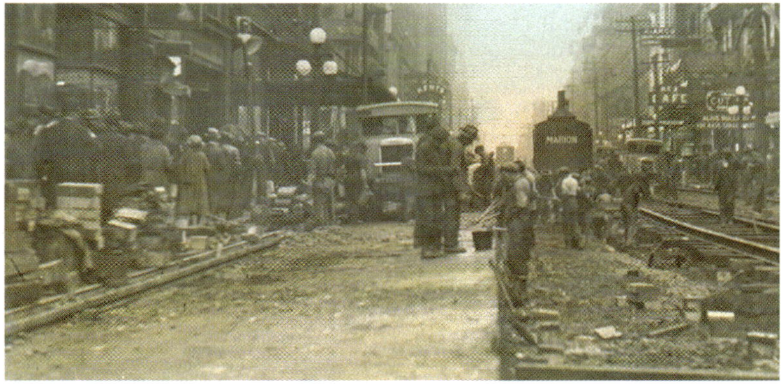

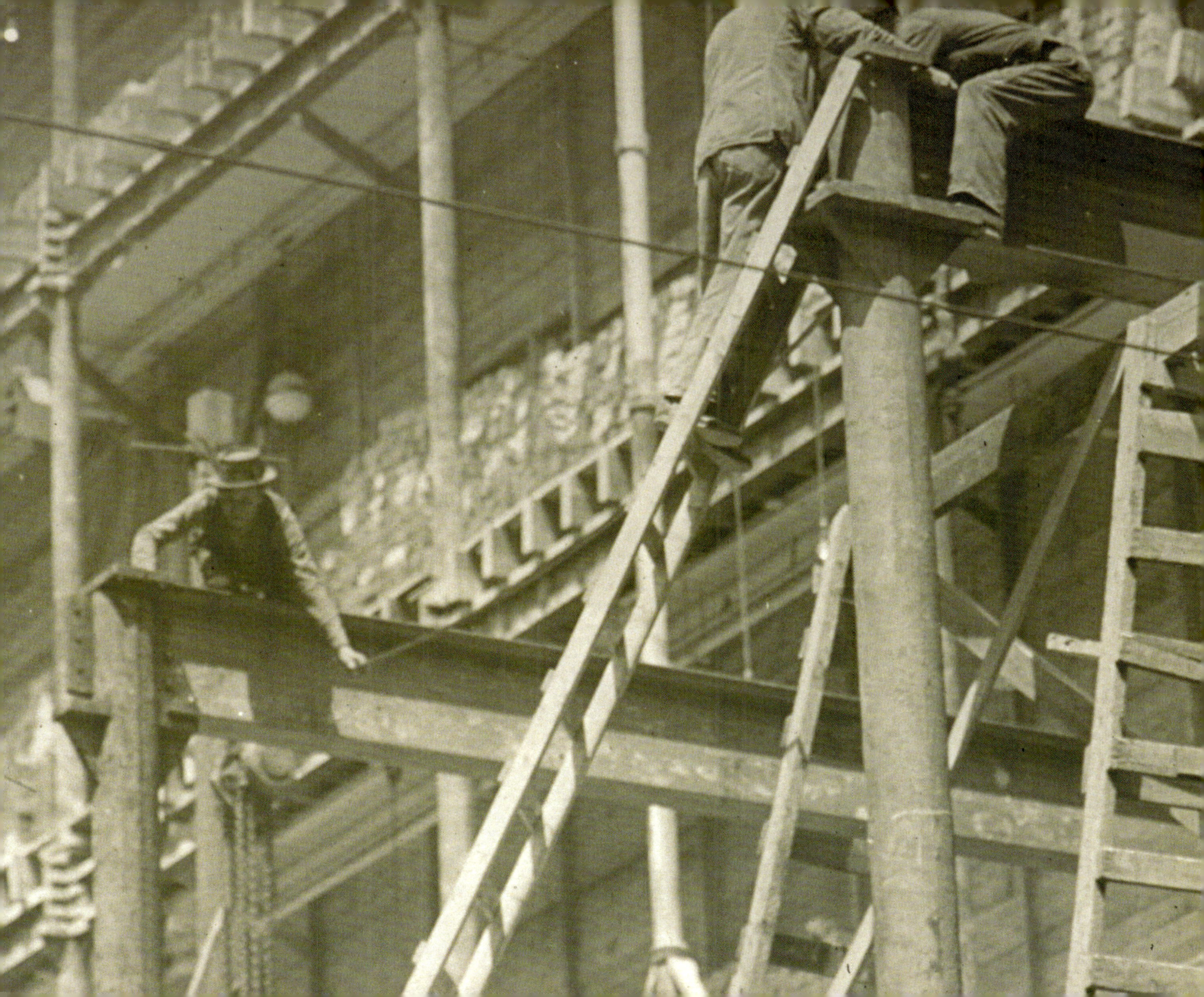

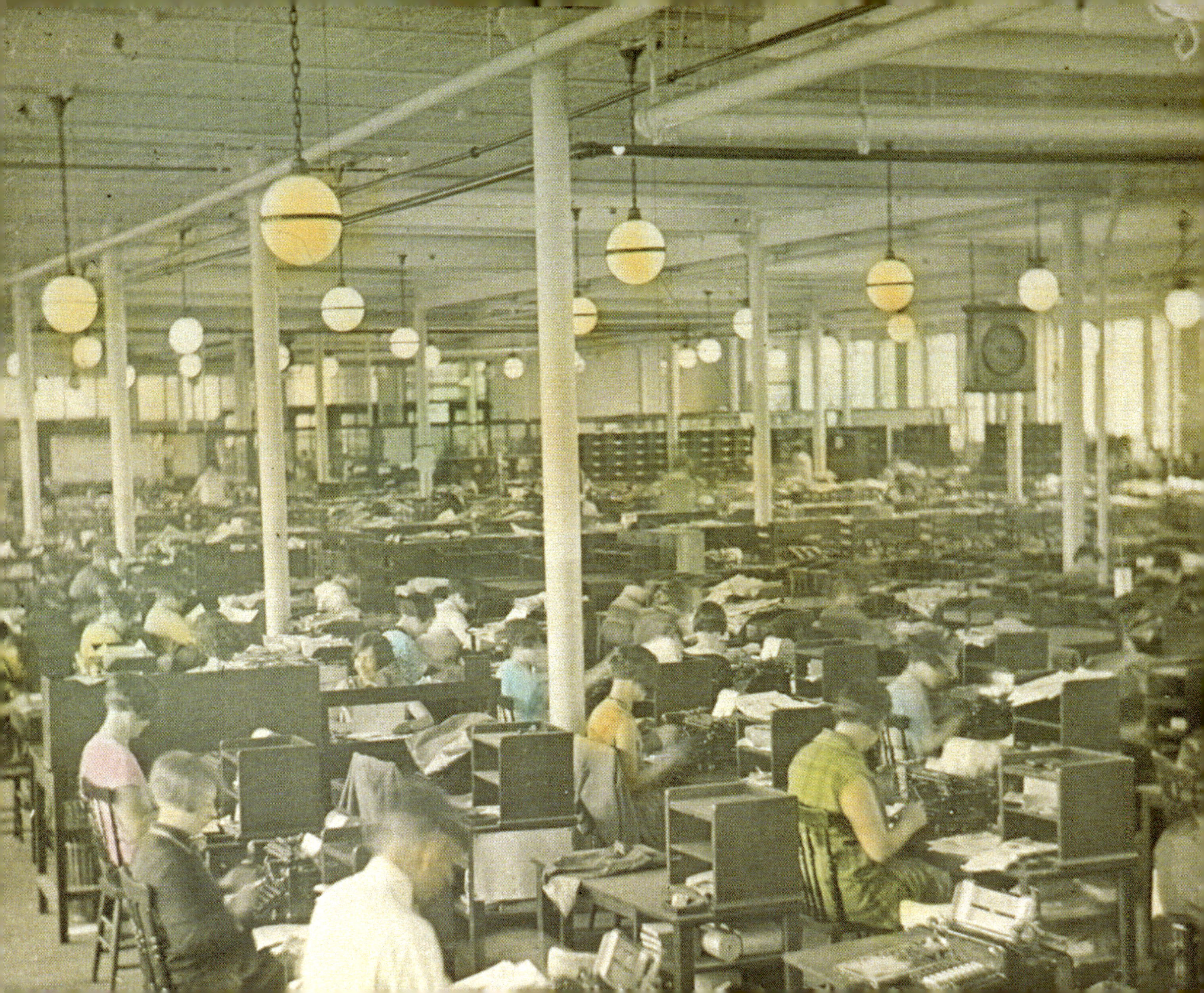

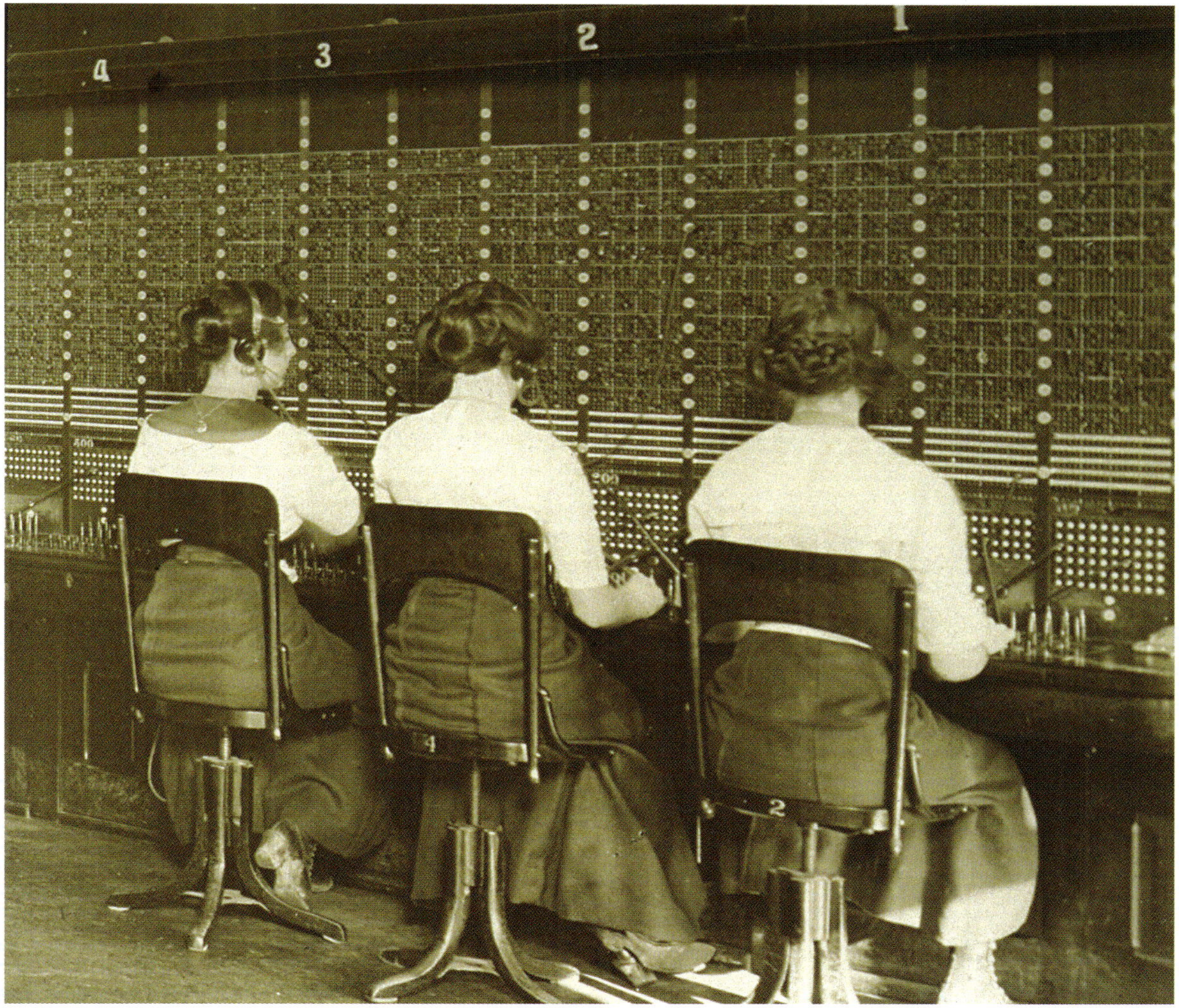

Left: *Clerks at Eaton's, 1927. Timothy Eaton opened his first store on Yonge Street in 1869; by the 1920s, Eaton's had anchored the main Toronto shopping district at Yonge and Queen, where its factories and mail order departments (like this one) also thrived.*
Right: *Switchboard operators, circa 1915.*

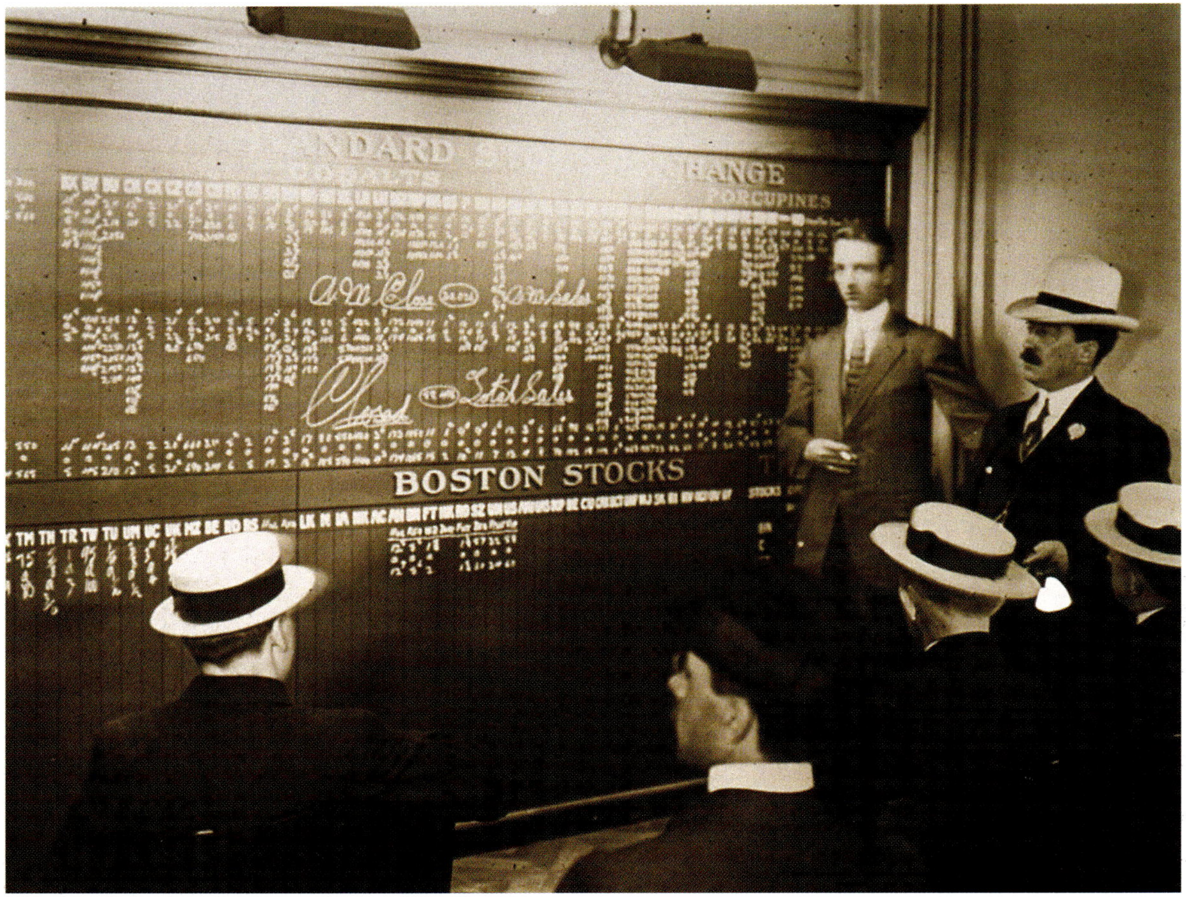

Left: *The Standard Stock Exchange at Scott and Wellington Streets, 1910. Stockbrokering began in Toronto in the 1870s. The Standard Stock Exchange opened in the 1890s.*
Far right: *Assembly line workers, circa 1910. By this time, the manufacturing industry had become Toronto's primary employer: 65,000 Torontonians (approximately twenty per cent of the total population) worked in factories.*

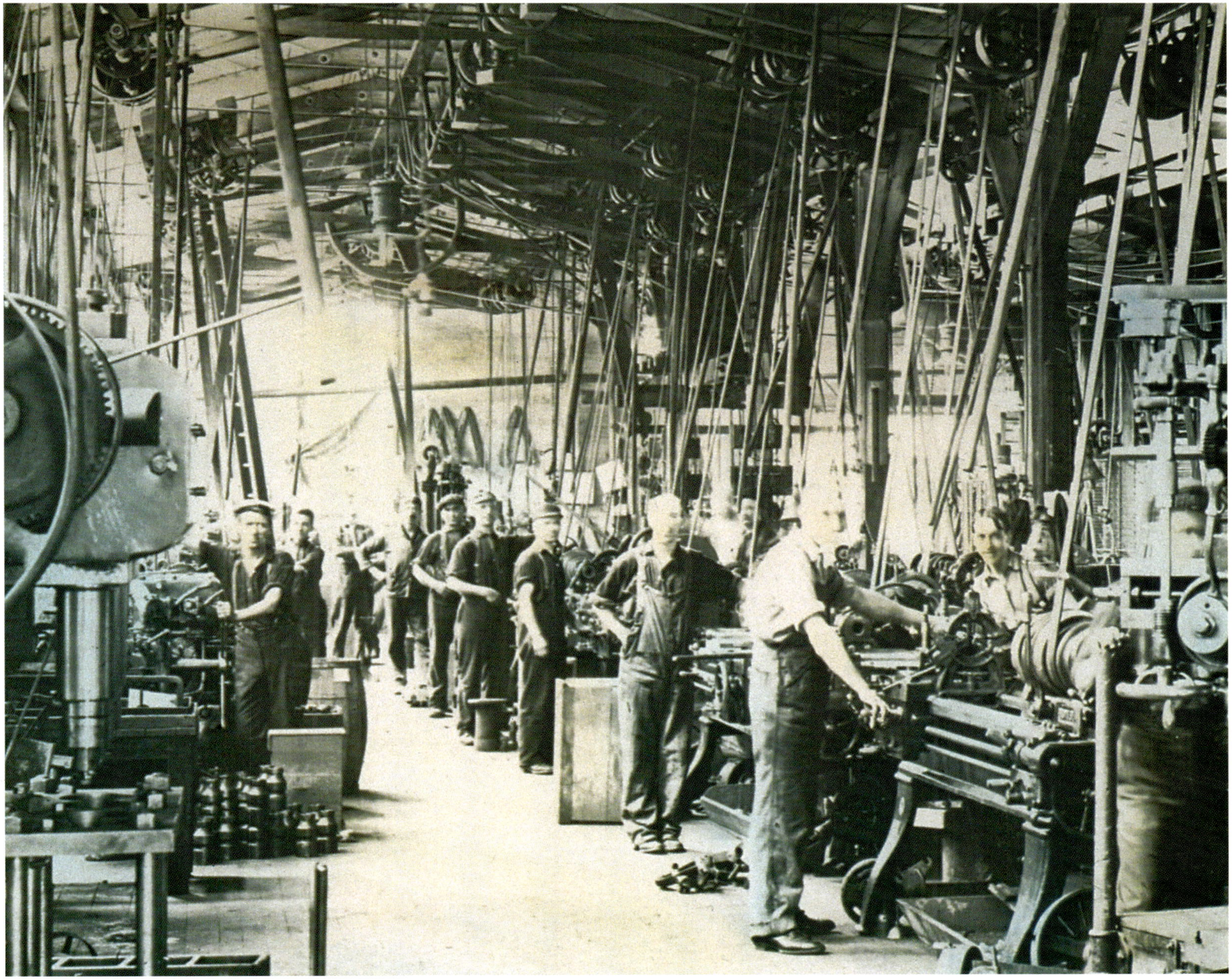

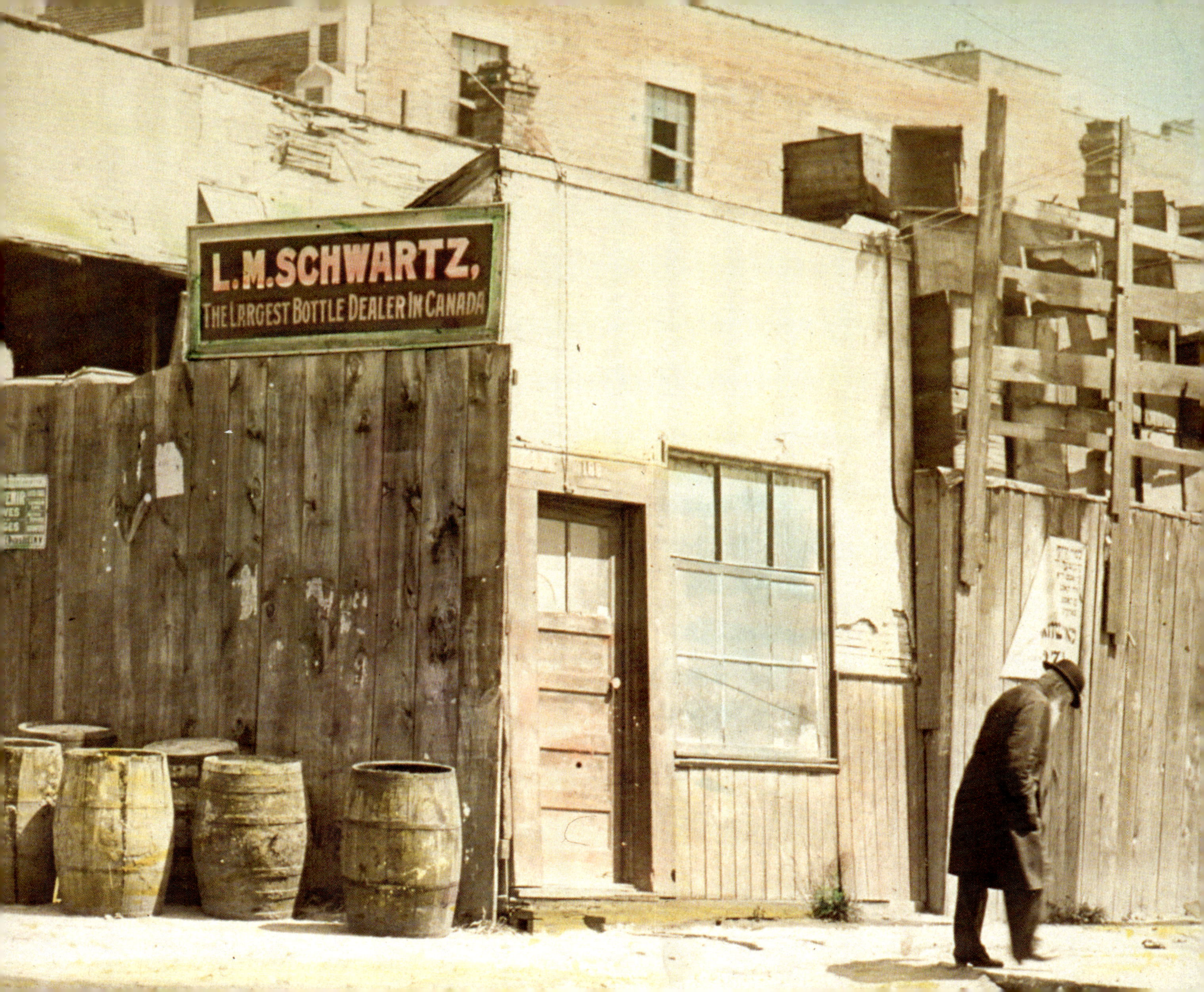
L.M.SCHWARTZ,
THE LARGEST BOTTLE DEALER IN CANADA

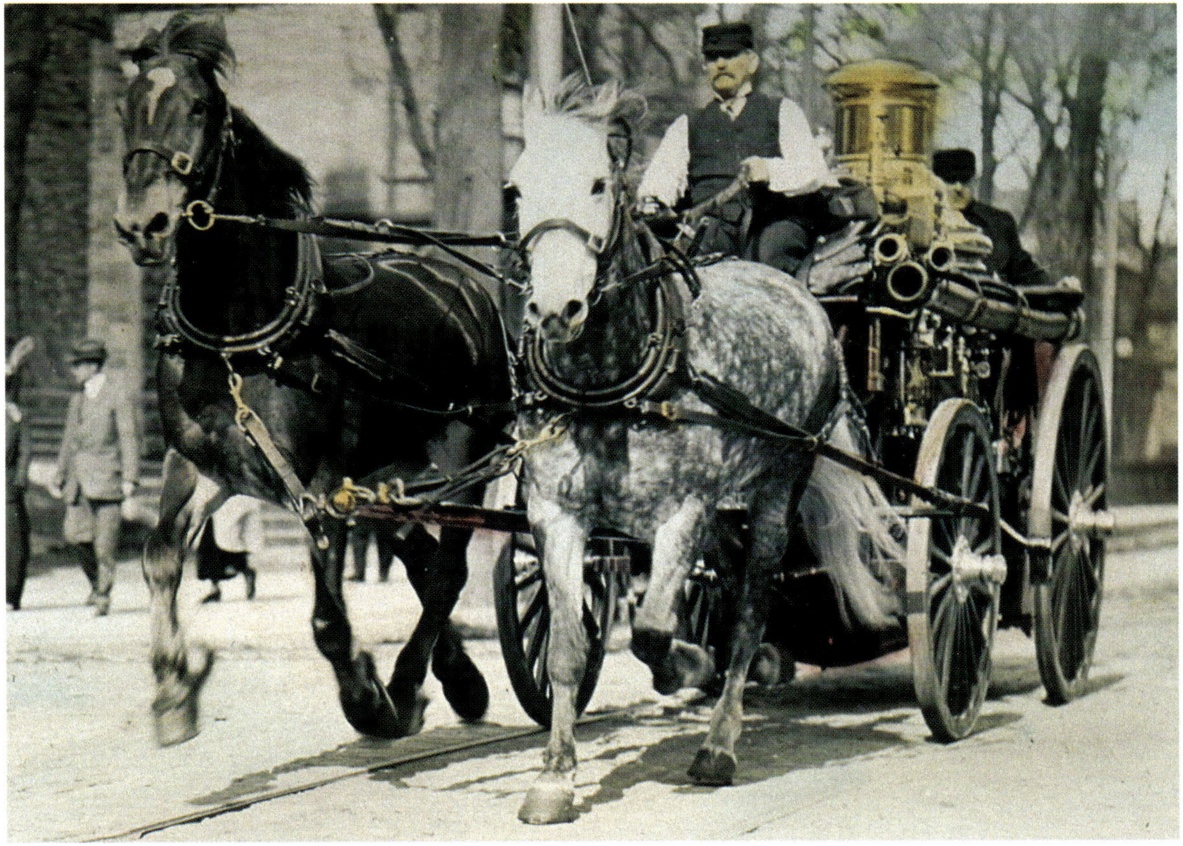

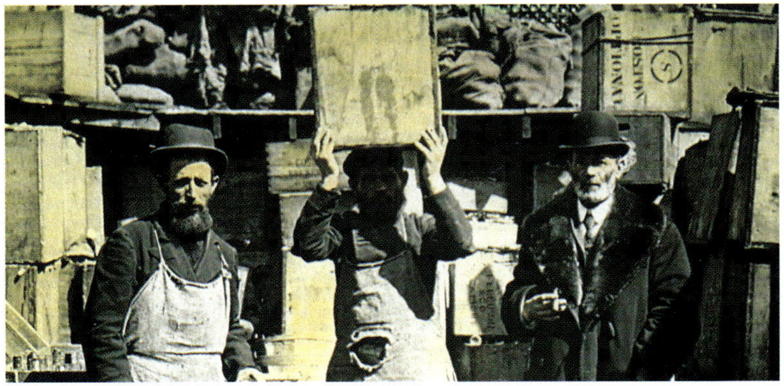

Left: *L.M. Schwartz's bottle dealership at Dundas and University (the Ward), 1907. Note the Hebraic script on the poster at right. Small industries like this laid the foundation for the shift of much of the Toronto Jewish community west to Spadina Avenue after 1911.* Above: *A horsedrawn steamer (fire engine) on Bloor Street, 1912. The Toronto Fire Department put its first motorized truck into service in 1911, but horsedrawn engines would not disappear until the 1930s.* Right: *Inside a bottling works, circa 1910.*

Right: *St. James' Anglican Cathedral, King Street East, 1927. The former religious bastion of the Family Compact has the tallest spire in Canada (just over 93 metres), but was overshadowed in the twenties by the eighteen-storey addition to the King Edward Hotel. This image was taken from its roof.*
Far right: *The provincial Normal School (or Teachers' College), north of Gerrard Street, 1922. Founded by Egerton Ryerson and opened in 1852, the school was the central feature of St. James's Square, an open space bounded by Gould, Victoria, Gerrard, and Church Streets. Today, only a fragment of the façade remains, trapped in the quadrangle of Ryerson University.*

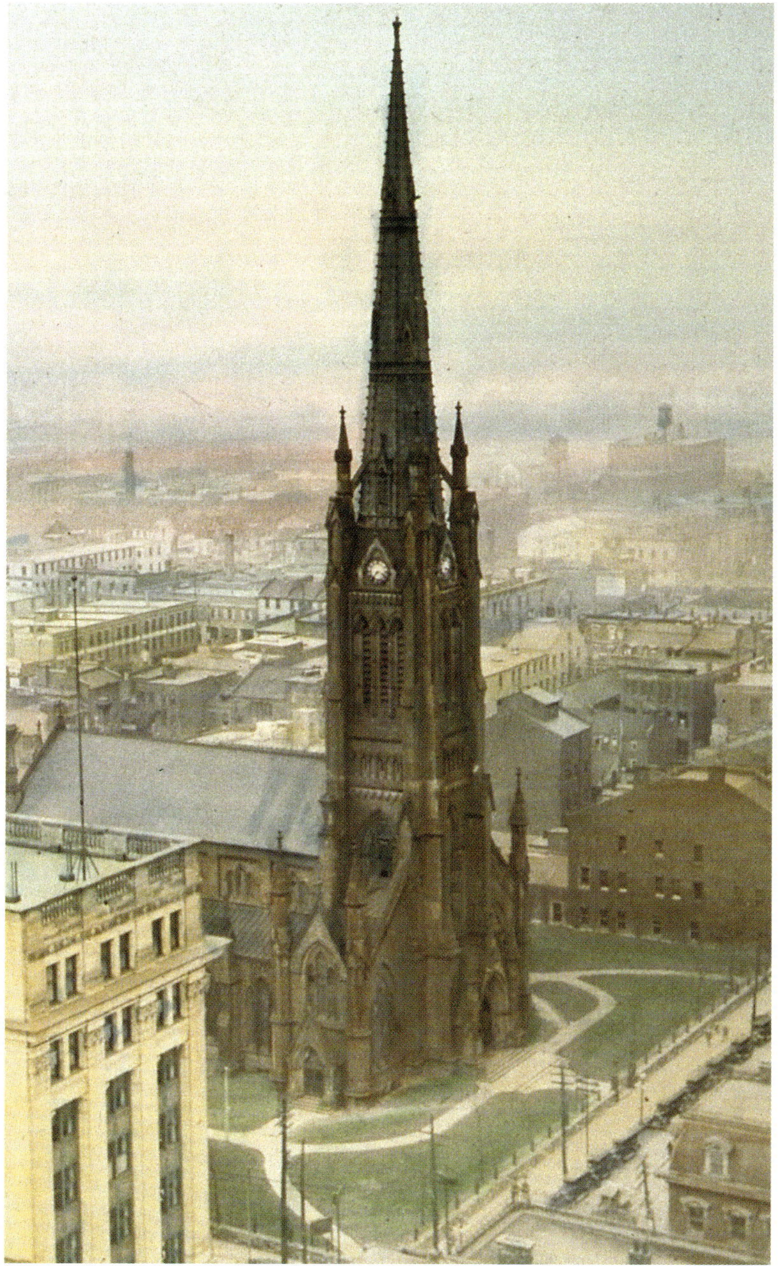

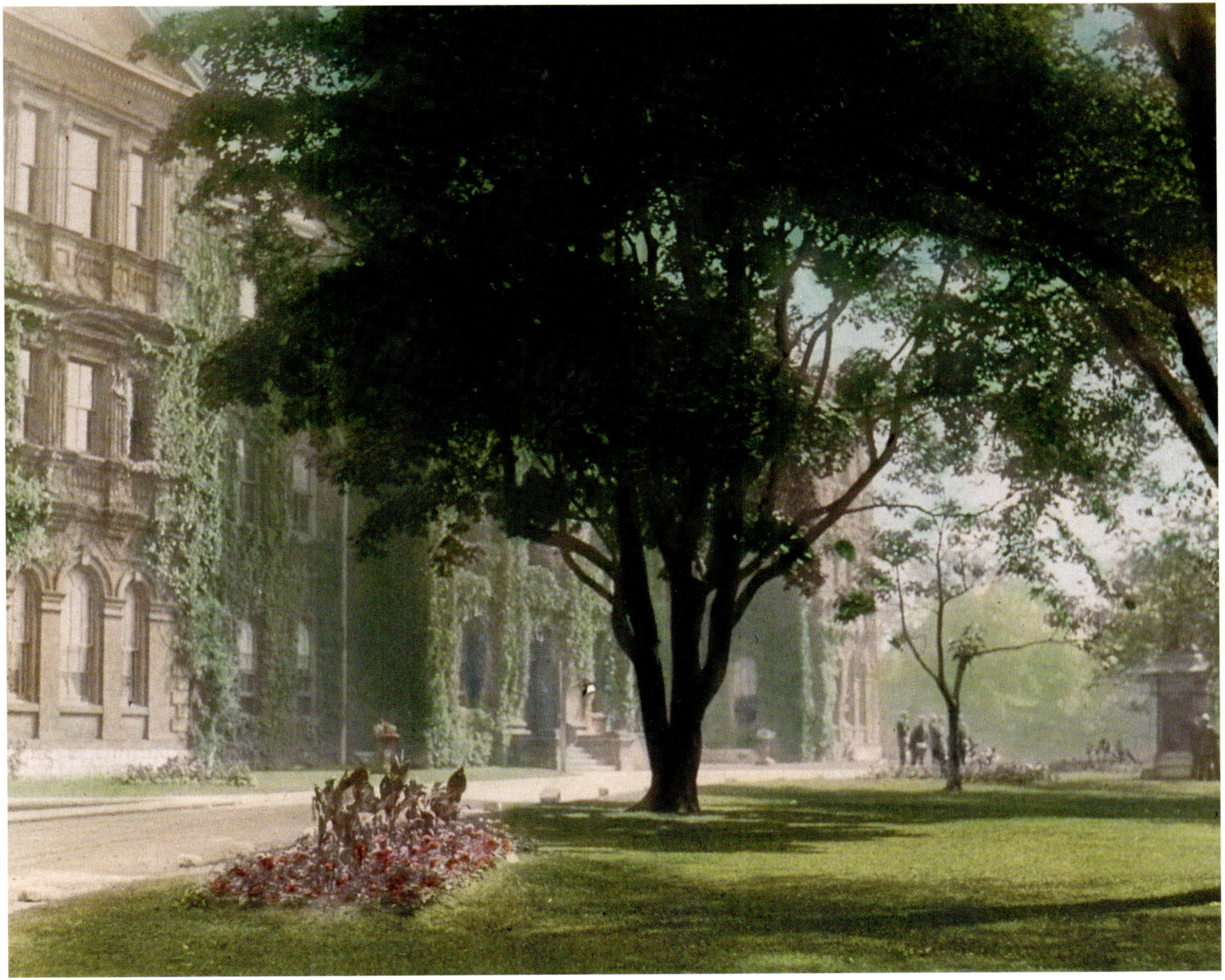

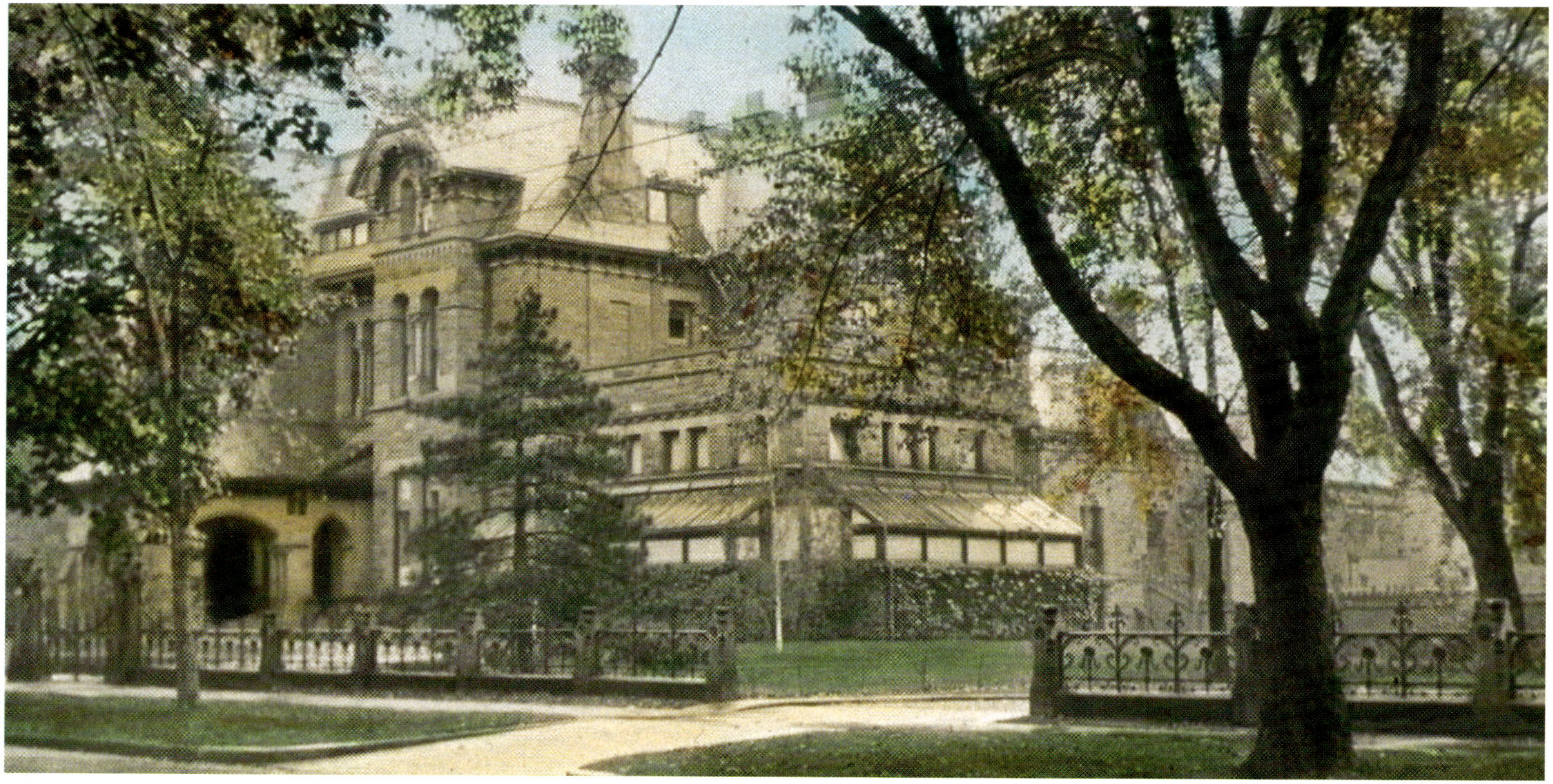

Above: *Barnardo Boys' Home, Jarvis Street, 1922. Dr. Thomas Barnardo sent destitute British children overseas to various homes such as this. He was himself a photographer, taking a picture of every child entrusted to his care.* Right: *Art Gallery of Ontario, Dundas Street West, 1926.* Far right: *Osgoode Hall, Queen Street and University Avenue, circa 1920. The home of the Law Society of Upper Canada was built in three stages in 1829, 1844, and 1857. Its impressive iron gates, shown here, were erected in 1866 and designed by William G. Storm. The grounds remain little changed from James' times.*

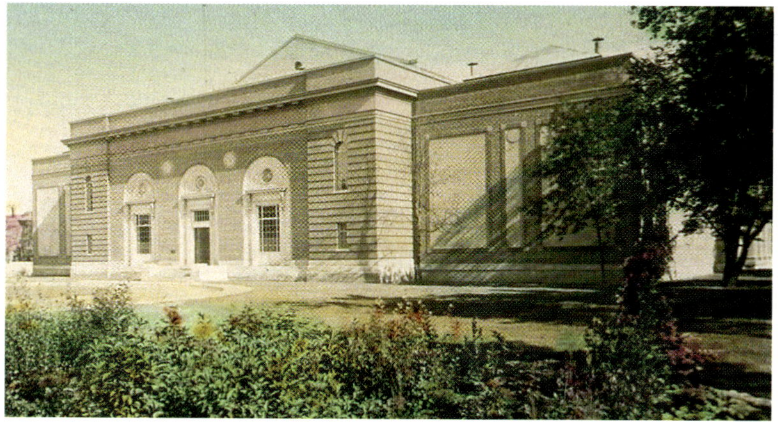

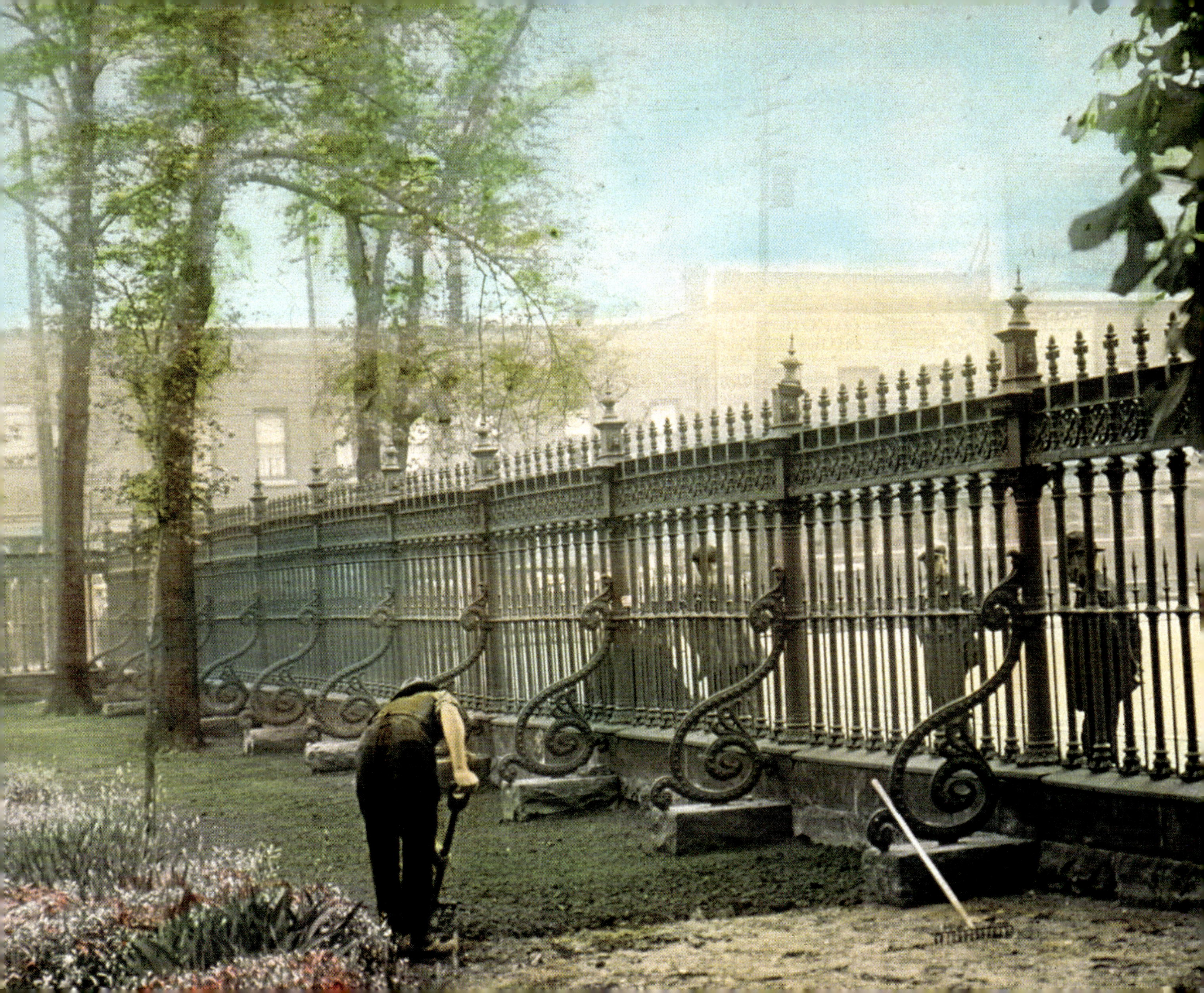

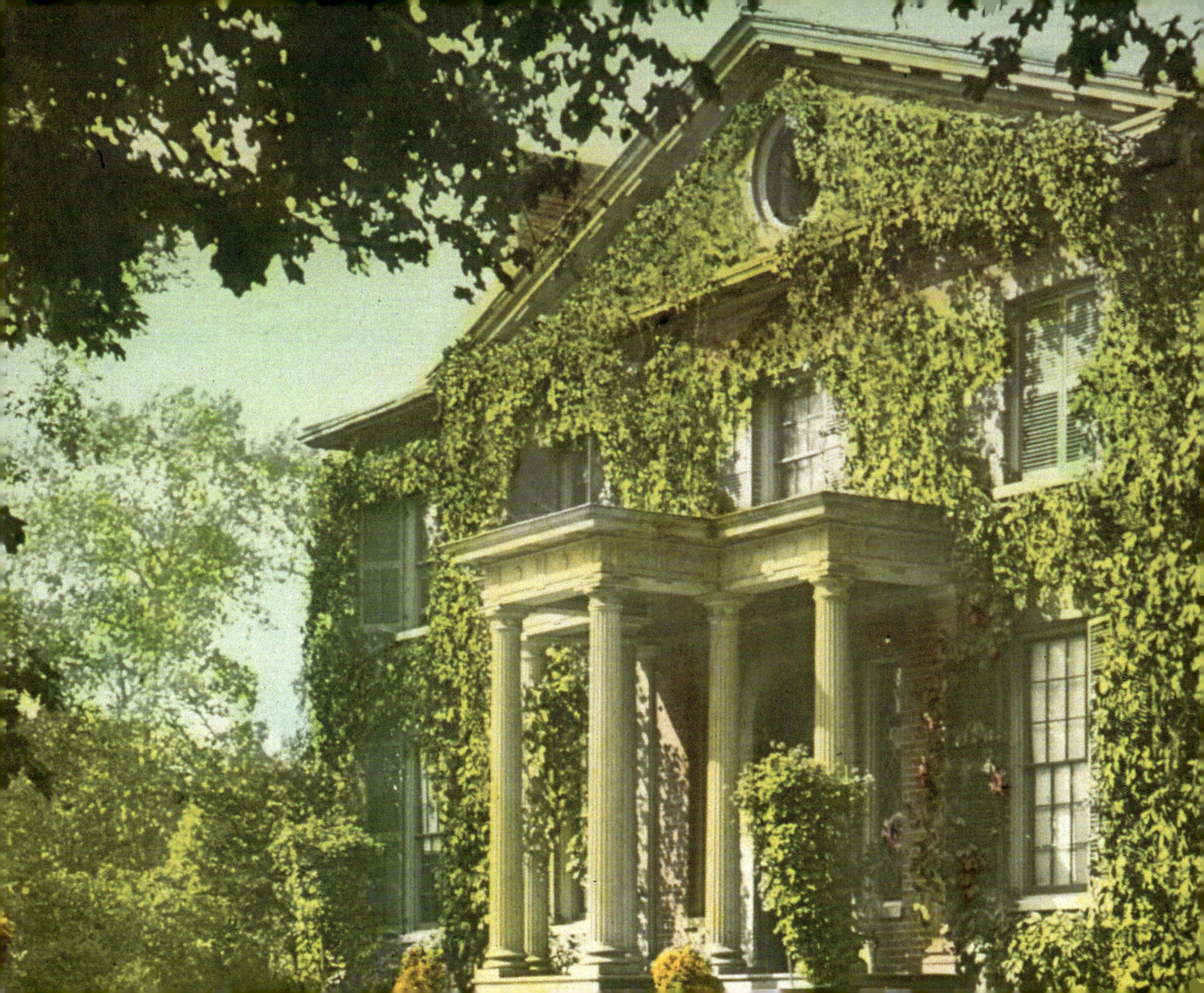

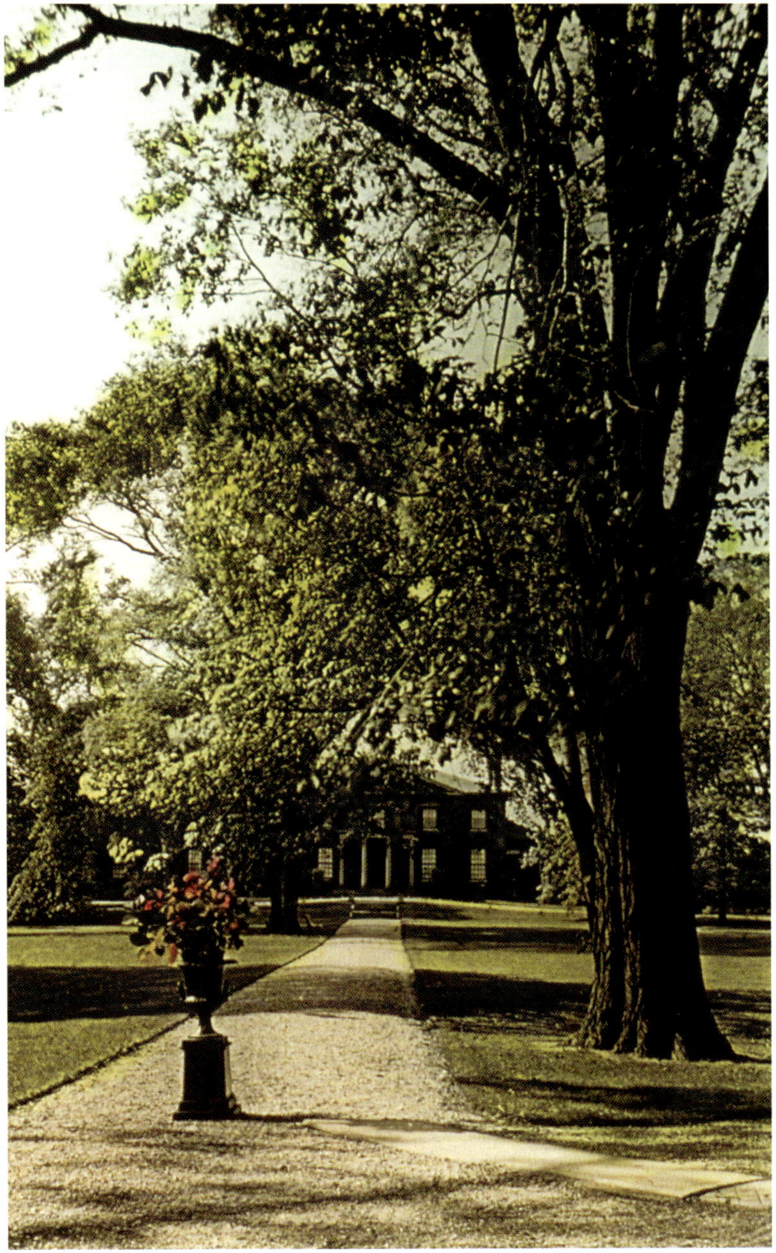

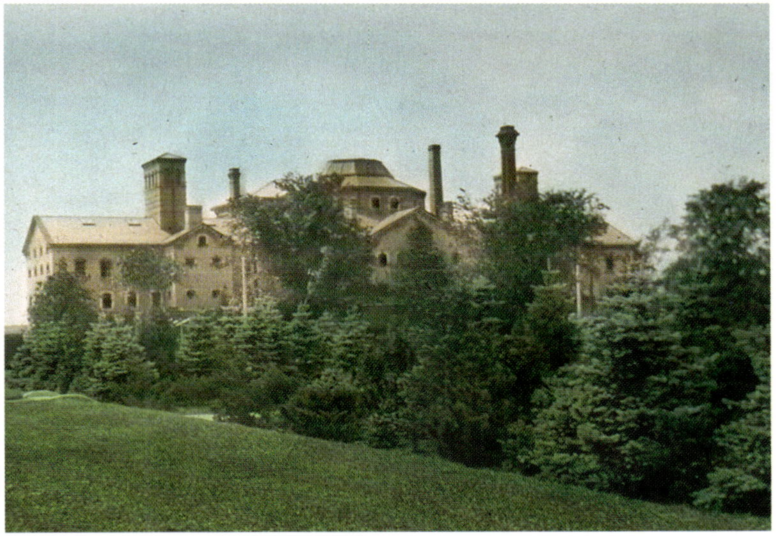

Far left: *The Grange, north of Queen at John, circa 1920. The stone porch was added by Dr. Goldwin Smith, who was resident until his death in 1910. Smith was an ardent, active social reformer and supporter of the University of Toronto. He willed the house to the Art Museum of Toronto, and it now forms part of the Art Gallery of Ontario.* Left: *Approach to the Grange, 1909. Built for the Boulton family in 1817, the Grange epitomized the landed gentry aspirations of the Toronto's early ruling elite.* Above: *Toronto Jail at the Don, 1922. The Don Jail, however dour it may seem to us, was a progressive model for its time (1858). Its palatial aspect is well brought out by this view of its north face.*

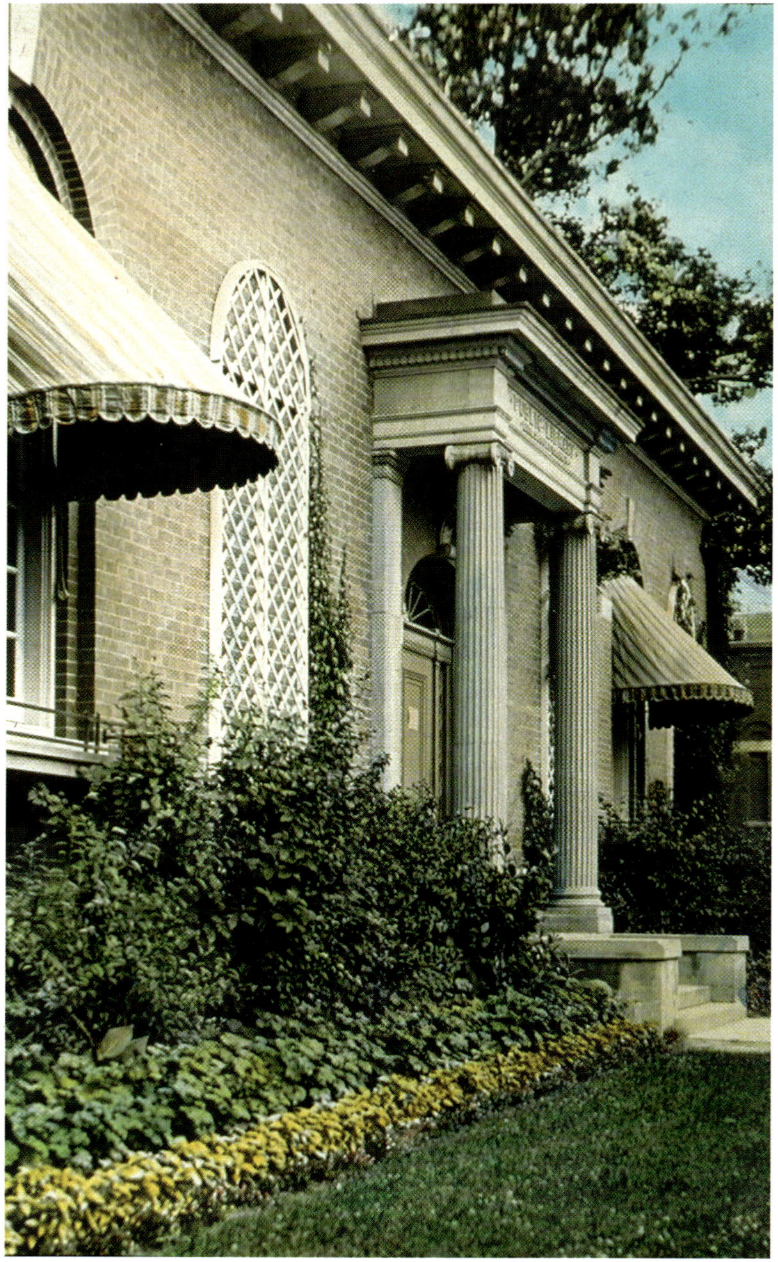

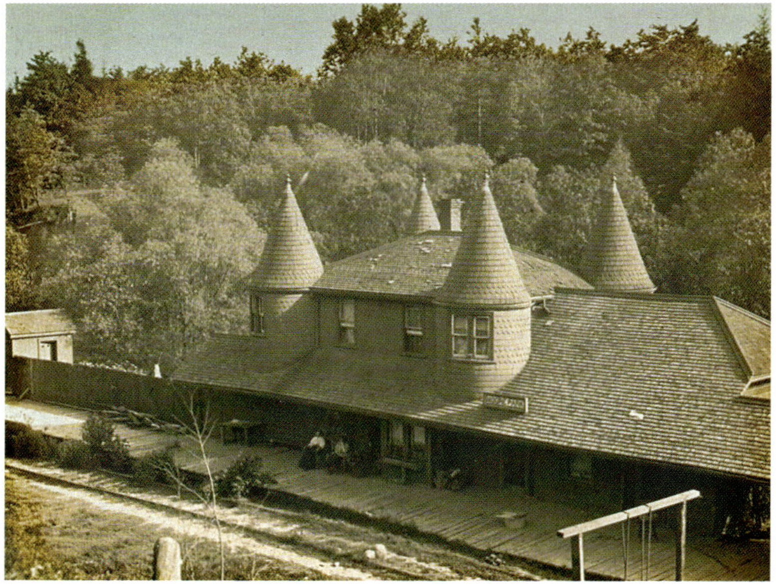

Left: *Dufferin Street Library, 1926. This branch was built as a Carnegie library in 1921, replacing temporary quarters in Earlescourt Methodist Church.* Above: *Moore Park Station, south of Moore Avenue, 1909. Moore Park was built along the Belt Line, which provided early commuter service for Toronto's new suburbs to the north and west in the early 1890s. By 1894, however, economic depression and the Toronto Street Railway had driven the line out of business.* Right: *University Avenue, 1927. This view looks south from Queen's Park and the legislative buildings.*

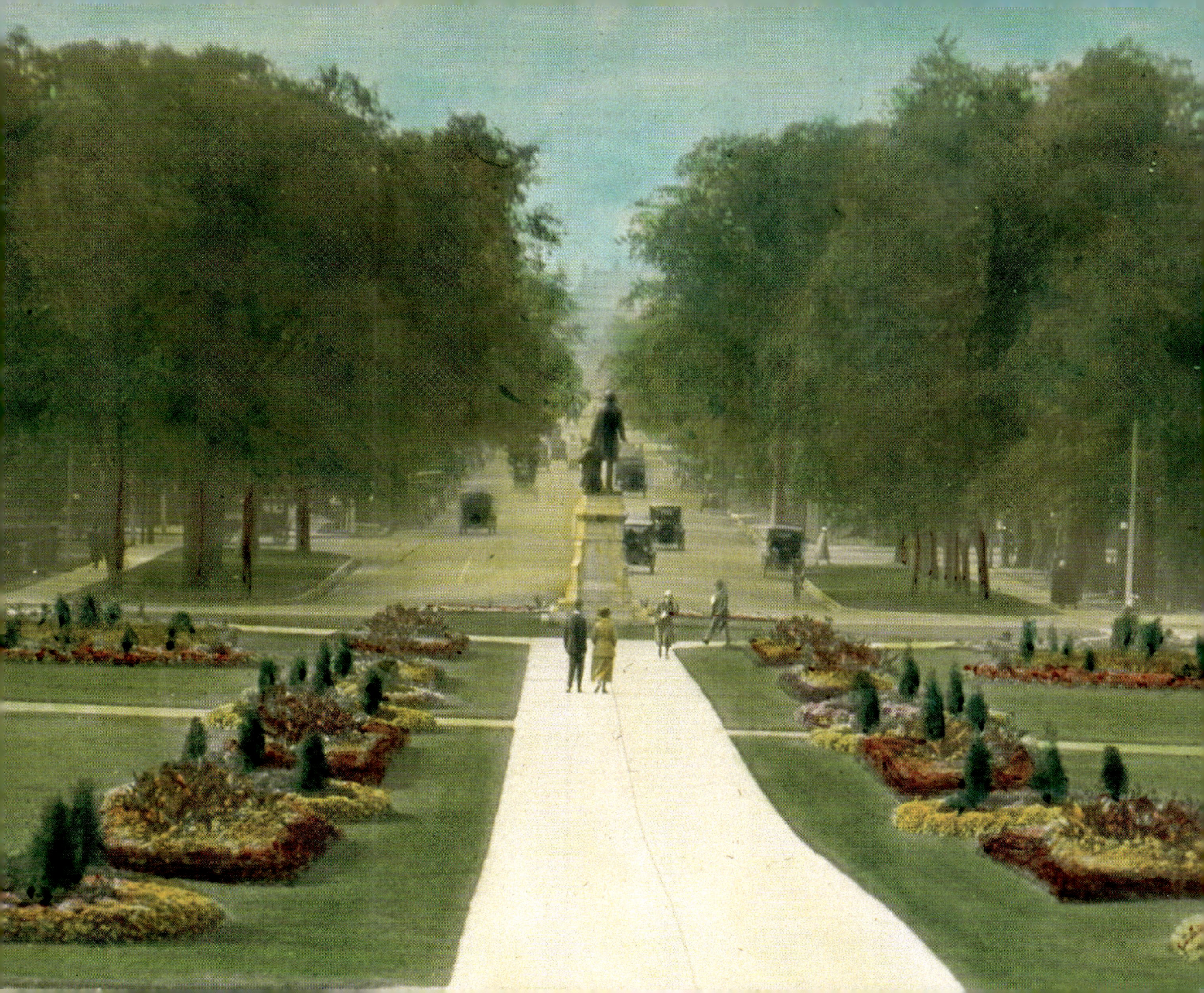

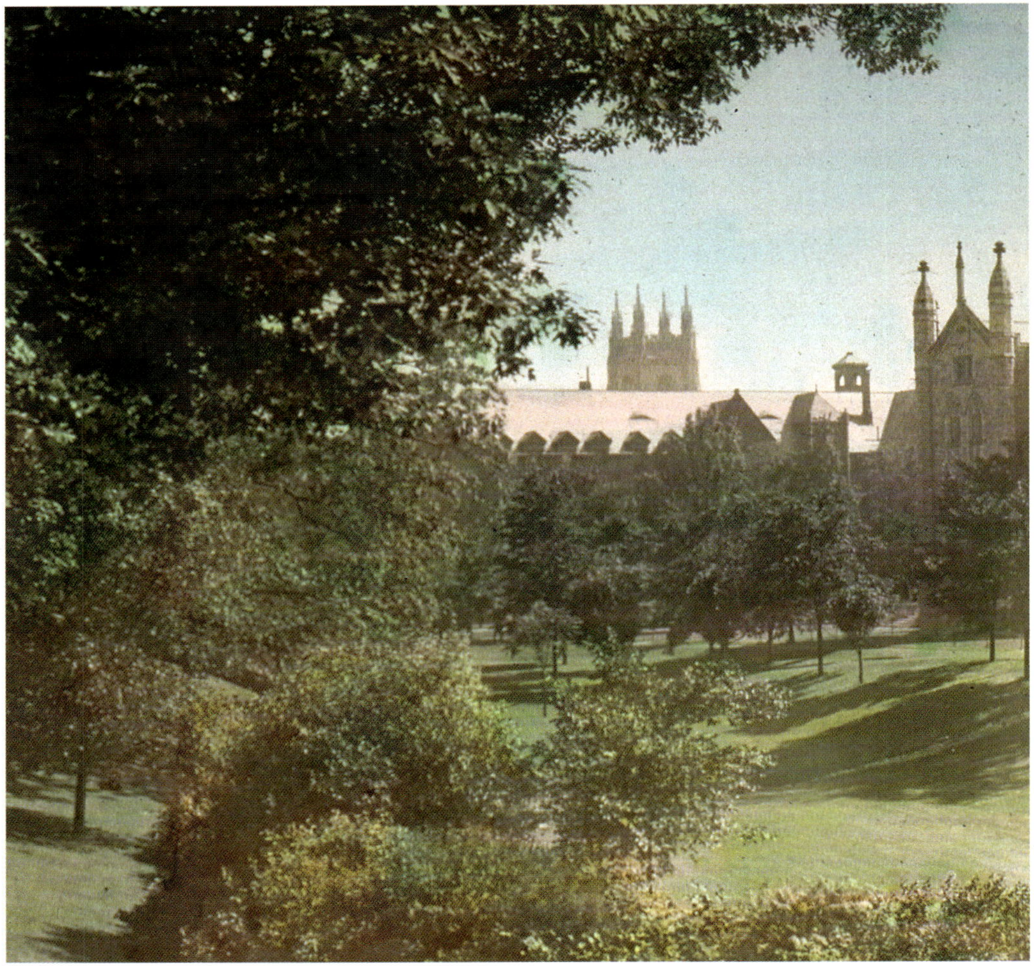

Left: *Philosopher's Walk, circa 1925. Trinity College (1925) and the Soldiers' Memorial Tower (1924) are in the distance.* Far right: *Victoria College Home for Women, now Falconer's Hall, part of the Faculty of Law.*

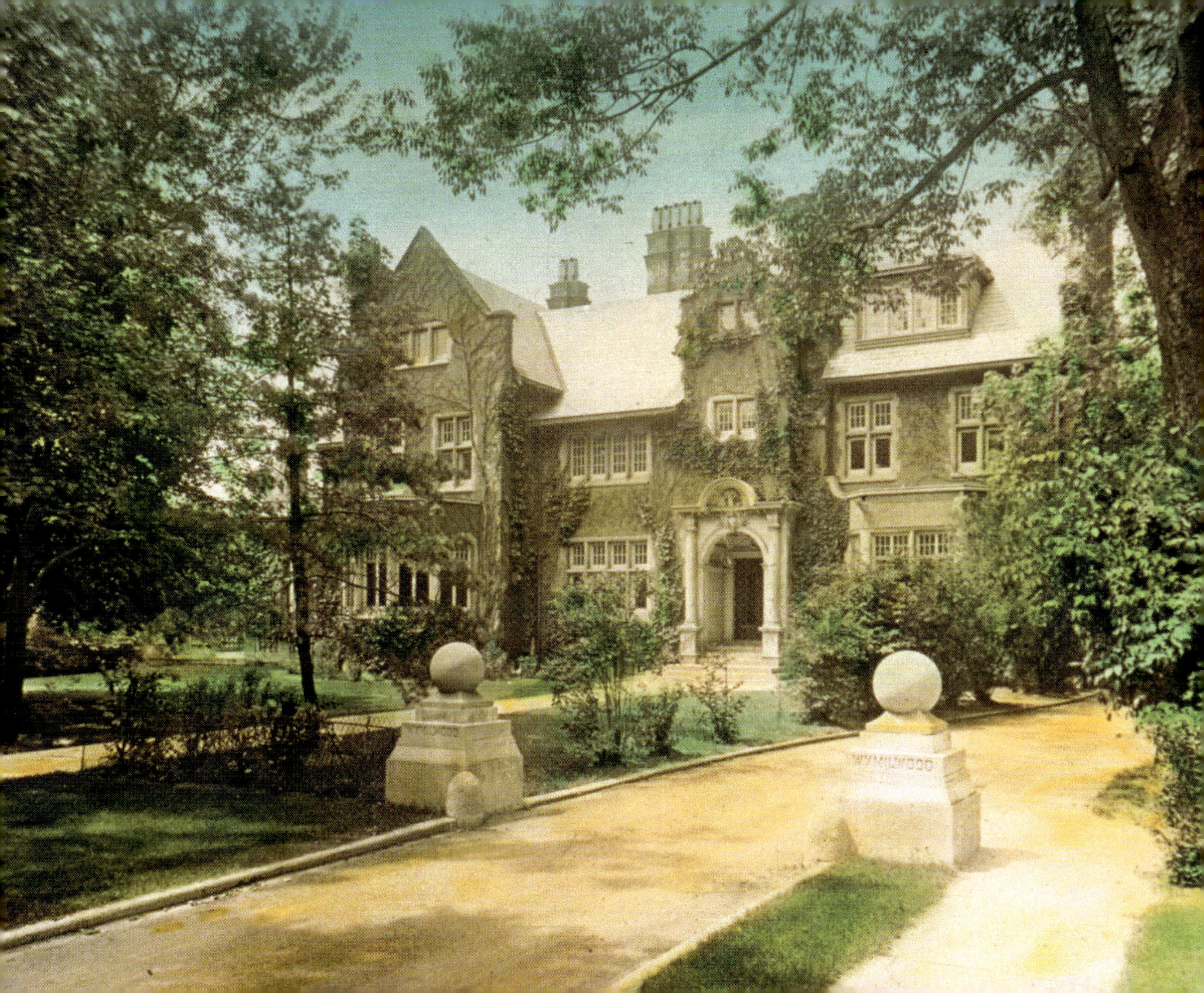

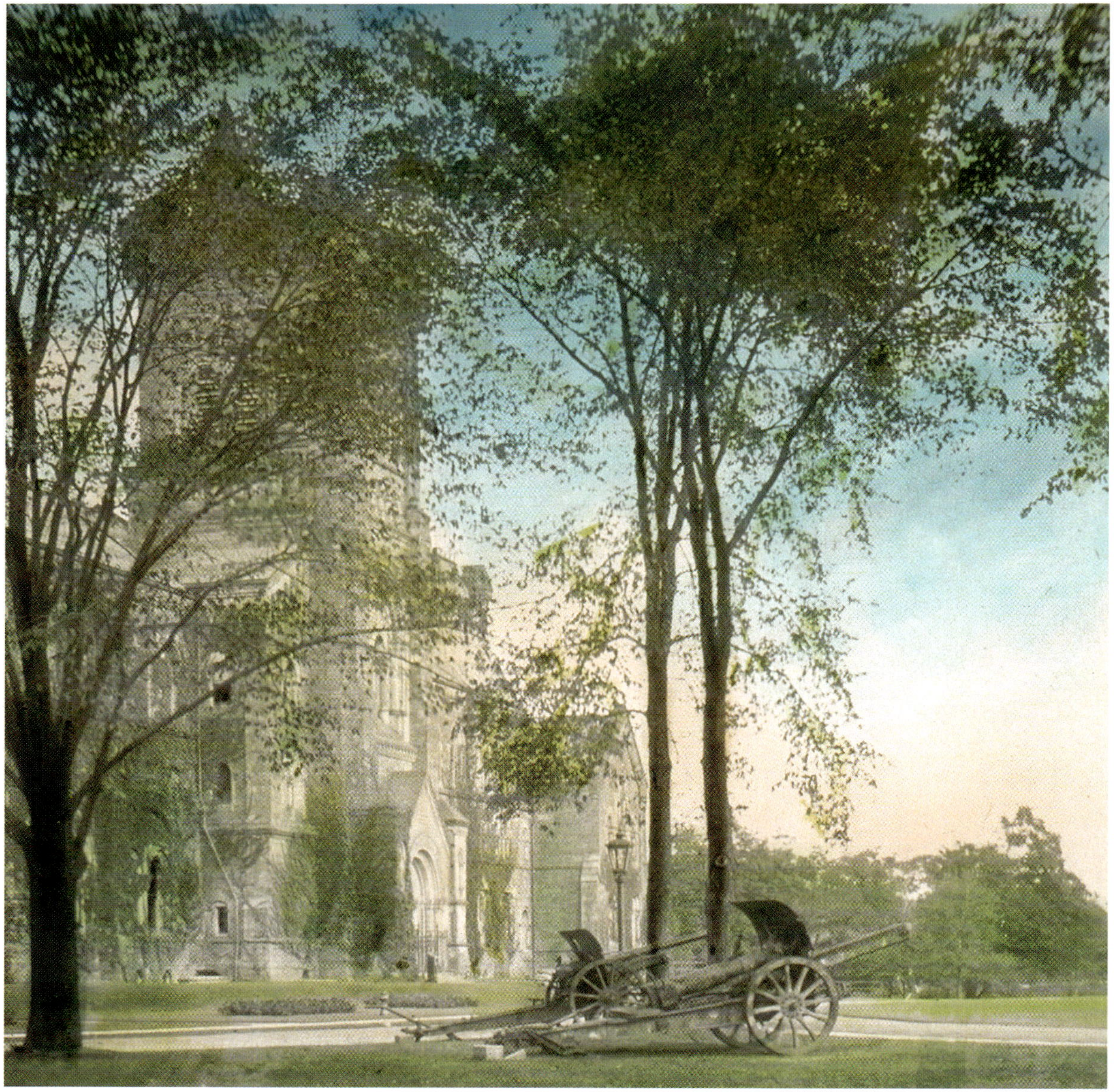

Left: *University College, circa 1920. During the first World War, the university grounds became an armed camp for officer training. The two field guns in the foreground are mementos.*

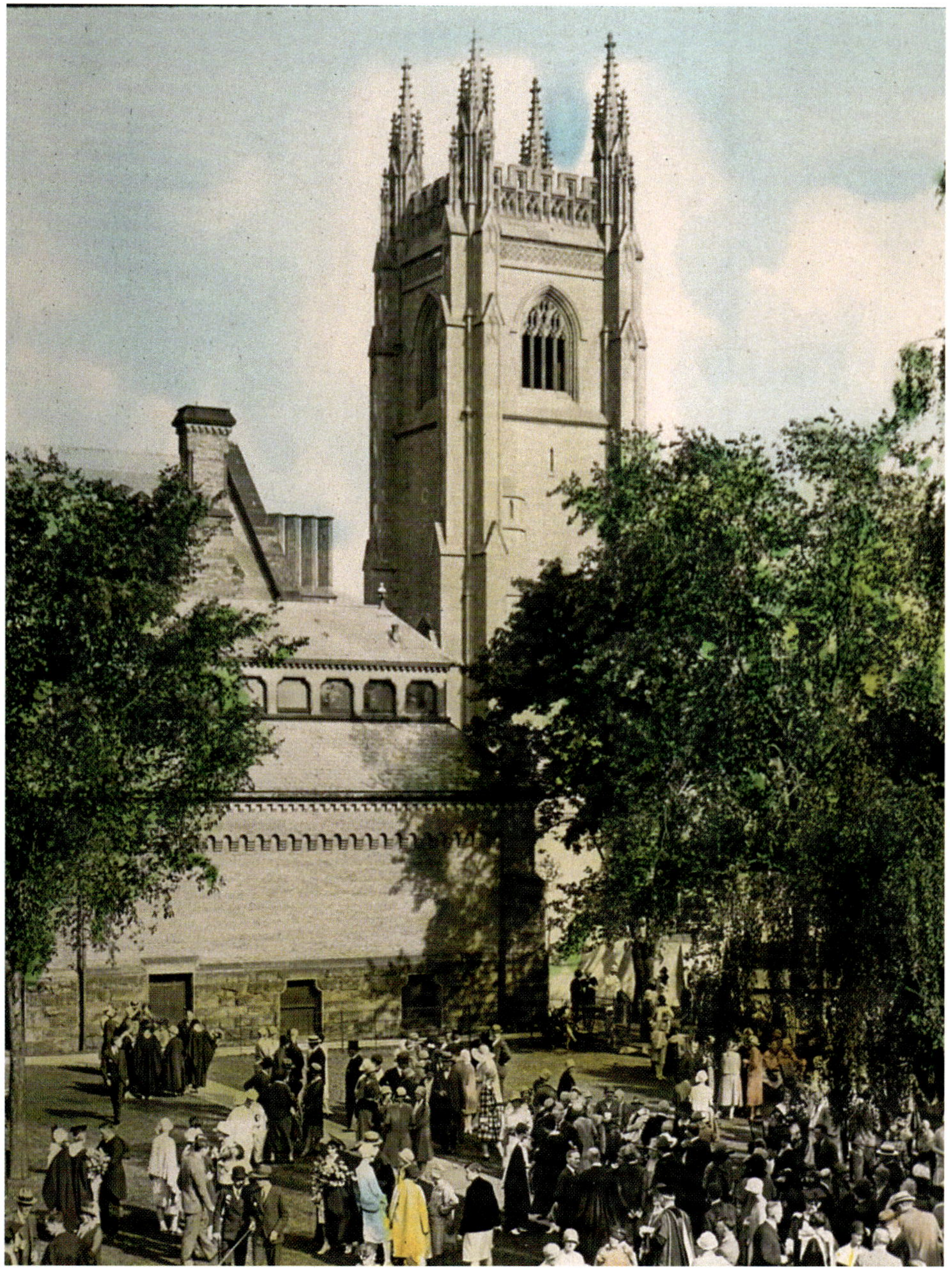

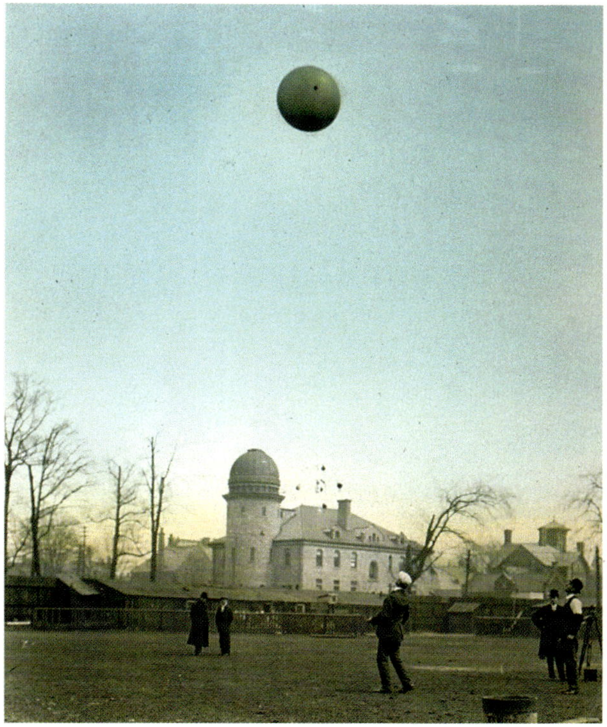

Left: *Hart House, 1927. Another gift to the university from the Masseys, Hart House contained recreational facilities, a theatre, billiards and a library. It also featured a shooting gallery, much used during the first World War. The newly completed Soldiers' Memorial Tower (1924) rises behind the gathering in this image.* Above: *Meteorological balloon, Varsity Stadium, 1908. The first balloon for weather studies is launched in view of the meteorology building.*

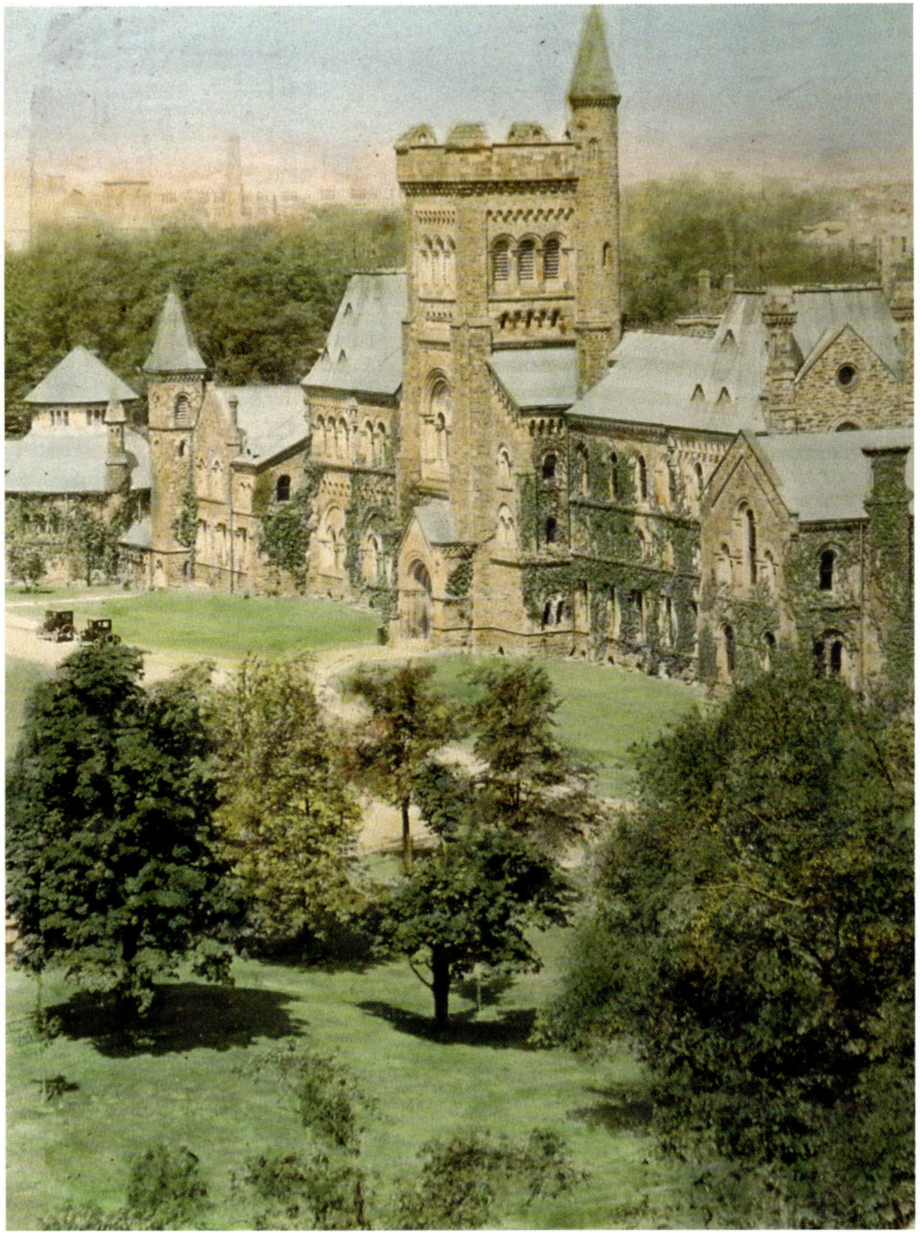

Left: *University College, 1926. Patricia McHugh calls this building "one of the most exciting, inventive structures ever created in Canada" for its wide variety of formal influences.*
Far right: *Bloor Street and Avenue Road, circa 1915. Lillian Massey Treble donated this Neo-Classical Revival building, constructed between 1908 and 1912, to educate women in domestic science, as well as to provide fitness facilities for women much as Hart House did for men. This magnificent structure now houses a clothing store.*

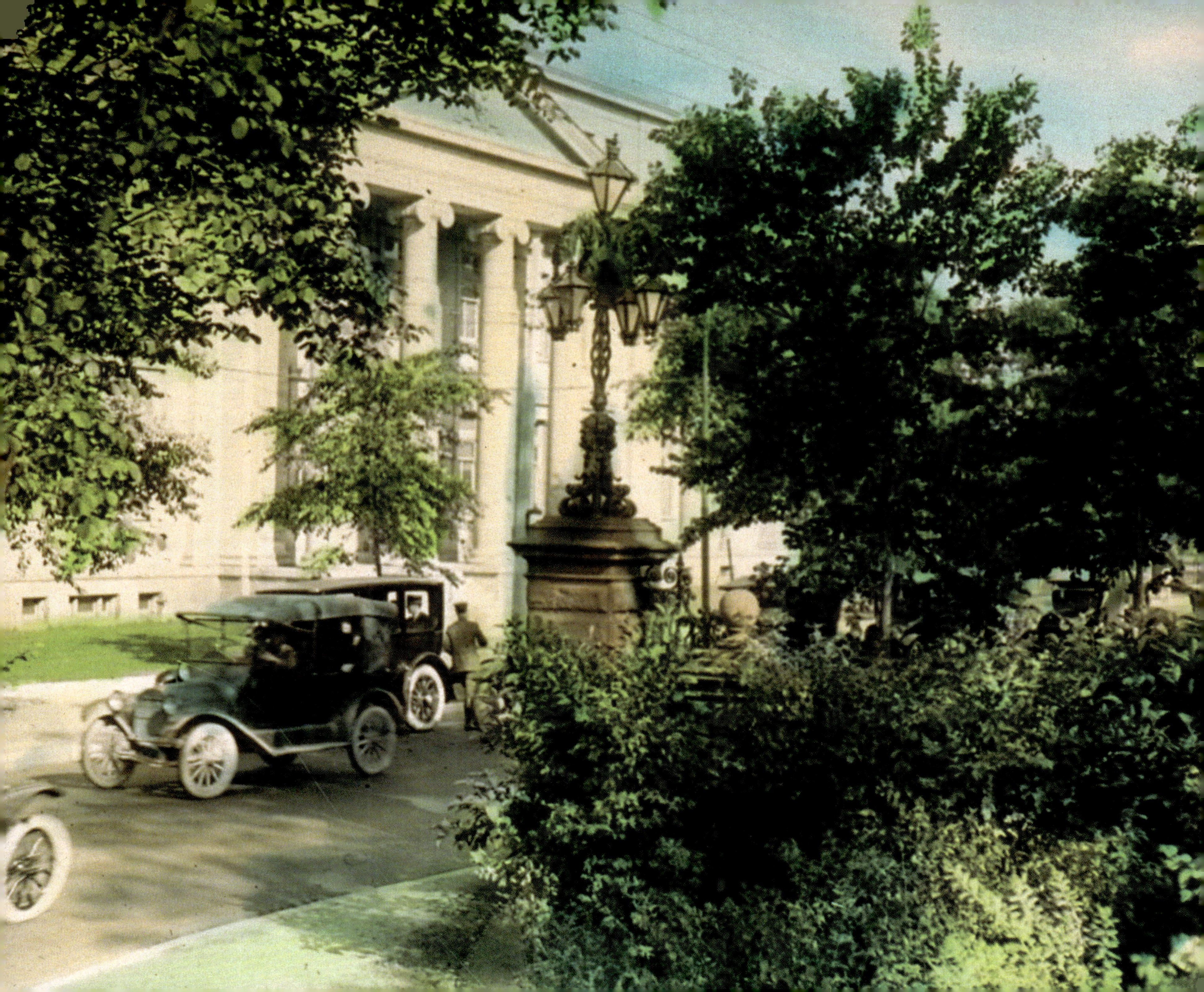

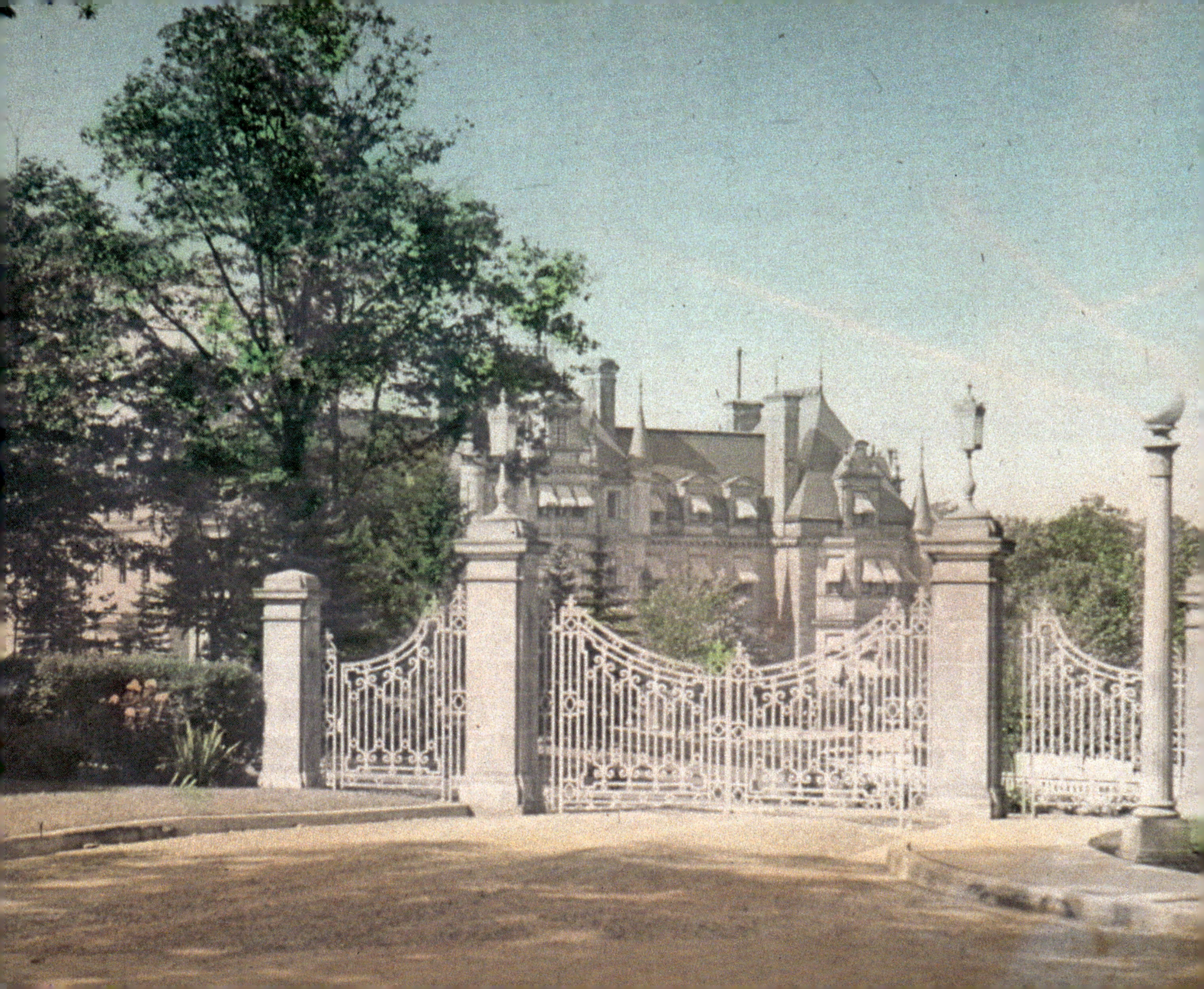

PEOPLE AND NEIGHBOURHOODS

Left: *Government House, Chorley Park, 1927. Chorley Park replaced the Government House of 1866 at Simcoe and King Streets. Located in Rosedale, it was built between 1911–1915 for over a million dollars — five times the amount budgeted.*

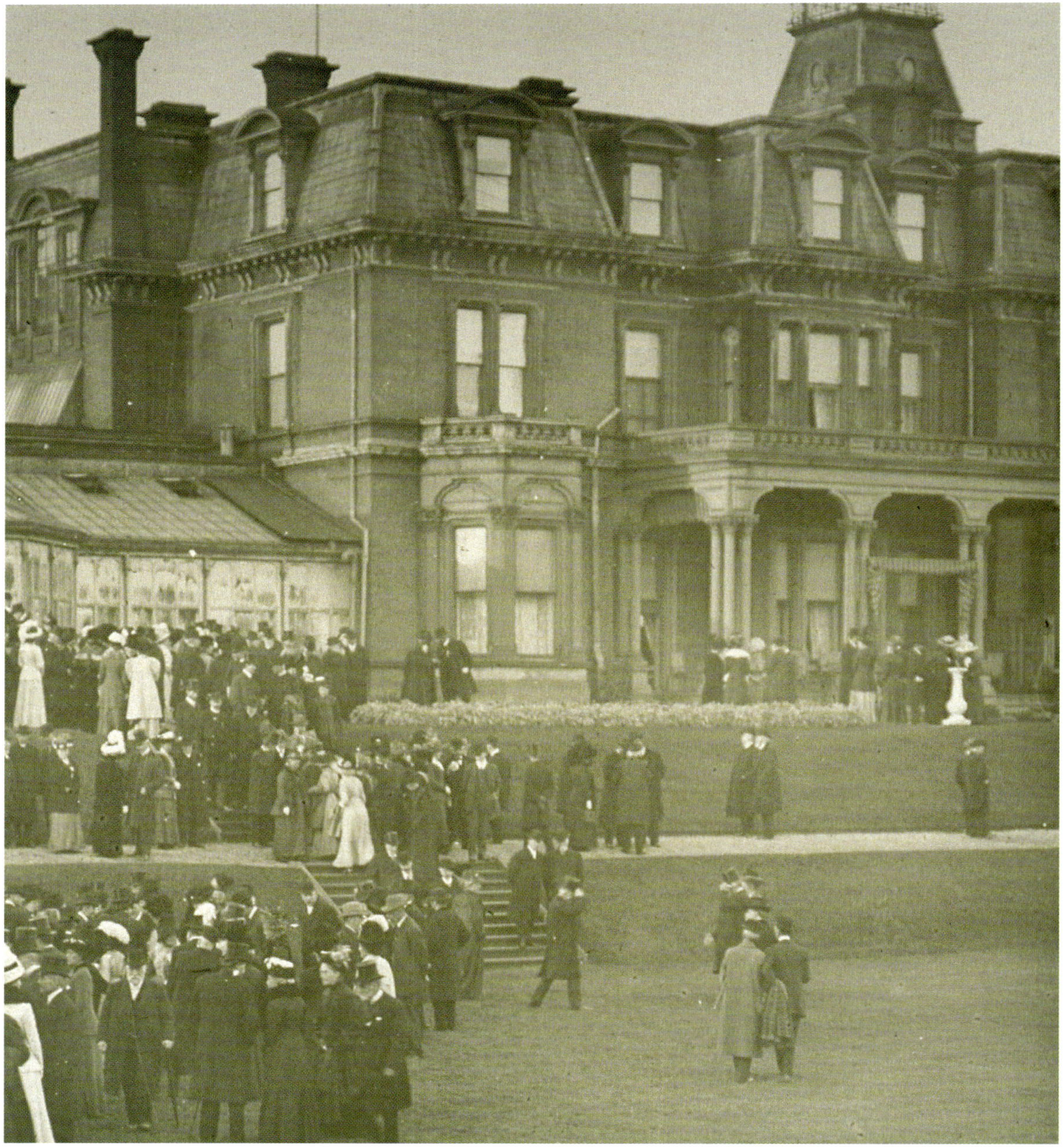

Right: *Garden party at Government House, circa 1910. This residence introduced the French Second Empire style to Toronto in 1866. Superceded by Chorley Park in 1912, the site was sold to the Canadian Pacific Railway, who replaced it with a freight and express building.*

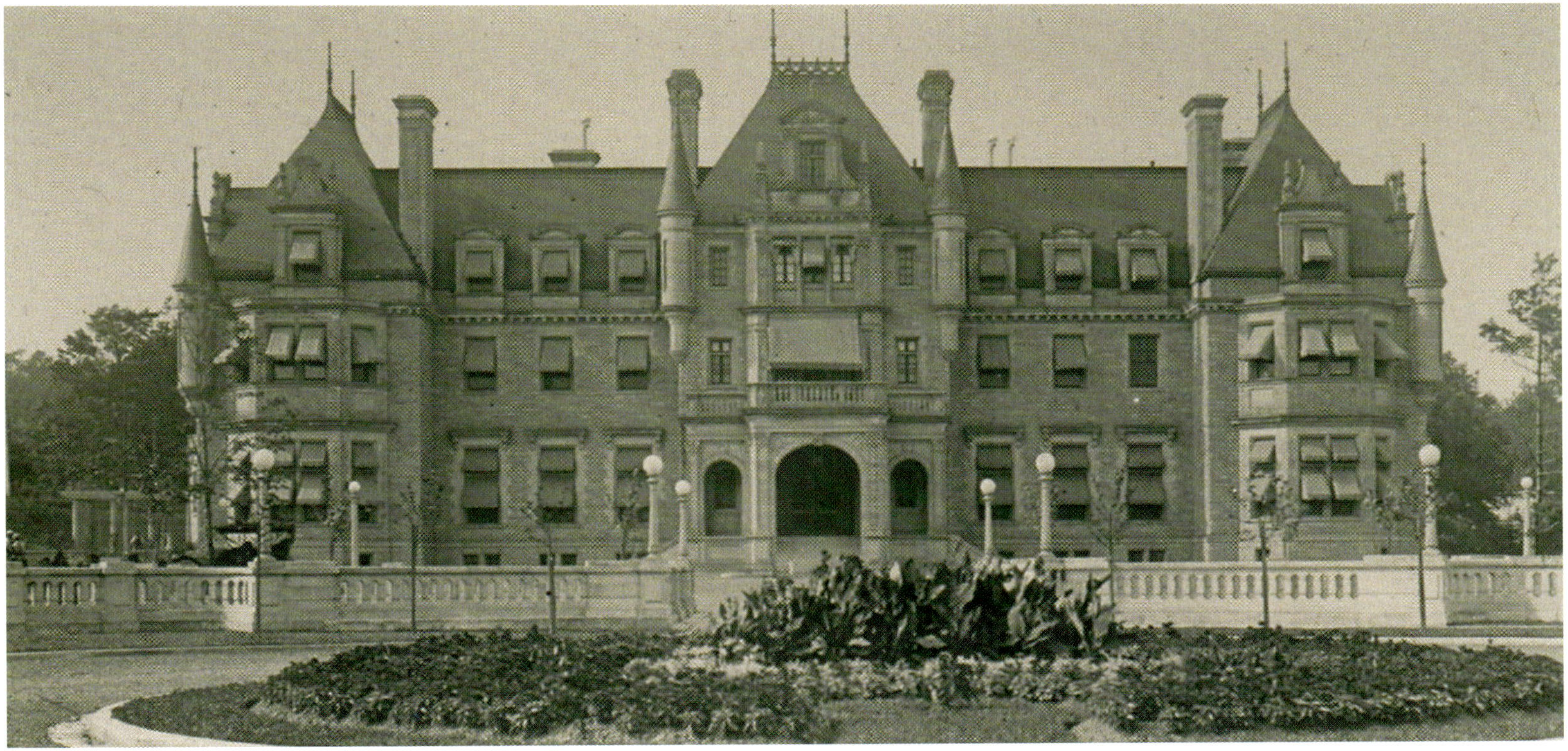

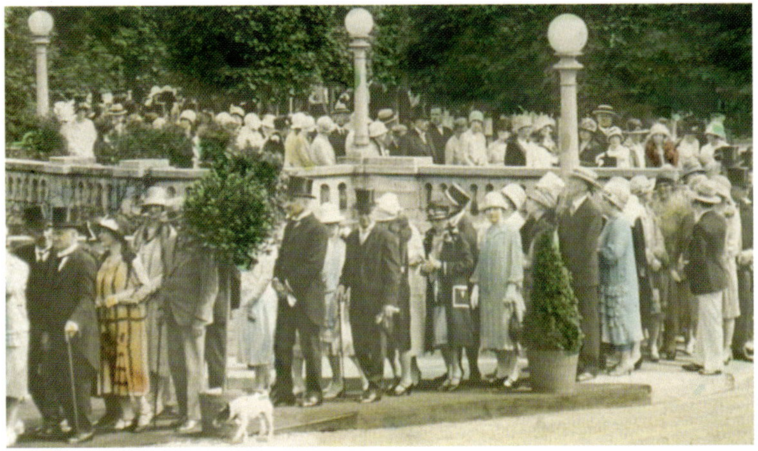

Above: *Chorley Park, circa 1925. The United Farmers of Ontario, no friends to privilege, forced Liberal Premier Mitchell Hepburn to close the Loire Valley-like château in 1937. Its contents were auctioned, the building became a military hospital, and was finally torn down to make way for more parkland in 1959.* Left: *Reception for the Prince of Wales, Chorley Park, 1919. Edward, Prince of Wales (later Edward VIII), made two tours of Canada, in 1919 and 1927. Dignified well-wishers line up to greet the Prince.*

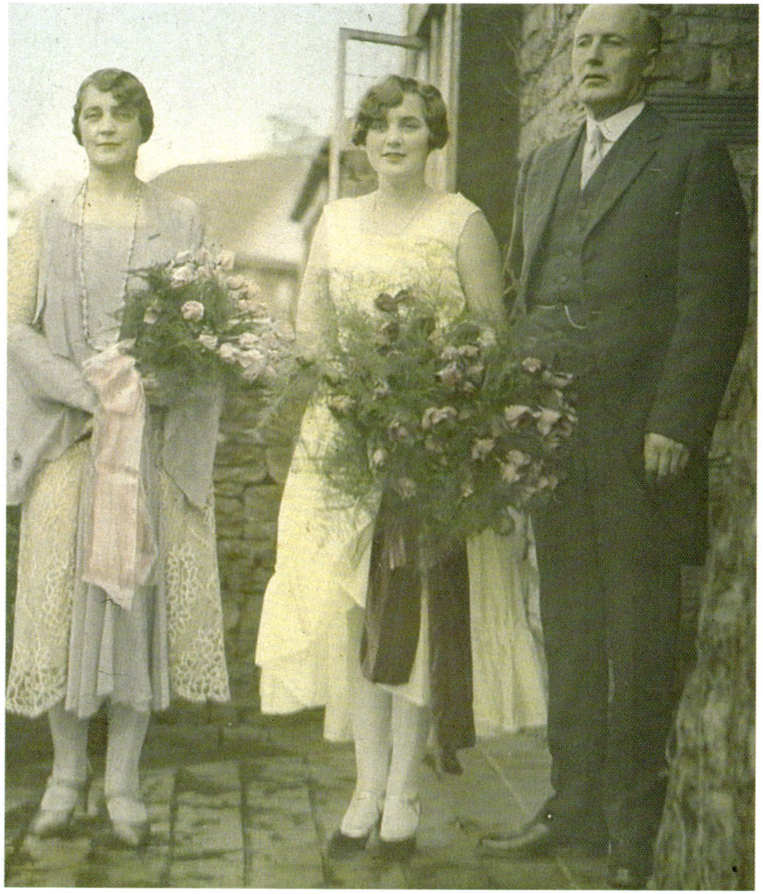

Left: *Authur Meighan with two debutantes, 1928. Canada's ninth prime minister, from 1920 to 1921, is here shown at a society gathering. Hoping to leave politics, Meighen would, in four years, be appointed to the Senate.* Far right: *Four wealthy young girls, circa 1920.*

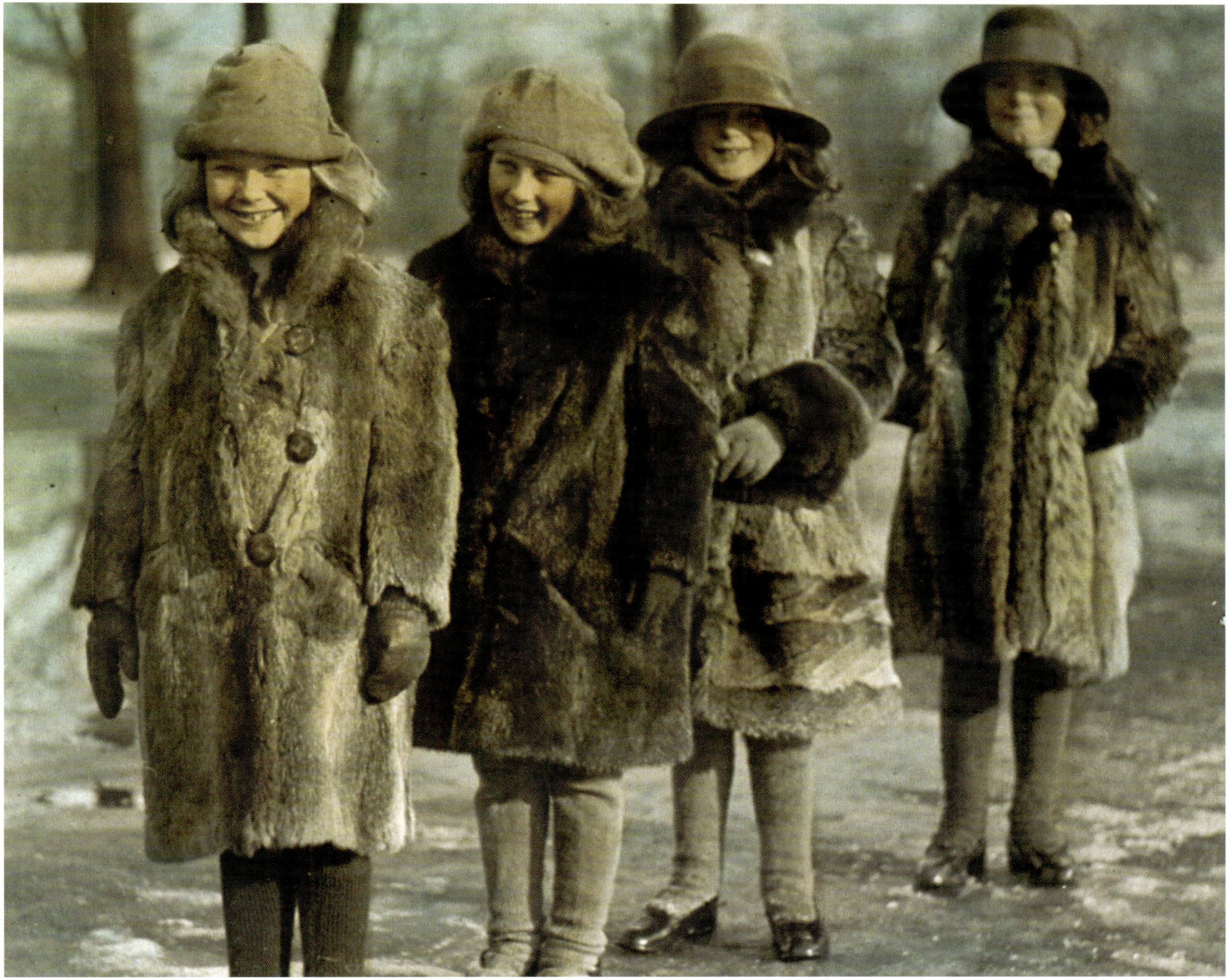

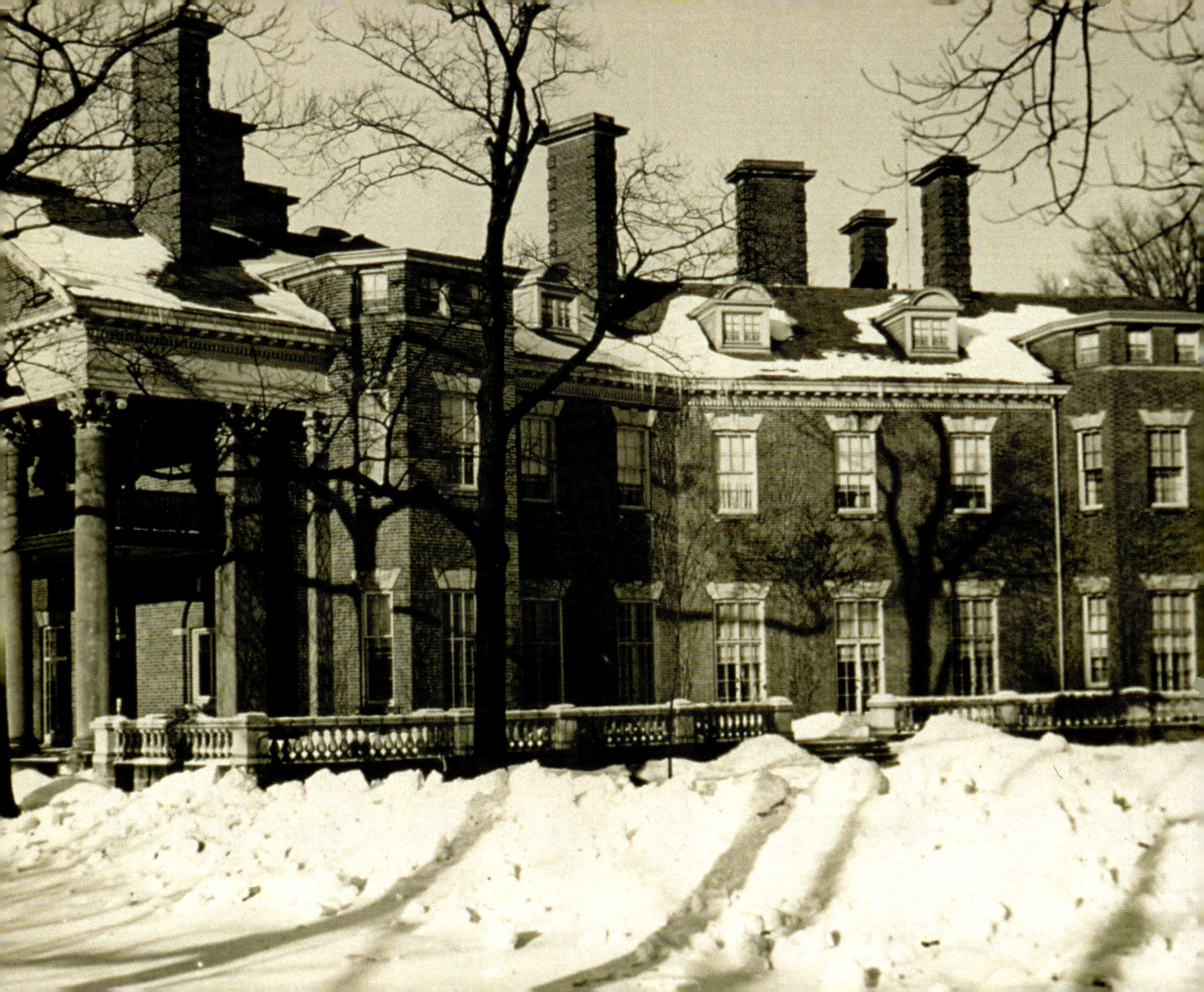

Left: *Flavelle House, Queen's Park, circa 1920. Sir Joseph Flavelle's mansion, "Holwood," was built in 1901–2 when Queen's Park was a residential quarter. The mansion is now part of the Faculty of Law at the University of Toronto.*
Right: *Flavelle House interior. Fabulously successful in business (a millionaire meat-packer, financier and part owner of the Robert Simpson Co.), Sir Joseph was turning much of his energies to charitable work and public service by the time he resided here.*

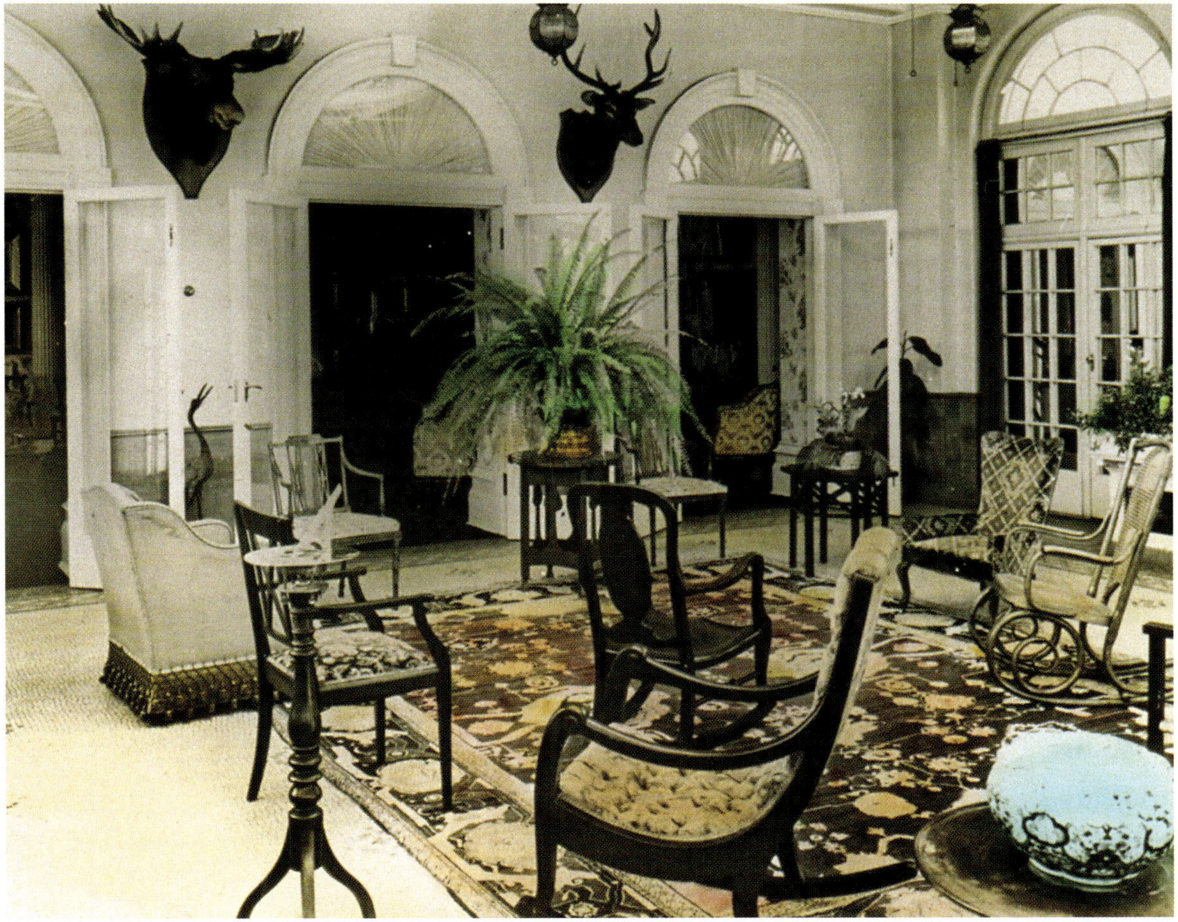

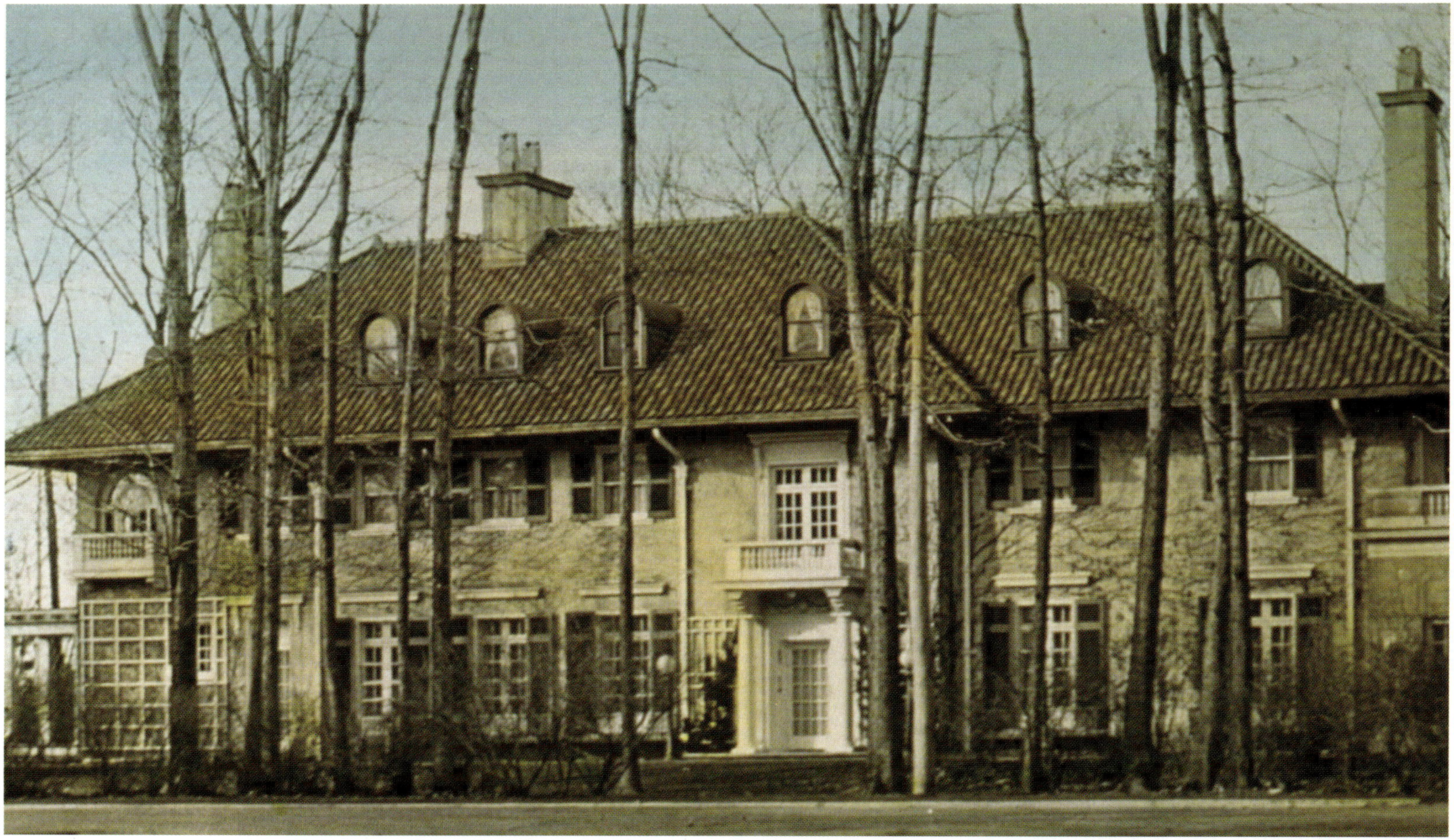

Above: *Lyndhurst Lodge, Front Street and Spadina. The lodge was built in 1837 for Vice-Chancellor (of the Court of Equity) Robert Jameson, and enlarged in 1844 by Frederick Widder of the Canada Company. Jameson was husband to Anna Jameson, author of* Winter Studies and Summer Rambles in Canada*. Lyndhurst was demolished in 1961.* The Globe and Mail *now occupies the site.* Far right: *Woodlawn, Jarvis Street, circa 1920. Originally the home of Sheriff Frederick William Jarvis, it was later renovated by Thomas Long, merchant, who gave it the Greek Revival portico shown here. Woodlawn was sold to the Toronto Board of Education in 1921 and demolished to make way for Jarvis Collegiate Institute.*

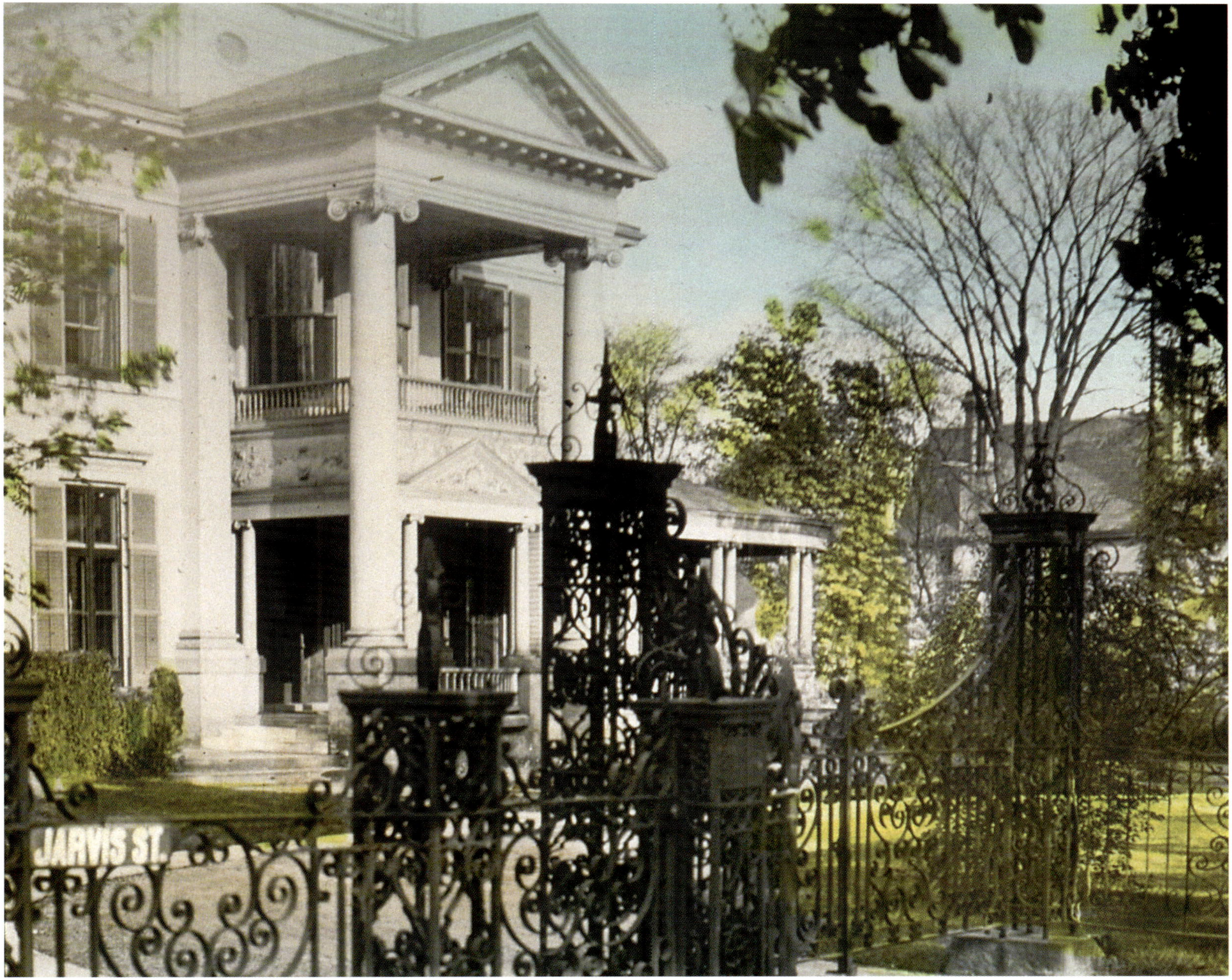
JARVIS ST.

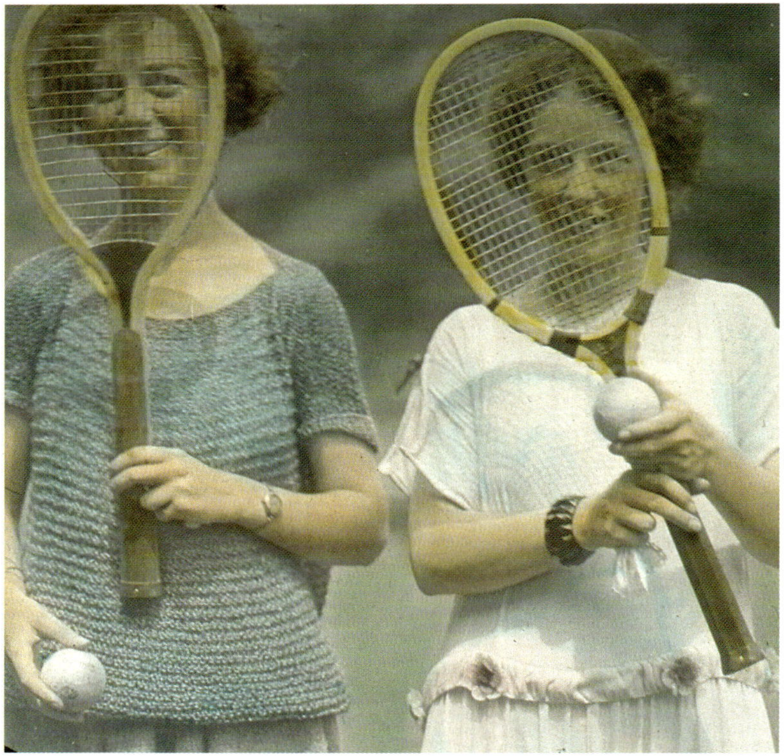

Left: *Two girls with tennis raquets, circa 1925. Lawn tennis became popular in Canada in the 1870s, and by 1890 the Canadian Lawn Tennis Association held its first championships in Toronto.* Far right: *Clifford Sifton and his wife, Sifton Estate on Lawrence Avenue East, circa 1925. Sifton was one of the ablest politicians of his day, and was responsible for the settlement of the Canadian West. He built his estate in 1923. It is now the Toronto French School.*

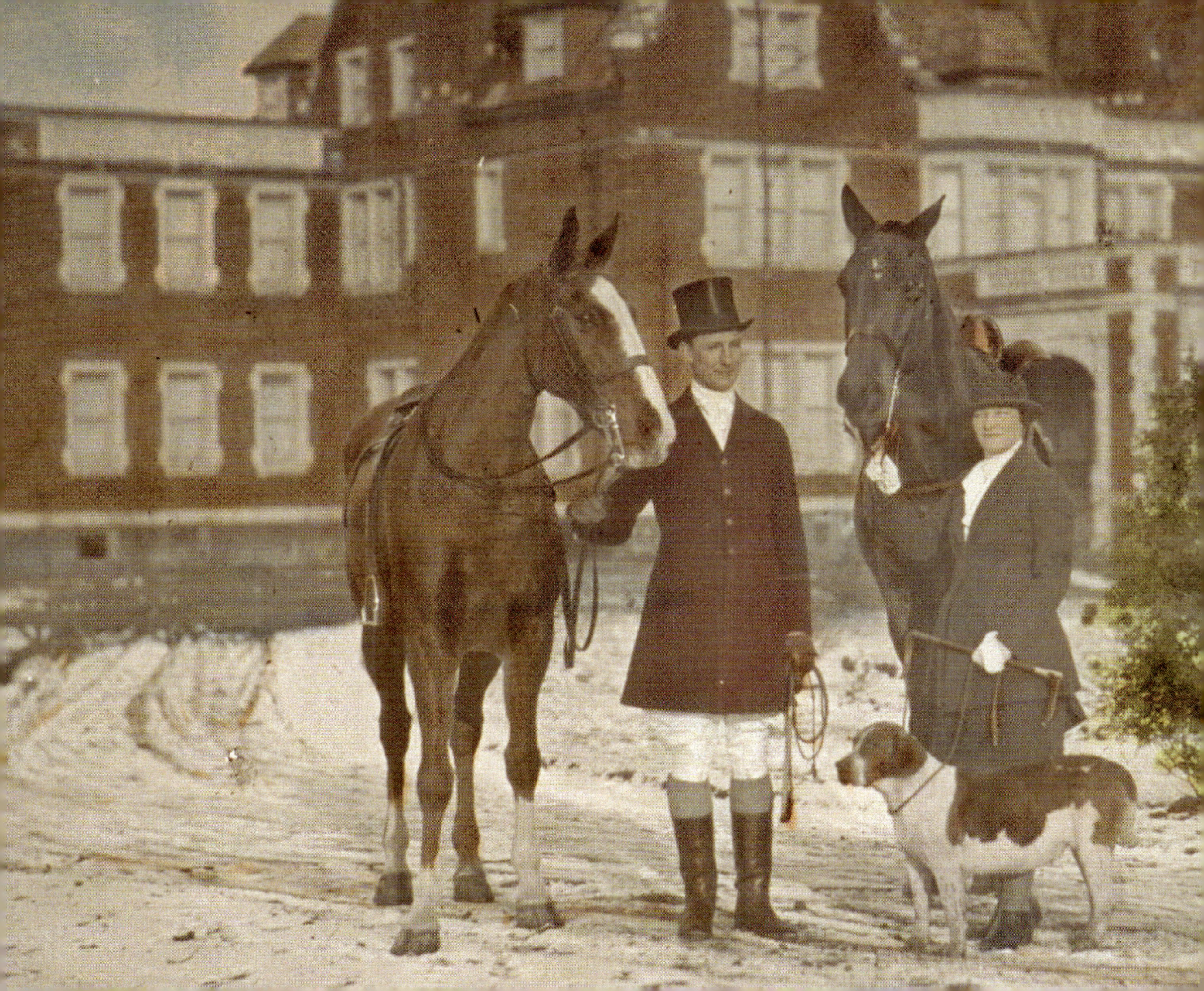

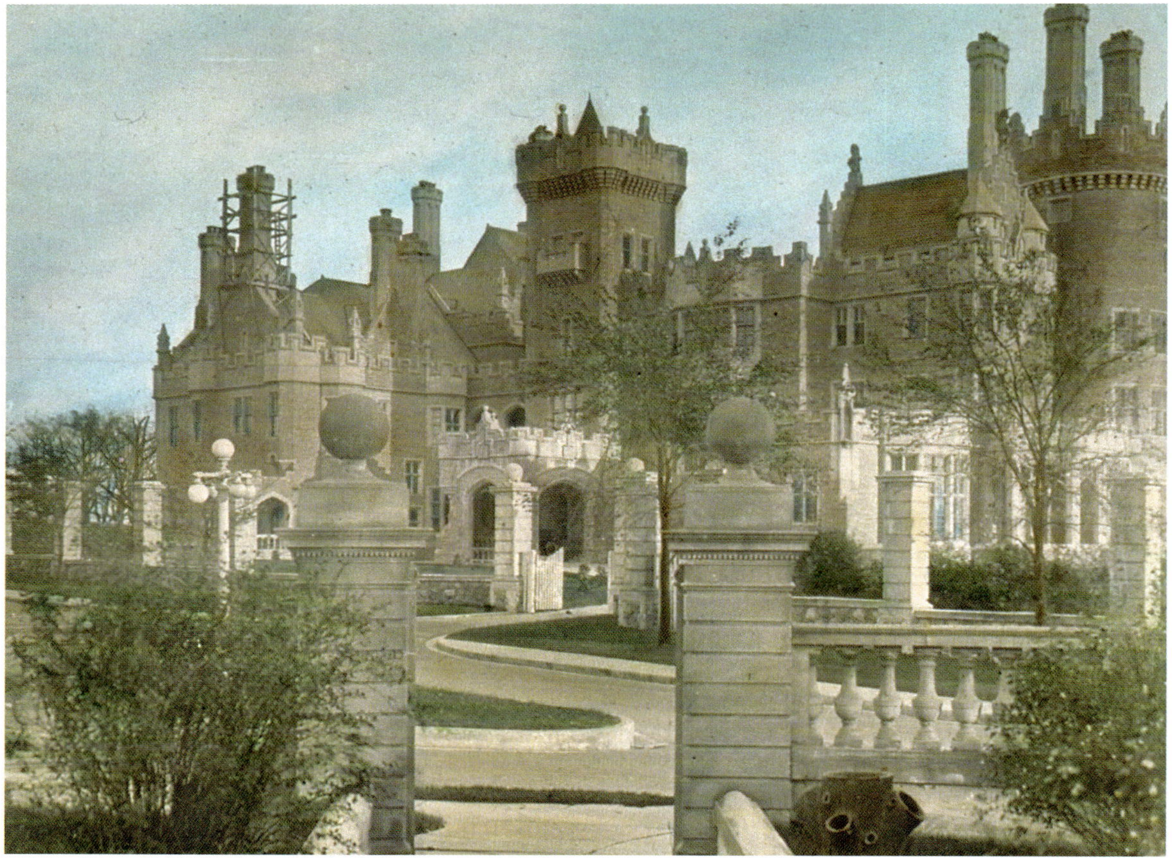

Left: *Casa Loma, Spadina Road, 1920. Sir Henry Pellatt lived in this fortress-like home with his wife Mary from 1914 to 1923, when business failures forced him out. Casa Loma became a hotel for a short time, and then was saved and preserved by the Kiwanis Club.* Far right: *The library, Casa Loma, 1922. Sir Henry took especial pride in his library, which had a floor strong enough to bear heavy guns, as he was hoping to make part of his home into a military museum.*

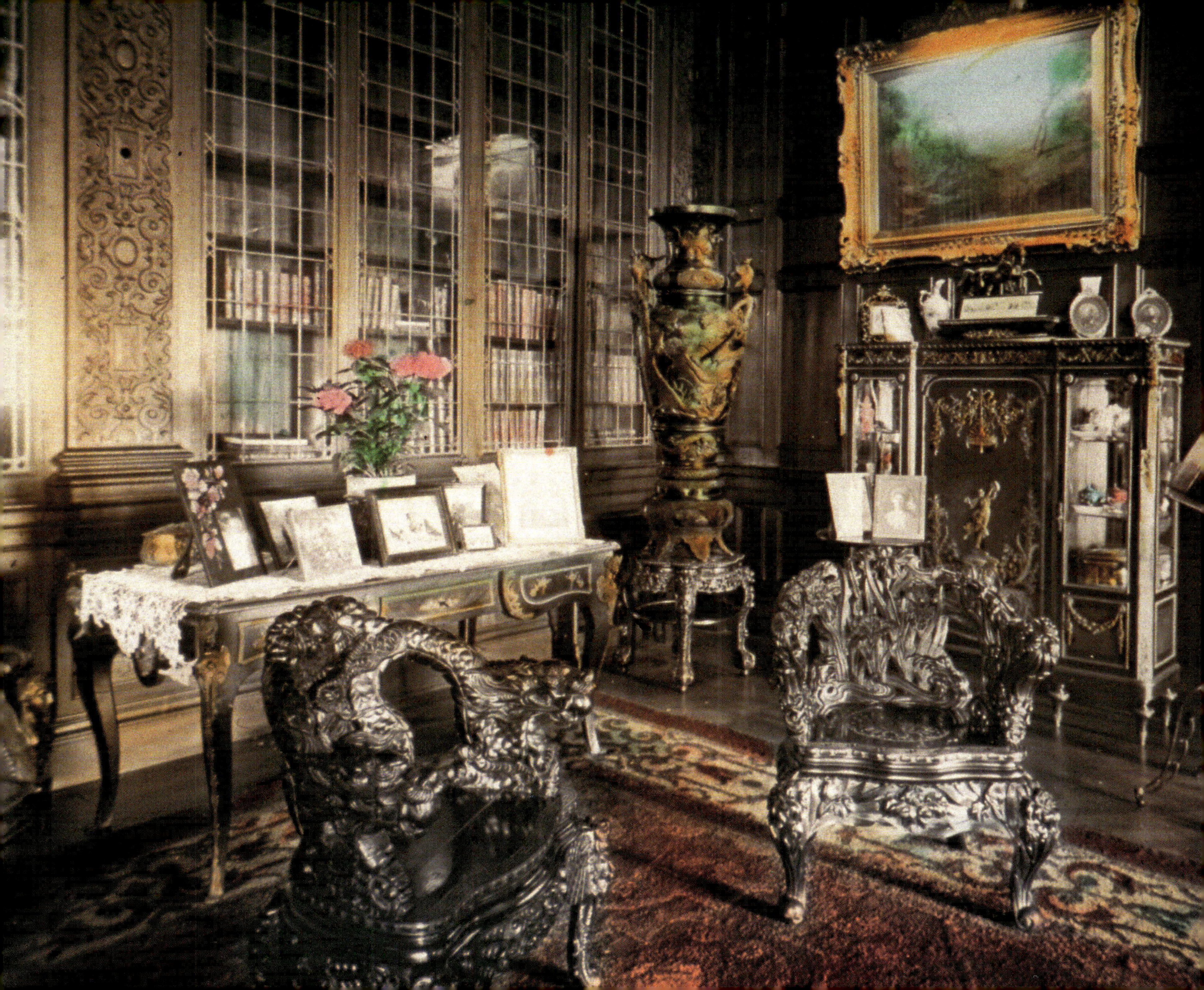

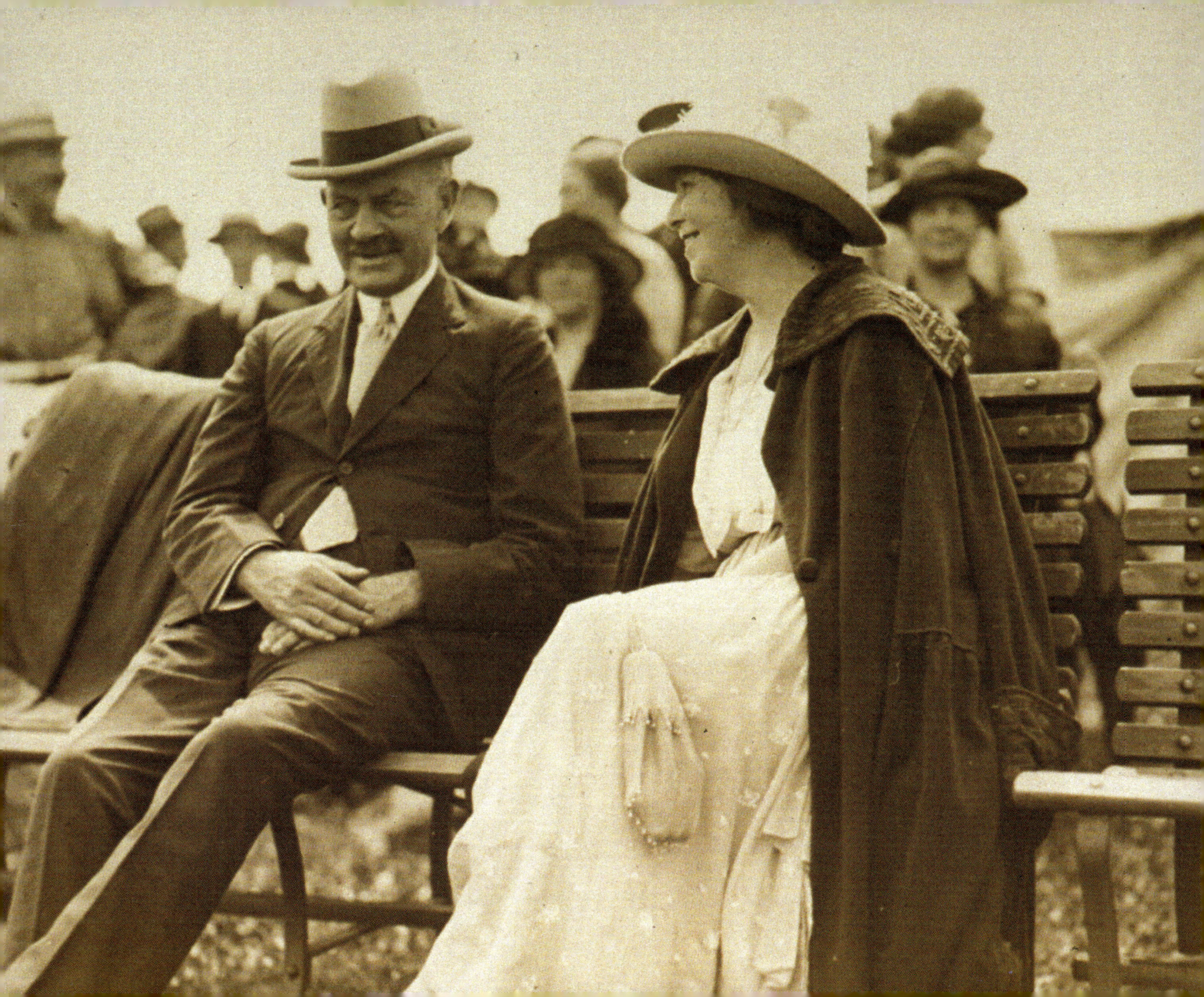

Far left: *Governor-General and Lady Byng, 1921. Viscount Byng of Vimy directed the famous attack by Canadian troops on Vimy Ridge in 1917 and was governor-general from 1921 to 1926. He was as sympathetic to Canada's poor as he had been respectful of its soldiers.* Right: *Norman Gooderham, 1922. The Gooderhams were a sailing family in addition to businessmen. Norman Gooderham won more international sailing competitions than any previous member of the Royal Canadian Yacht Club.*

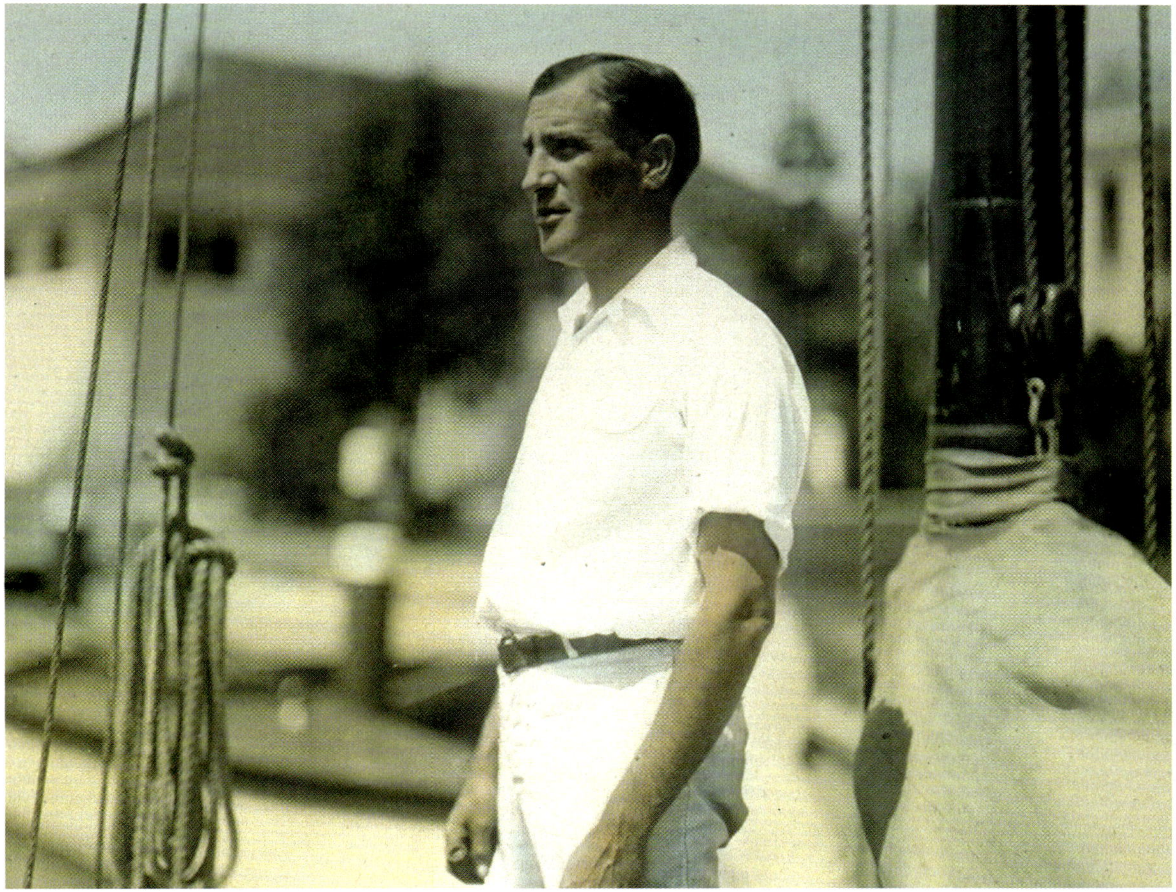

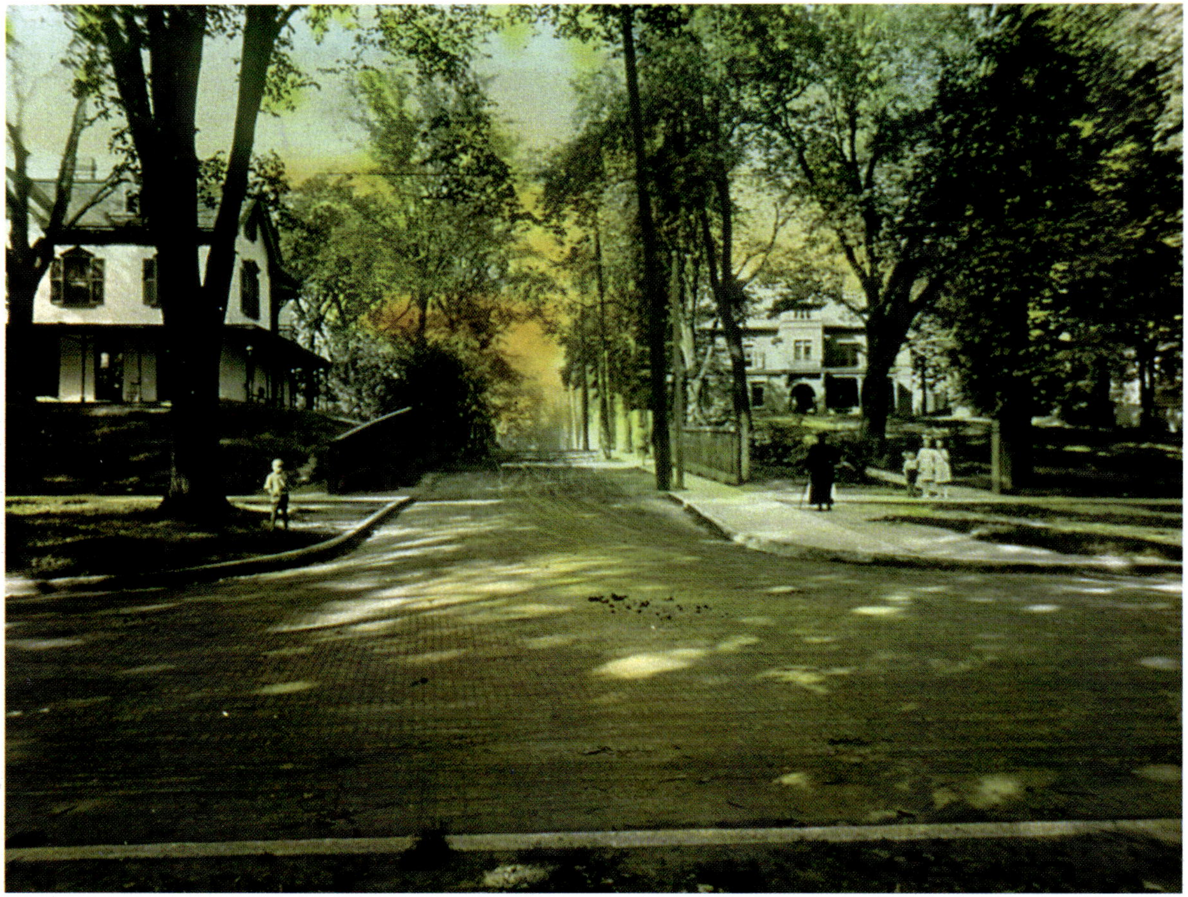

Left: *North Street, 1921. North Street is now part of Bay Street between St. Mary and Bloor.* Far right: *Garden, circa 1920.*

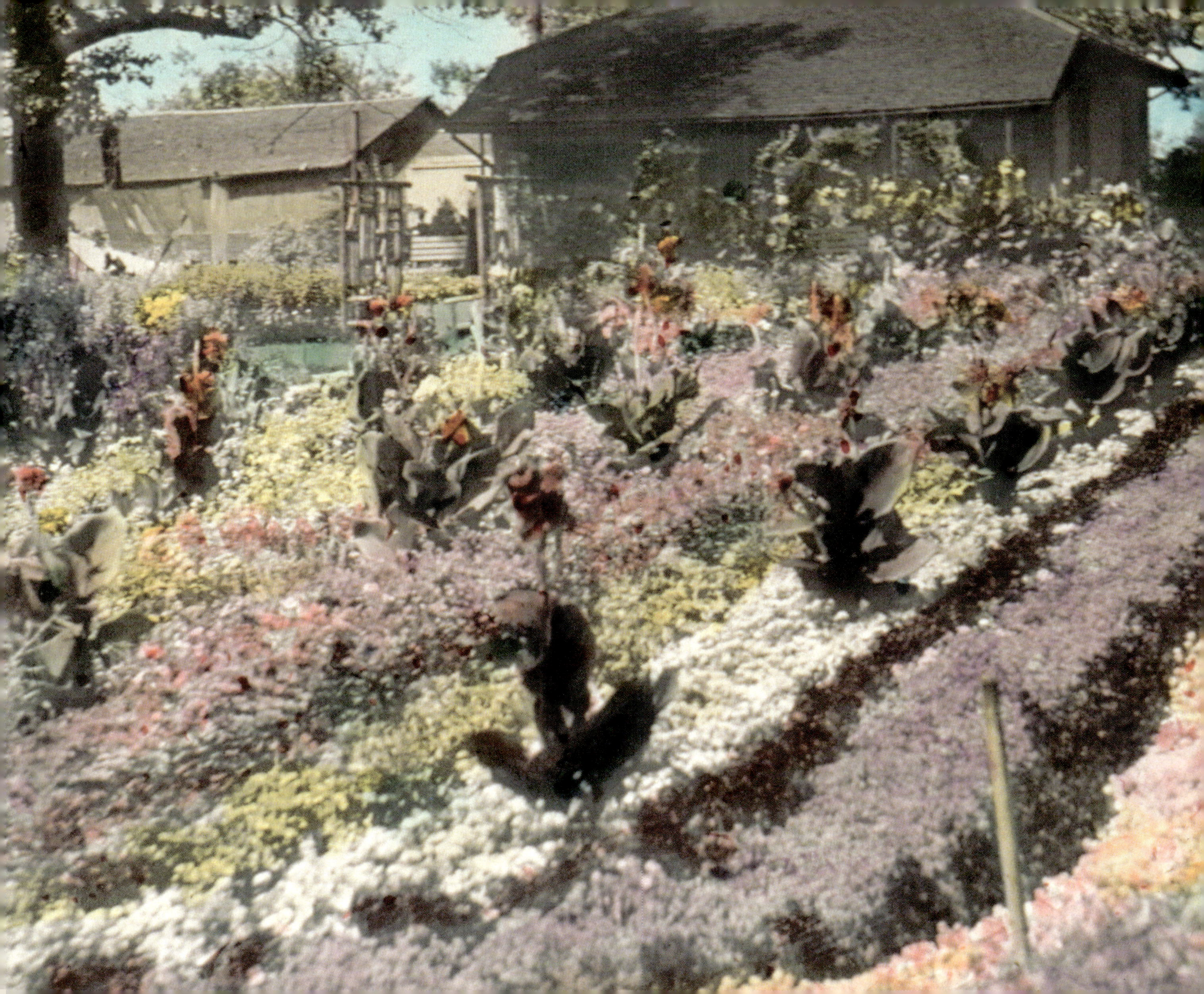

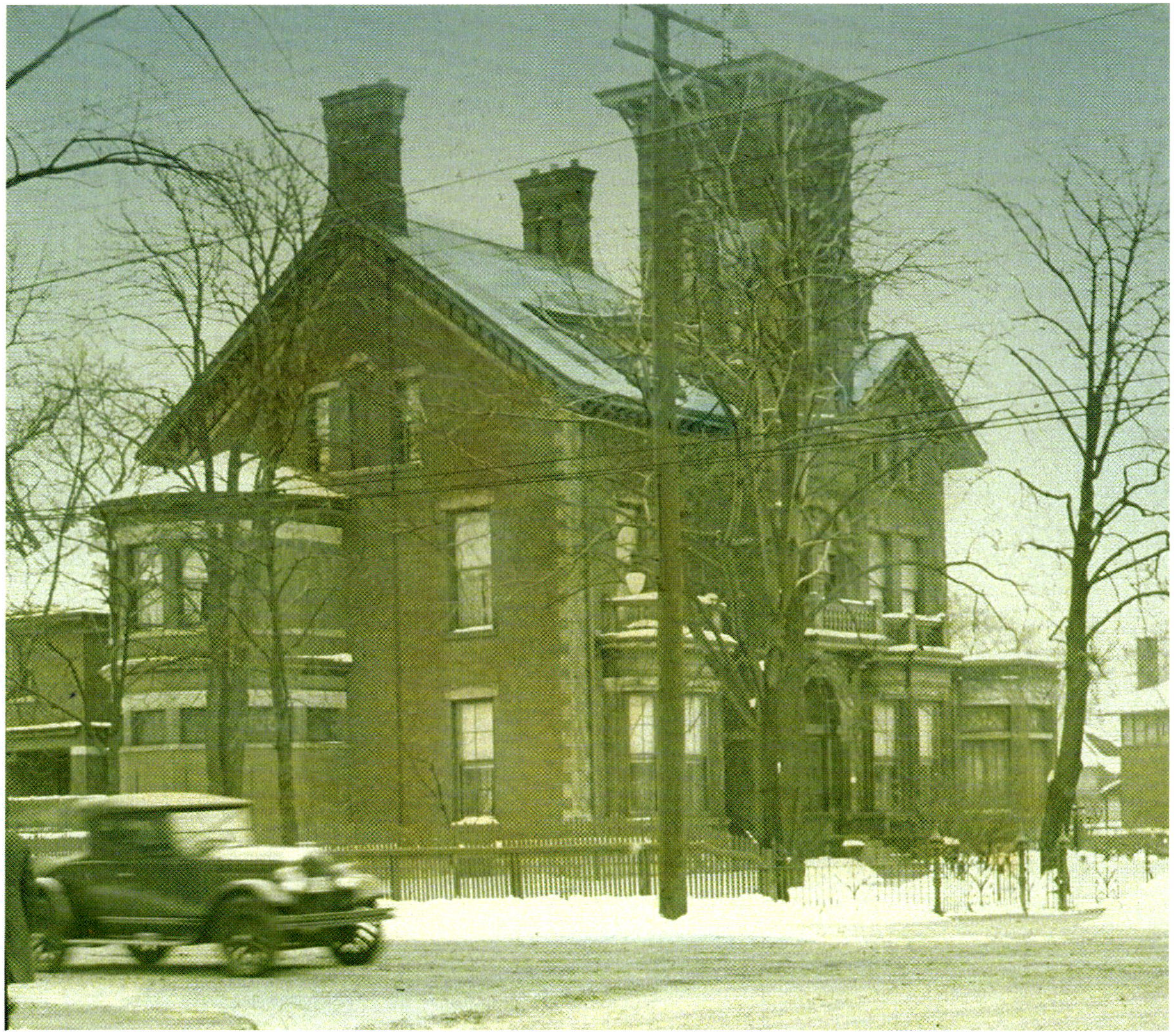

Left: *Old McDonald House, southeast corner of St. George and Bloor Streets, 1926.* Far right: *Girls in wagon, circa 1920s.*

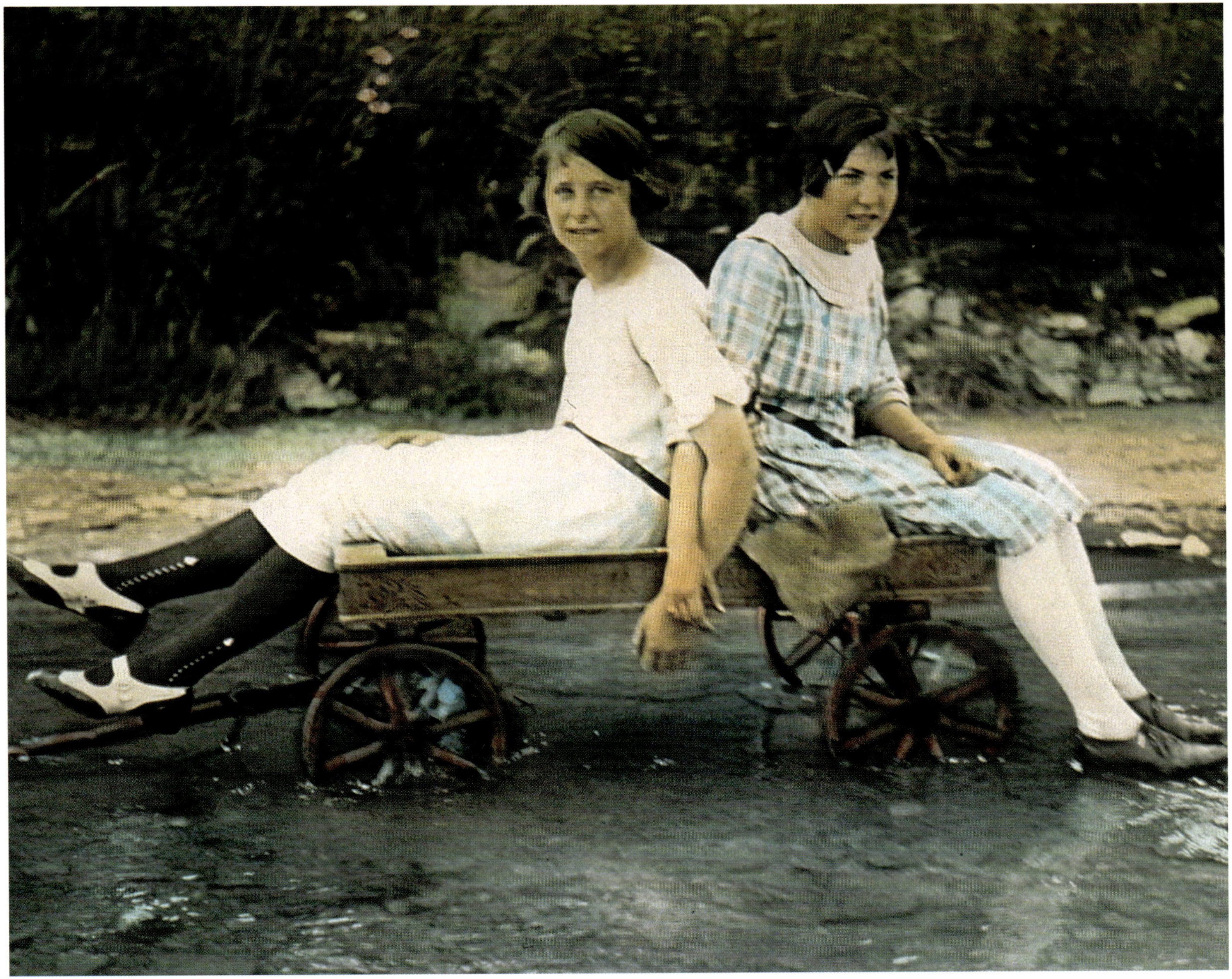

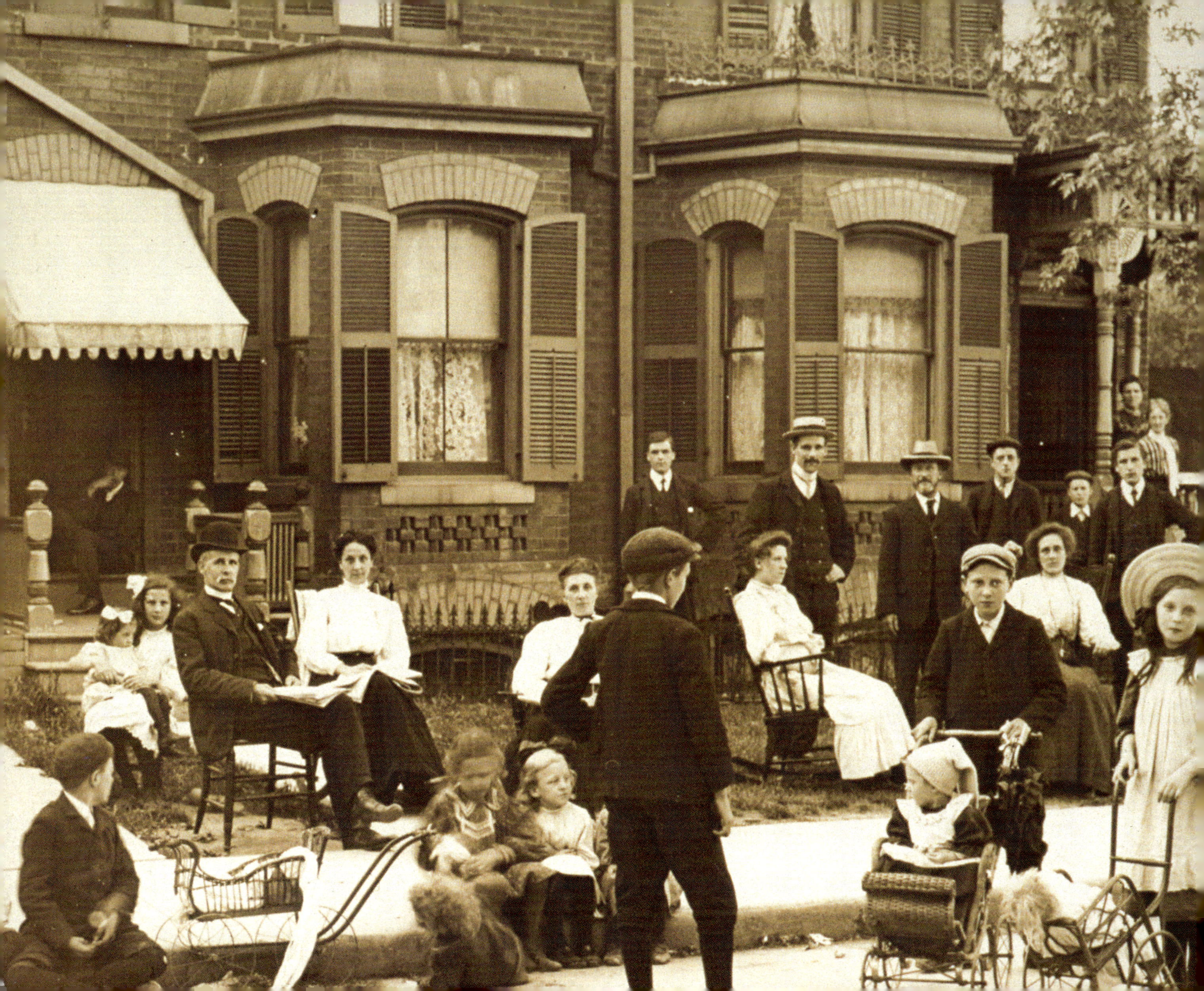

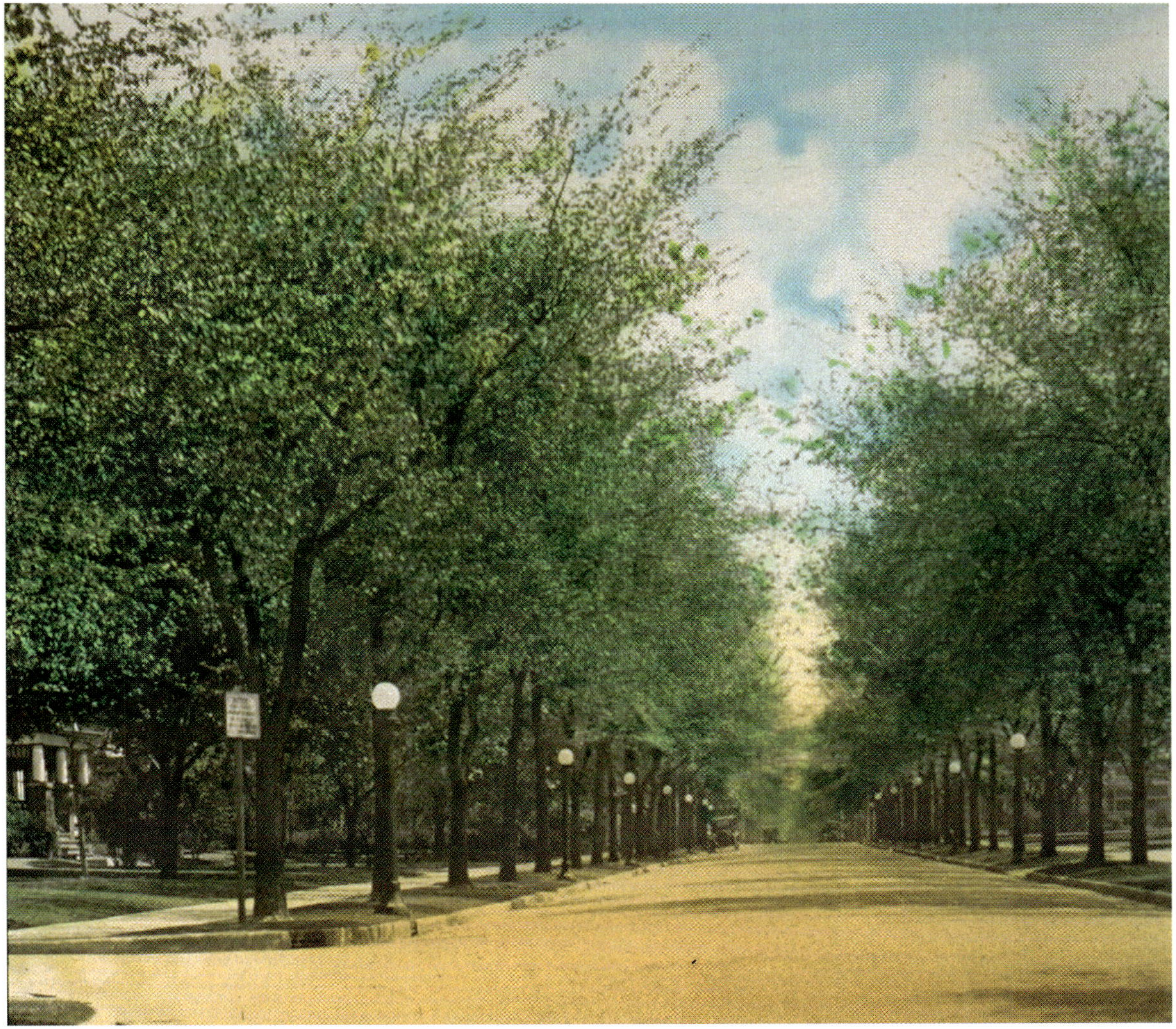

Far left: *The James family and neighbours, circa 1910.* Left: *High Park Avenue, 1927. The pedestrian lighting shown in this image was characteristic of many Toronto streets at the turn of the century, as were the gates that were just behind James when he took this photograph.*

The Poor

Right: *Man sleeping by the street, probably in the Ward, circa 1920.* Far right: *A line of children on tricycles at Major and Harbord Streets in 1920.*

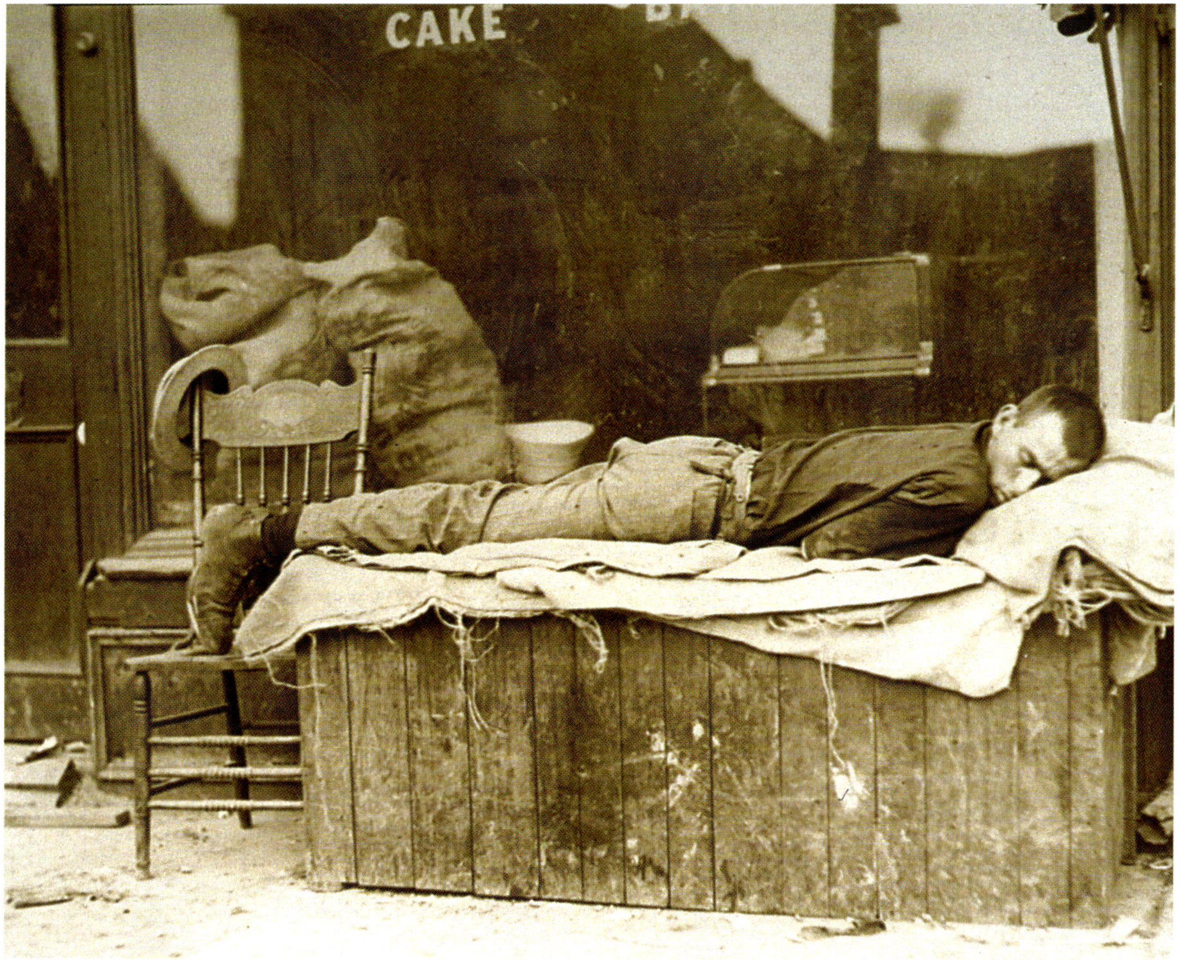

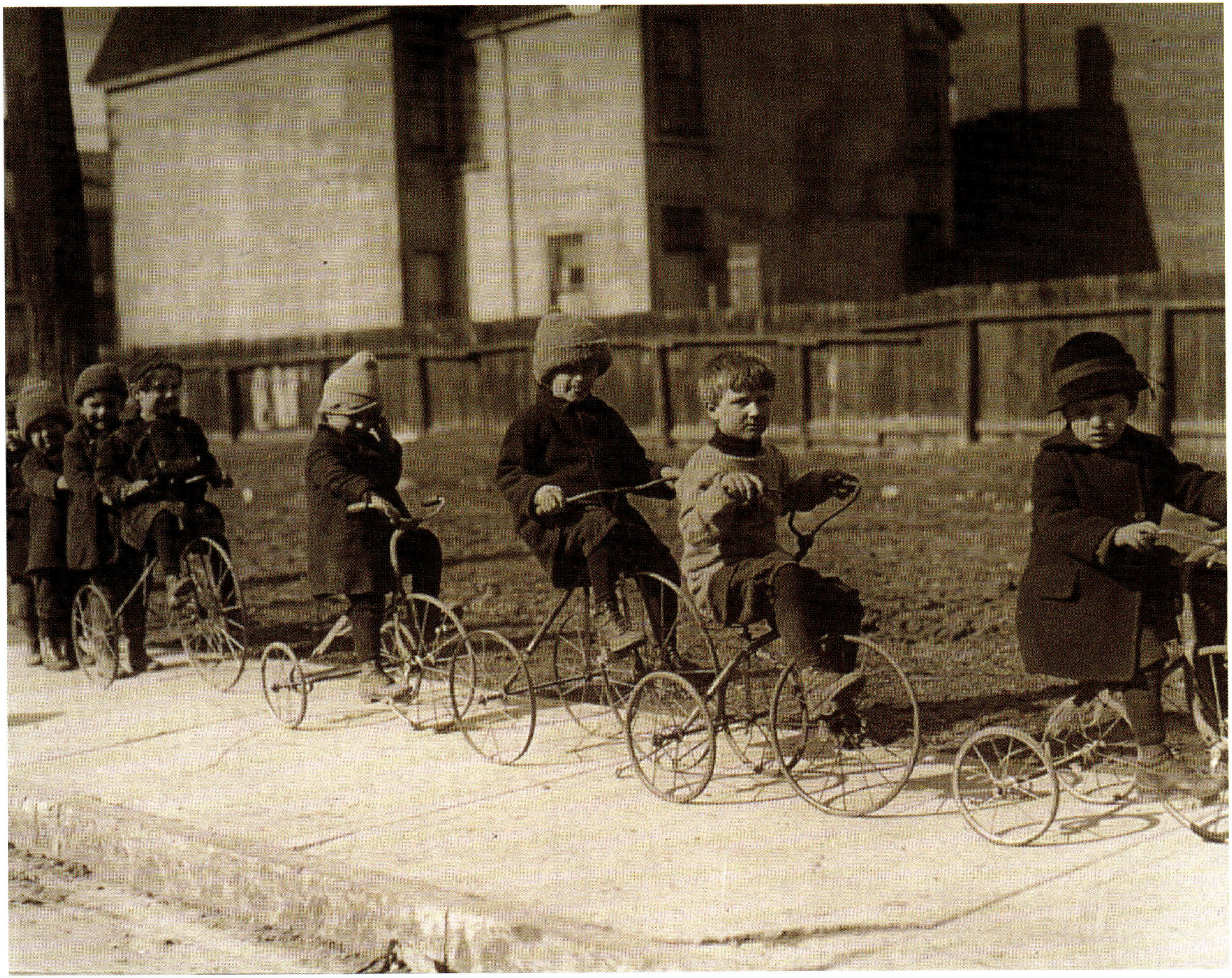

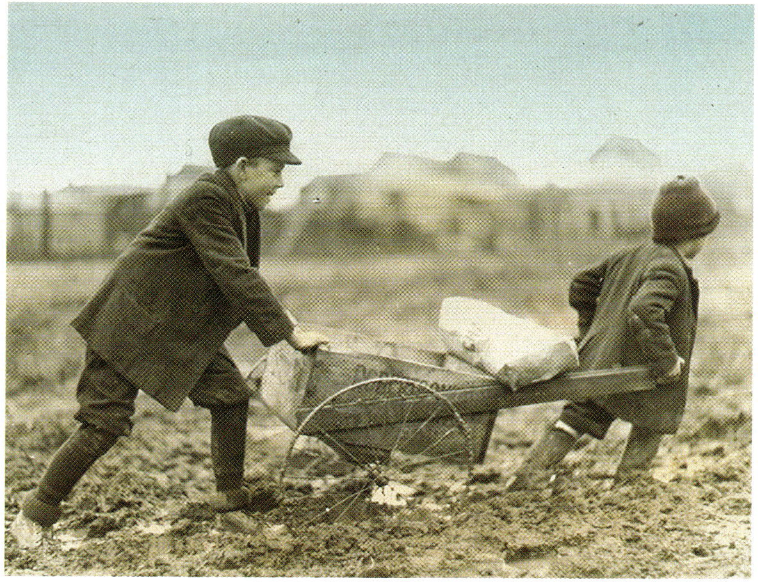

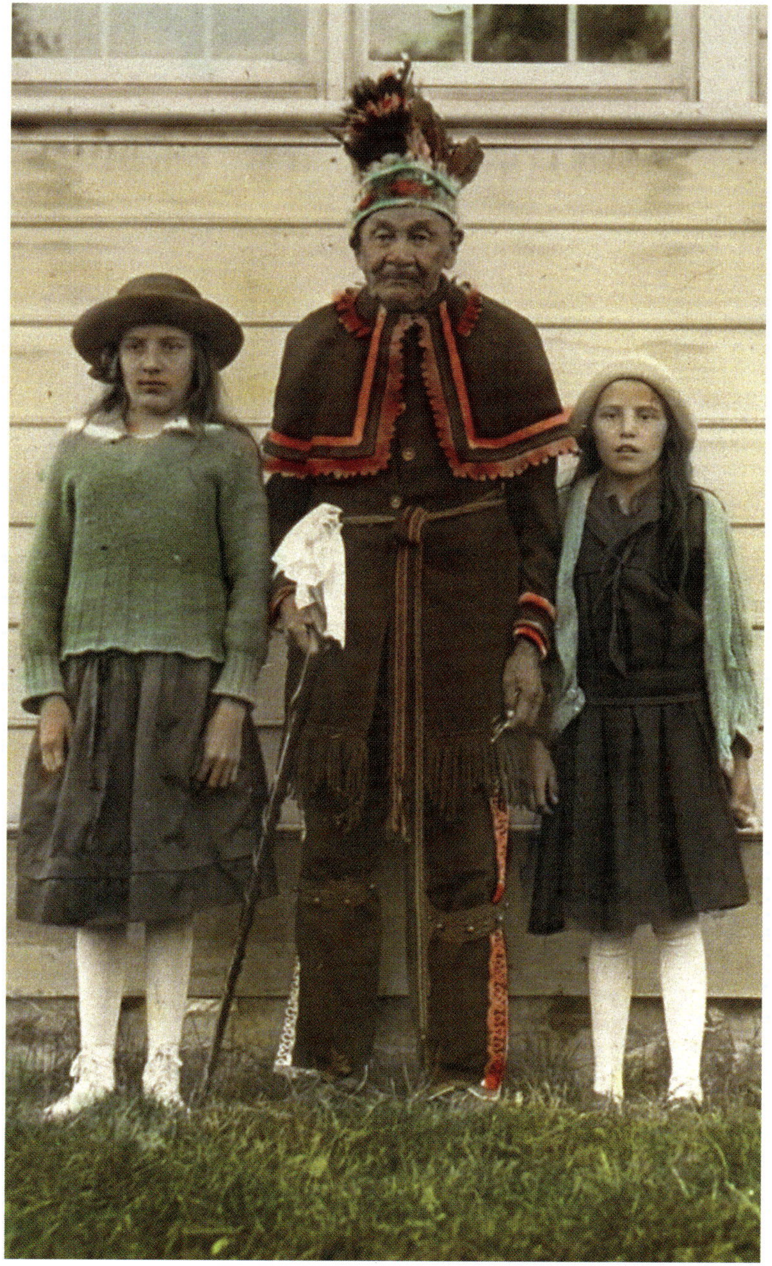

Above: *Earlescourt, circa 1915. Two boys push and pull a wagon through the mud. Earlescourt was annexed to Toronto in 1910 as the city bourgeoned outward. Lawren Harris called it "a picturesque semi-slum district west of Bathurst and south of Eglinton."* Right: *An Aboriginal man with two girls, circa 1920.* Far right: *Rolling bicycle rims on Chestnut Street, 1922.*

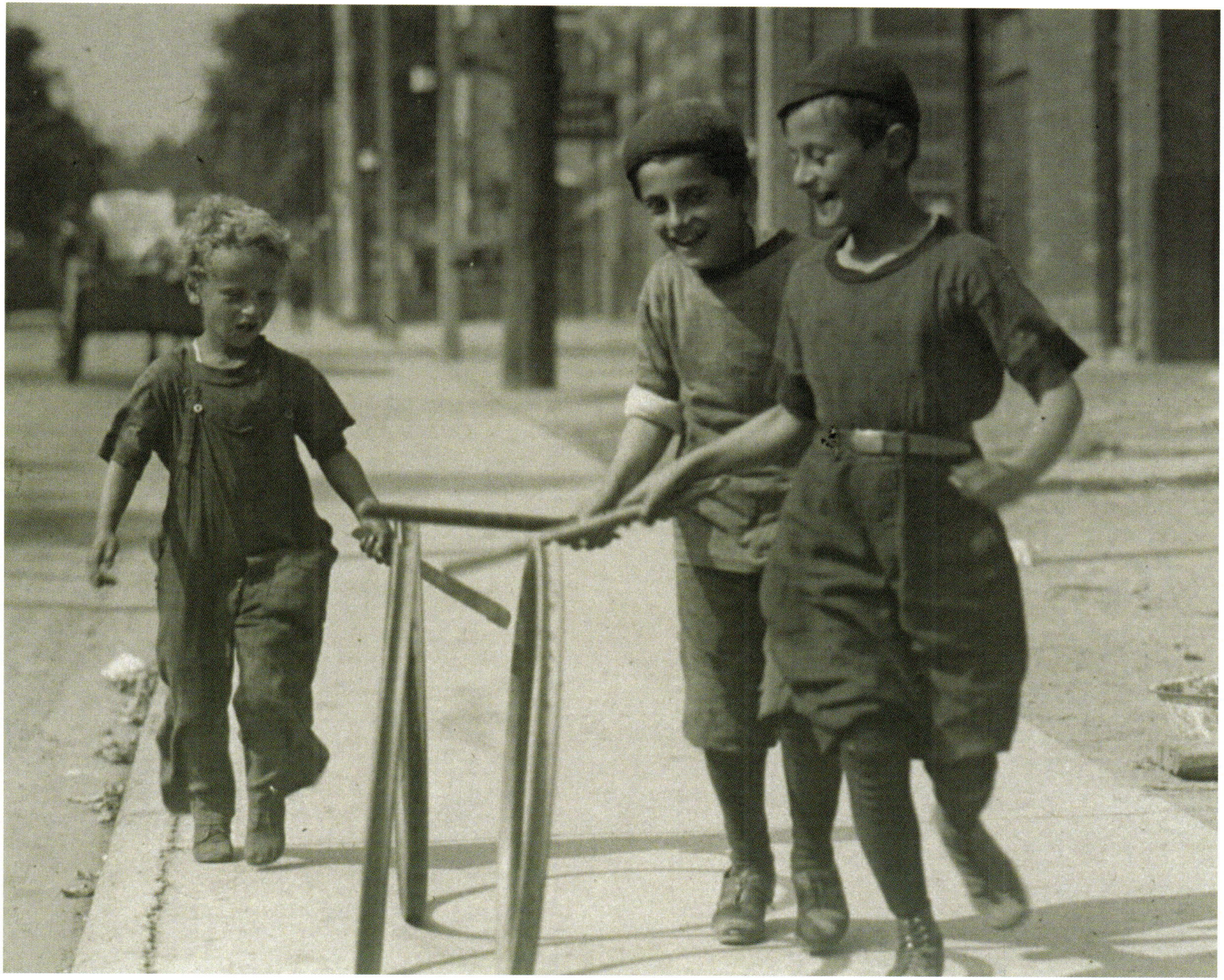

Right: *A man brings home a chicken, possibly in Kensington Market, circa 1912. The market was established by this time as a predominantly Jewish neighbourhood, west of the diminishing Ward.* Far right: *Agnes Street, the Ward, 1910. In James' early days in Toronto, many non-English-speaking newcomers to the city lived in St. John's Ward, later referred to simply as the Ward. It was bound by College, Dundas, University and Terauley (Bay) Streets. Agnes Street is now part of Dundas.*

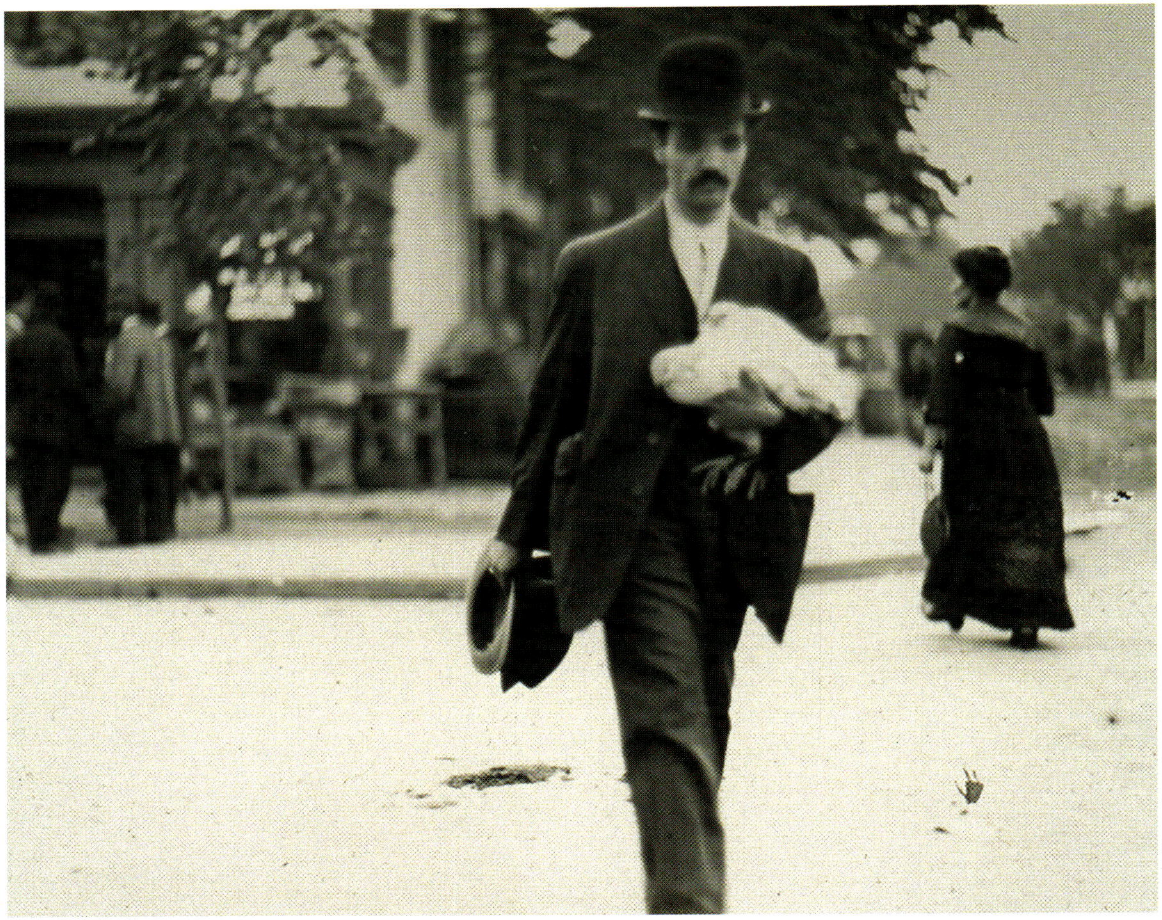

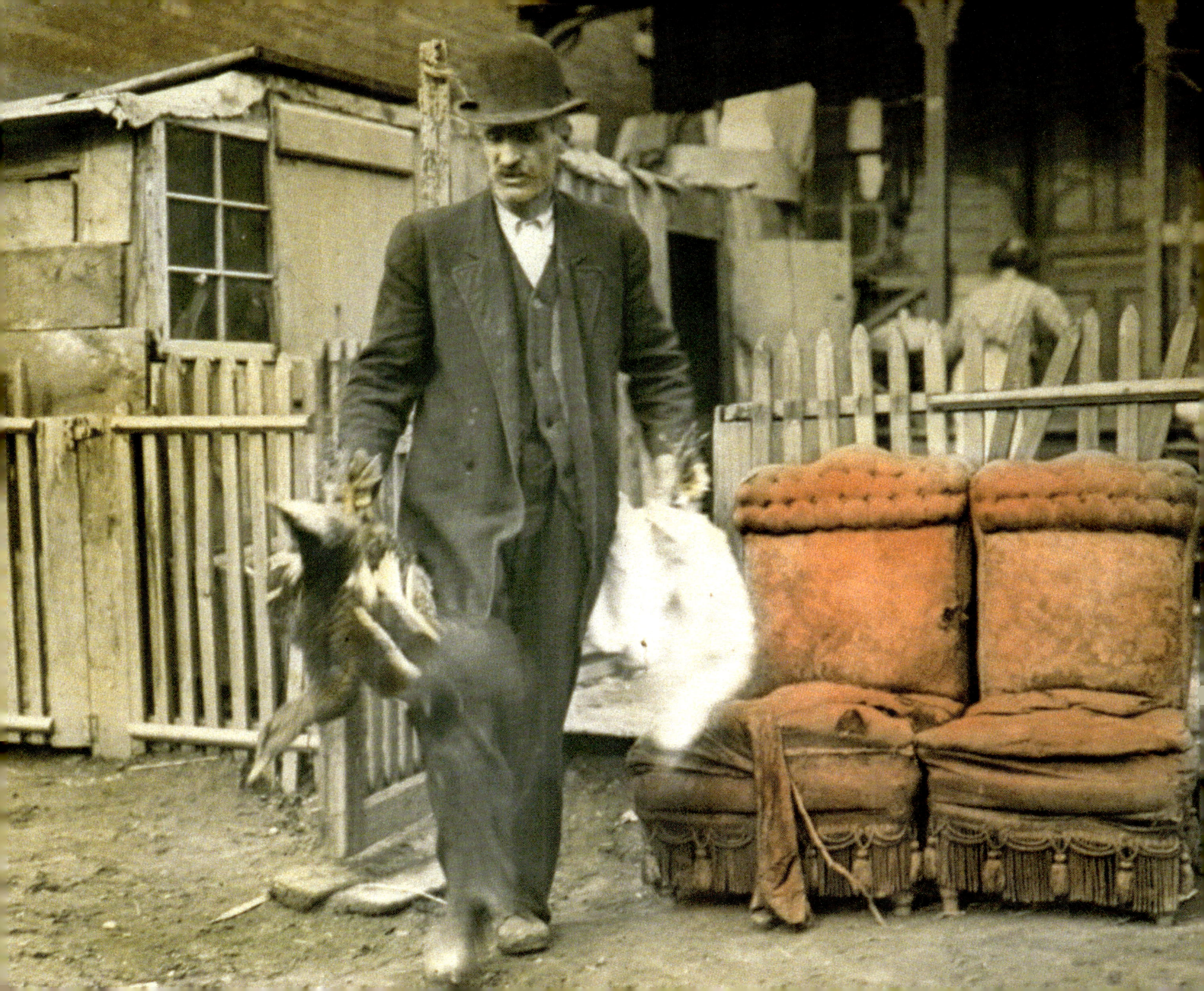

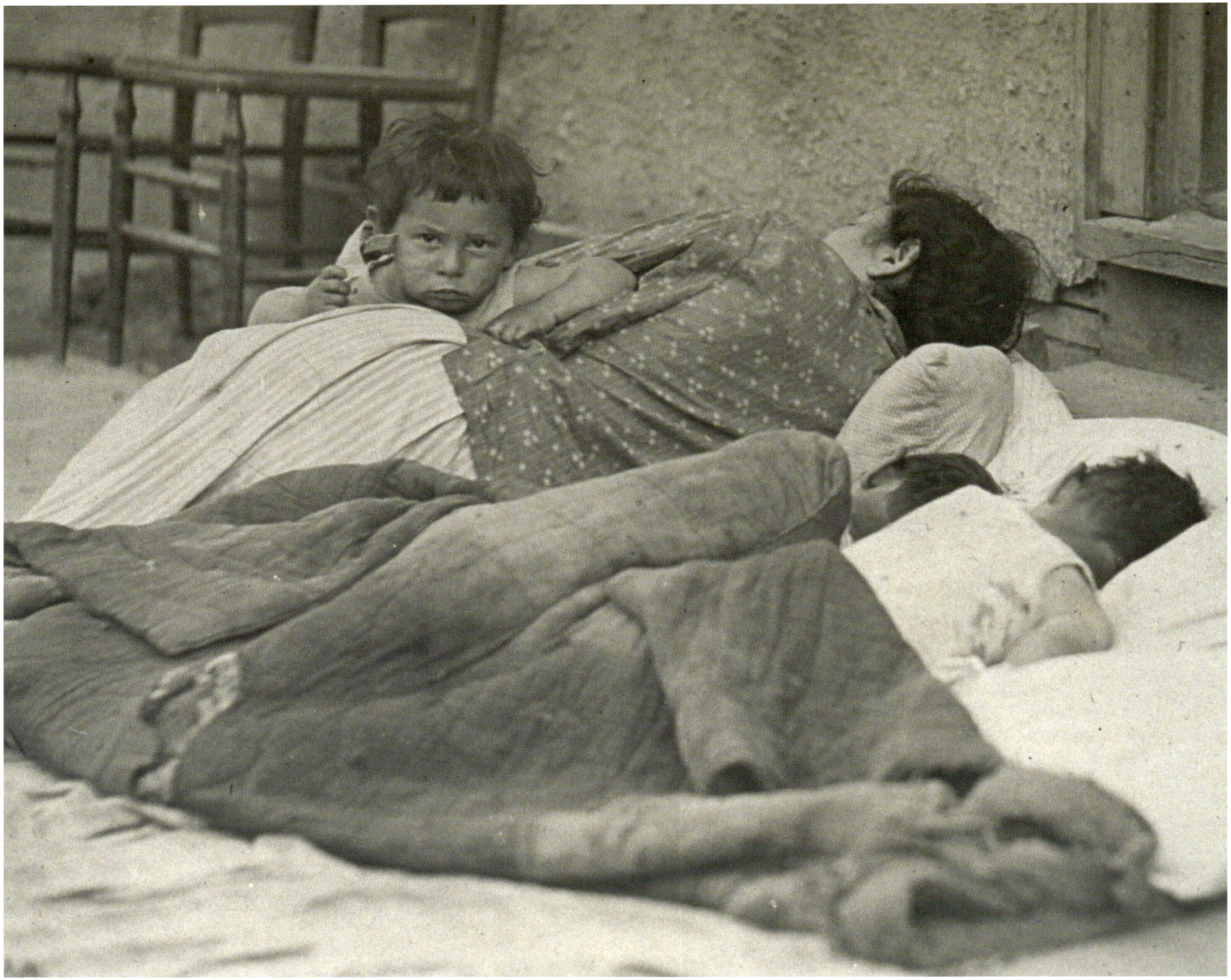

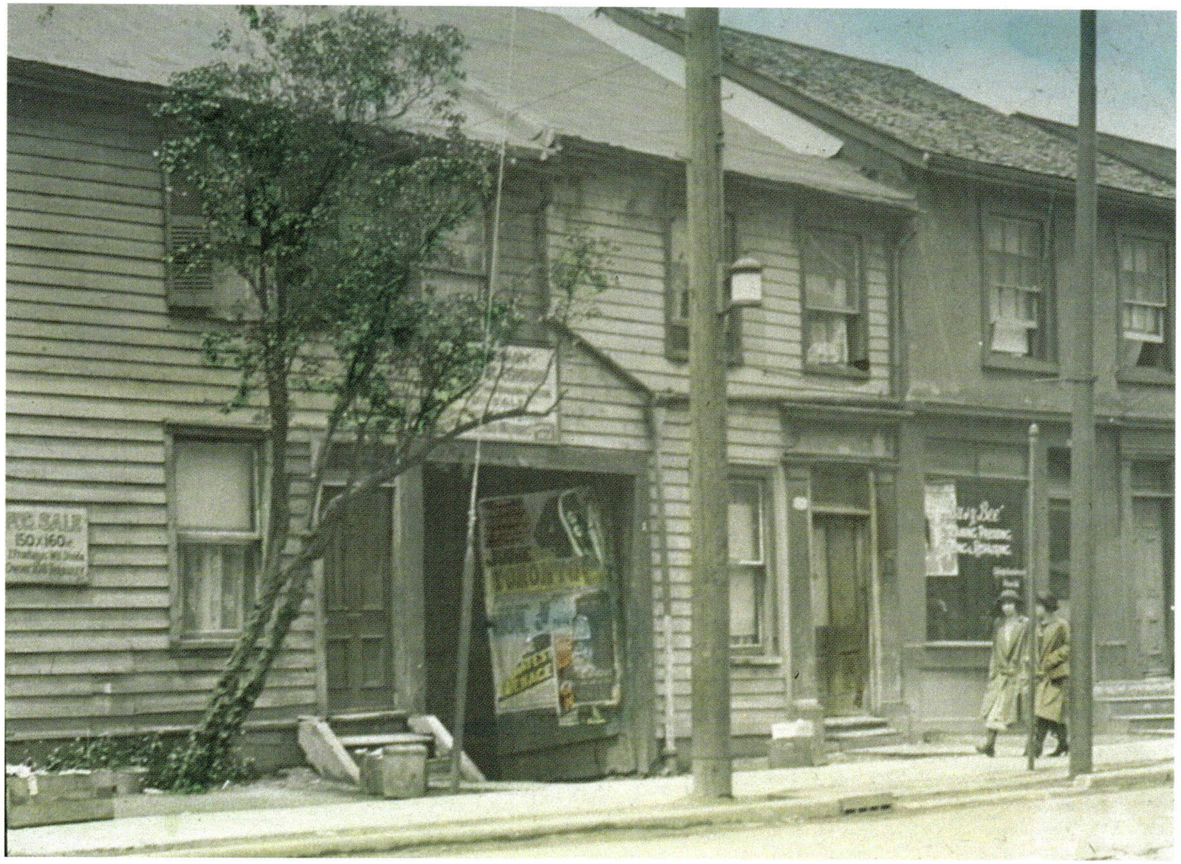

Far left: *A family sleeping in the street. By 1907, the Ward was being vilified by the press and colonized by charities. As J.M.S. Careless observed, however, "brothels and disorderly houses ... were largely found in poor, English-speaking inner districts ... all outside the Ward."* Left: *Old Terauley Street, circa 1920. Terauley ran between Queen and College where Bay Street is now. It was named after Terauley Cottage, the home of Dr. James Macauley, surgeon of the Queen's Rangers under Colonel Simcoe. The street became the western border of Macauley Town, Toronto's first suburb and, later, part of the Ward.*

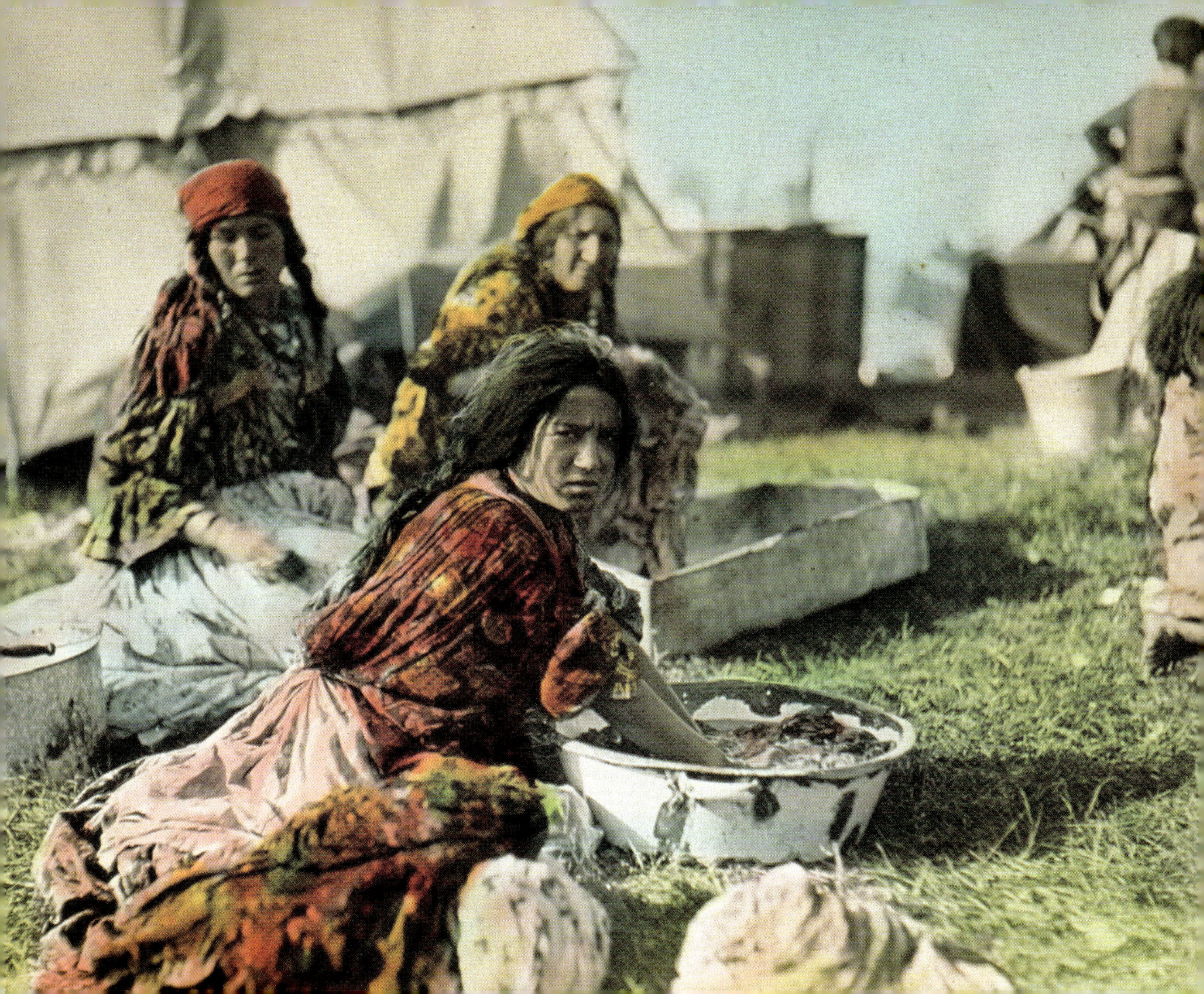

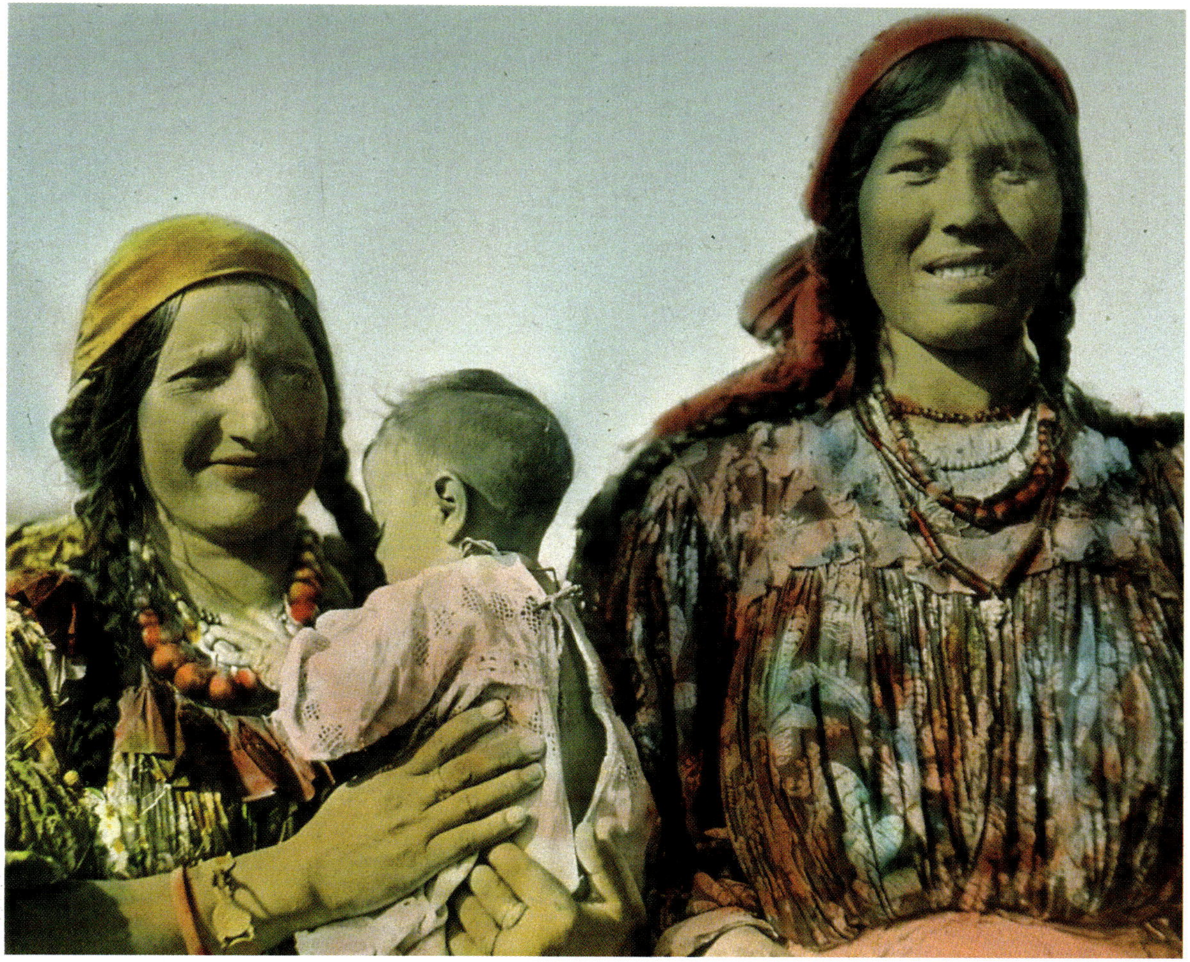

Left: “*Gypsy” camp, washday.*
Top: “*Gypsy” women with a child.*

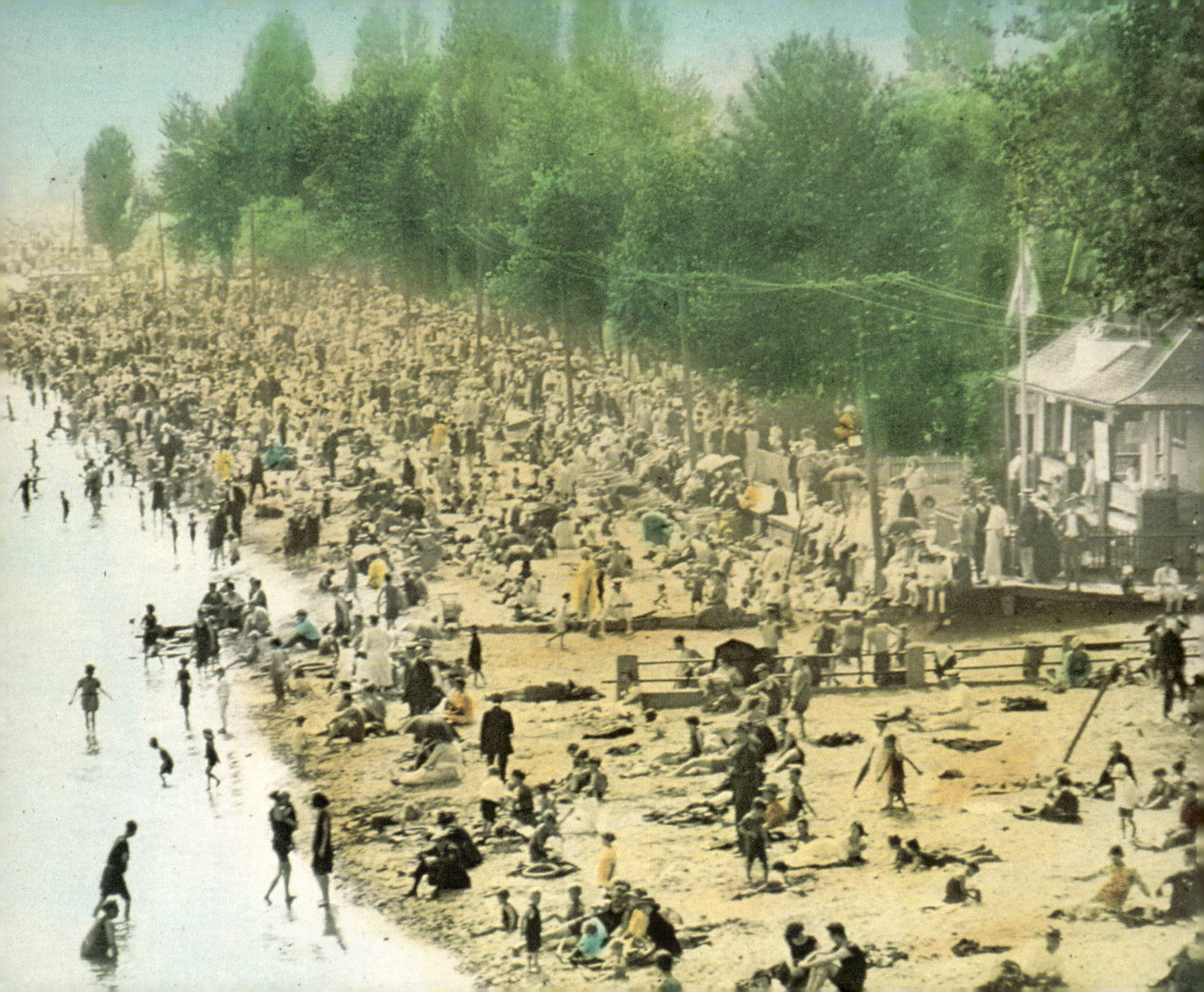

LEISURE

Left: *Bathers at Kew Beach, circa 1925. Kew Beach and Kew Gardens were purchased by the city in 1907 to provide a wide range of pleasures for Toronto residents, including lawn bowling, tennis, and swimming.*

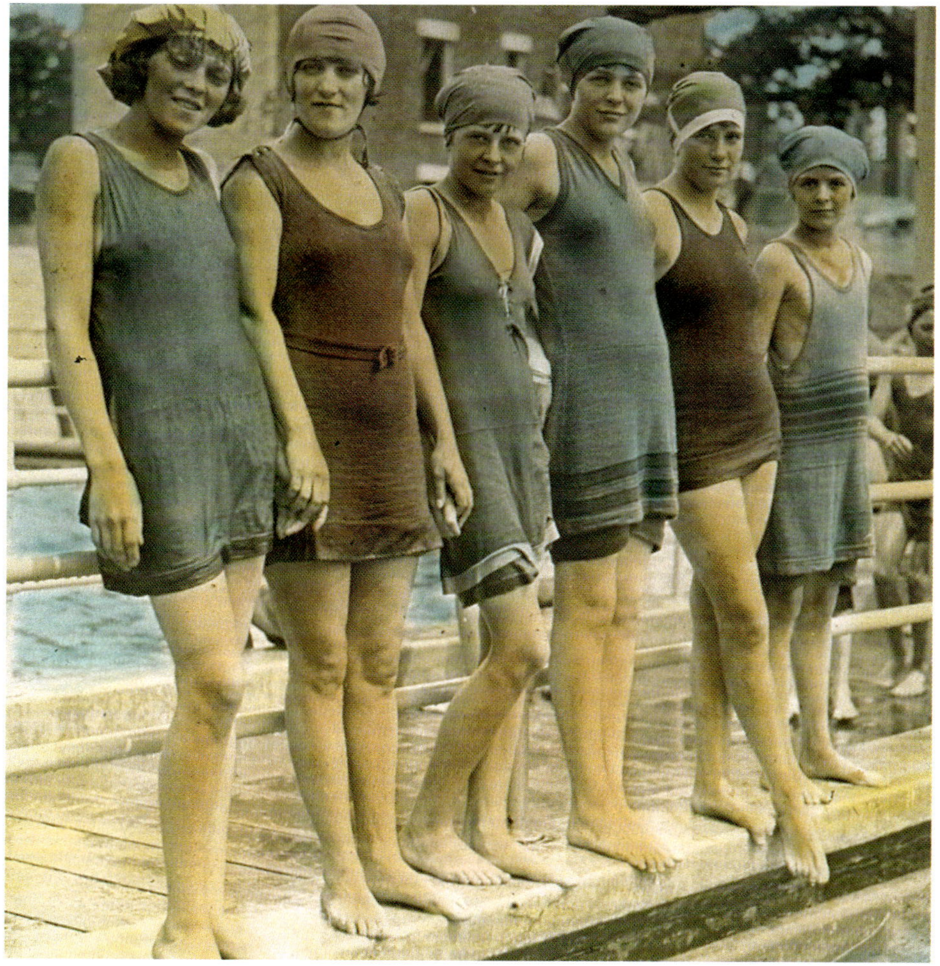

Left: *Young swimmers, 1920s.*
Far right: *Sunnyside Beach, 1923. The Sunnyside Bathing Pavilion, at left, opened in 1922. Attractions such as a rollercoaster and a ferris wheel, plus the boardwalk, made this reclaimed patch of land in the Humber Bay into "the poor man's Riviera."*

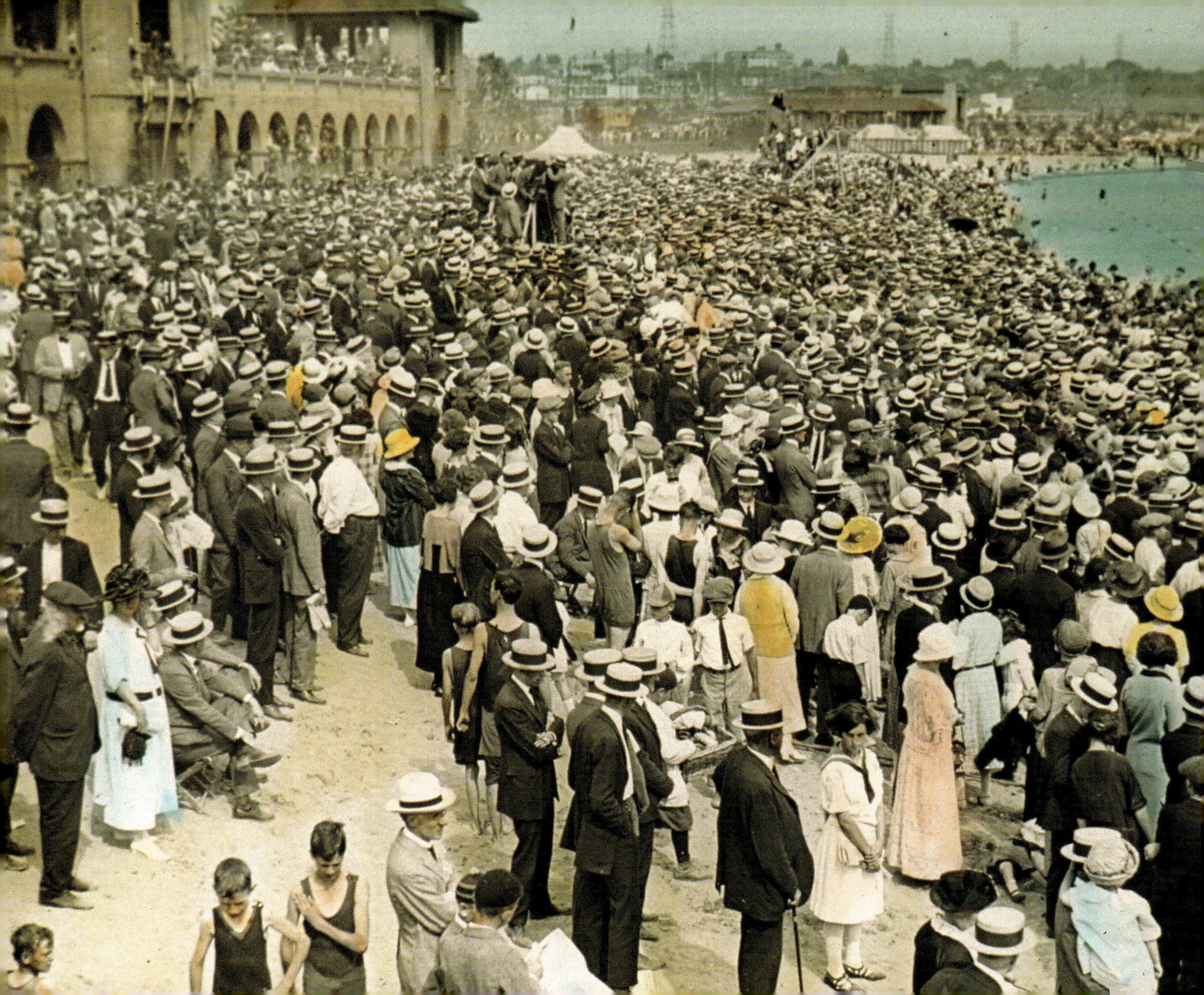

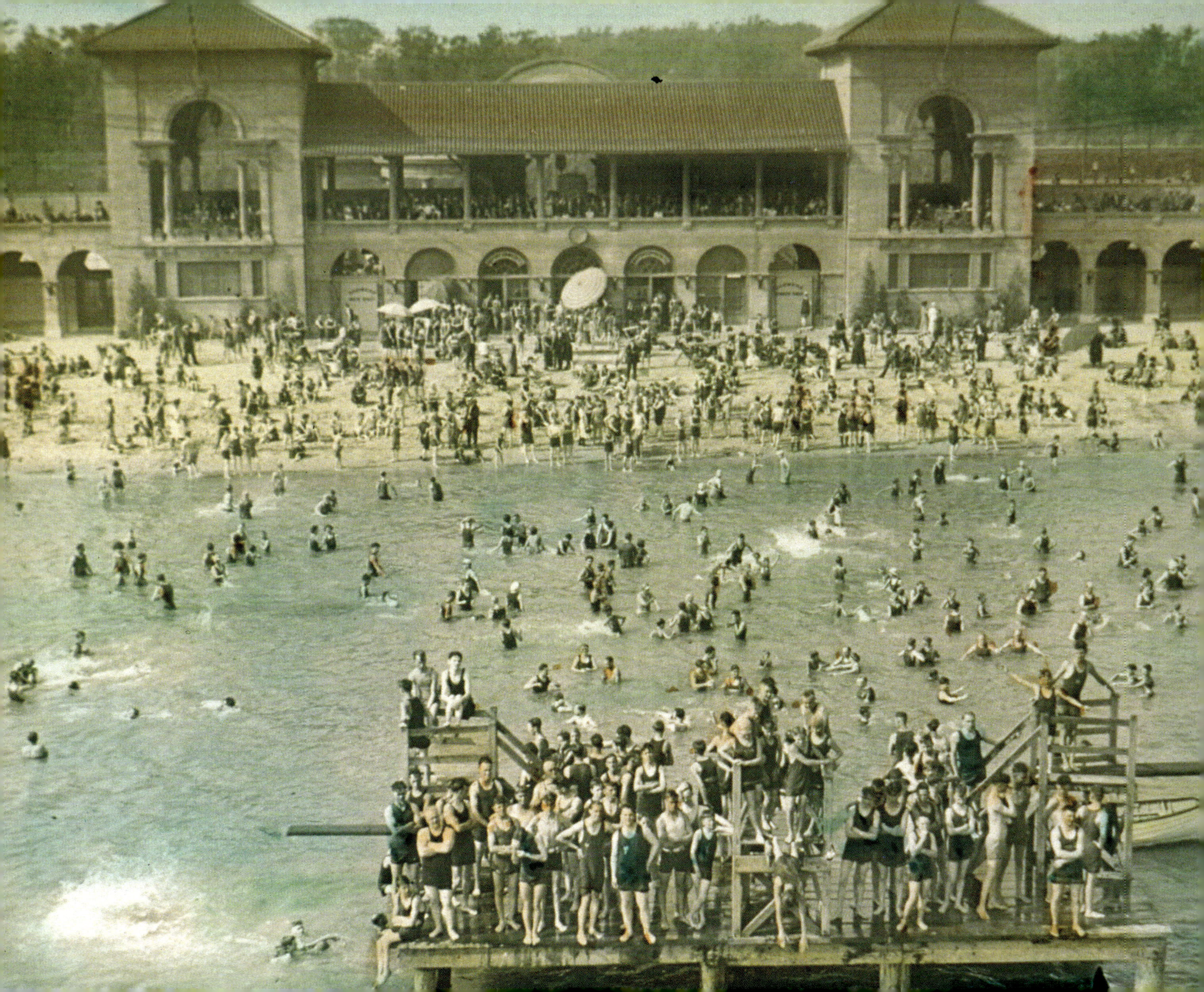

Far left: *Sunnyside Bathing Pavilion, 1923. The Toronto Harbour Commissioners transformed Sunnyside in the early twenties, erecting a breakwater to protect swimmers and small boats, an amusement park, and the bathing pavilion, which still stands.* Right: *Swimming lesson, circa 1920. These boys are at the Don Free Bathing Station, just north of the Prince Edward (Bloor Street) Viaduct. Free bathing services were City Council's first recreation program for children, starting in 1897.*

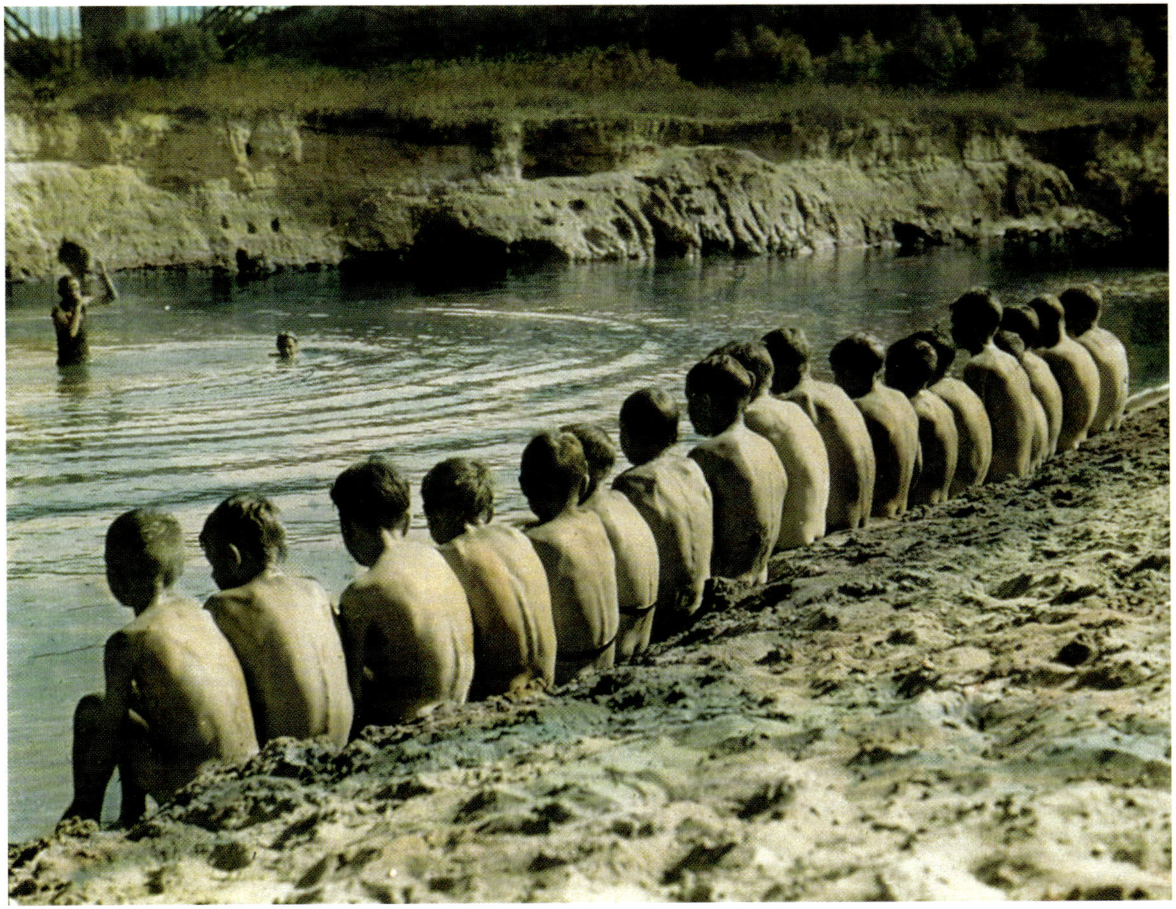

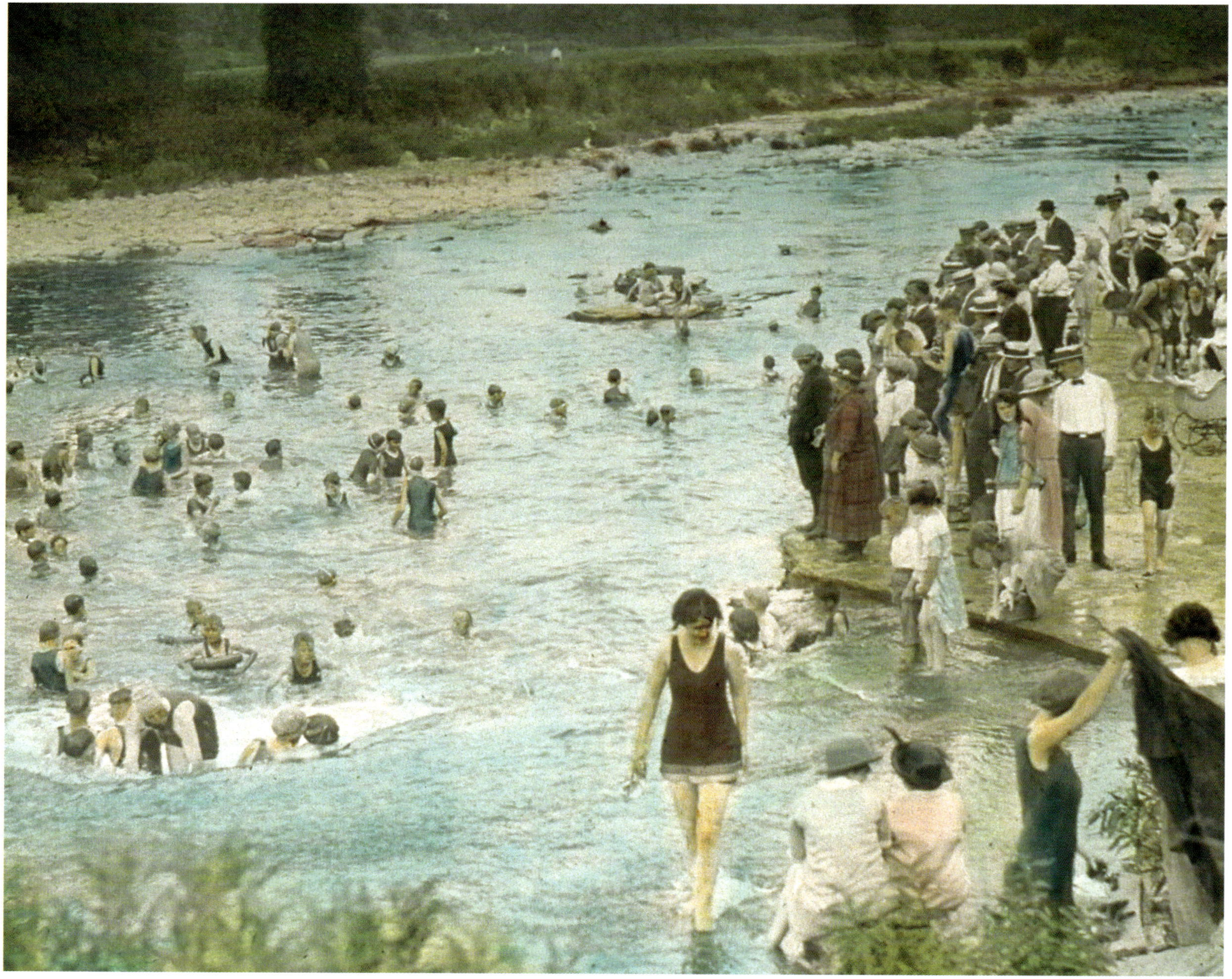

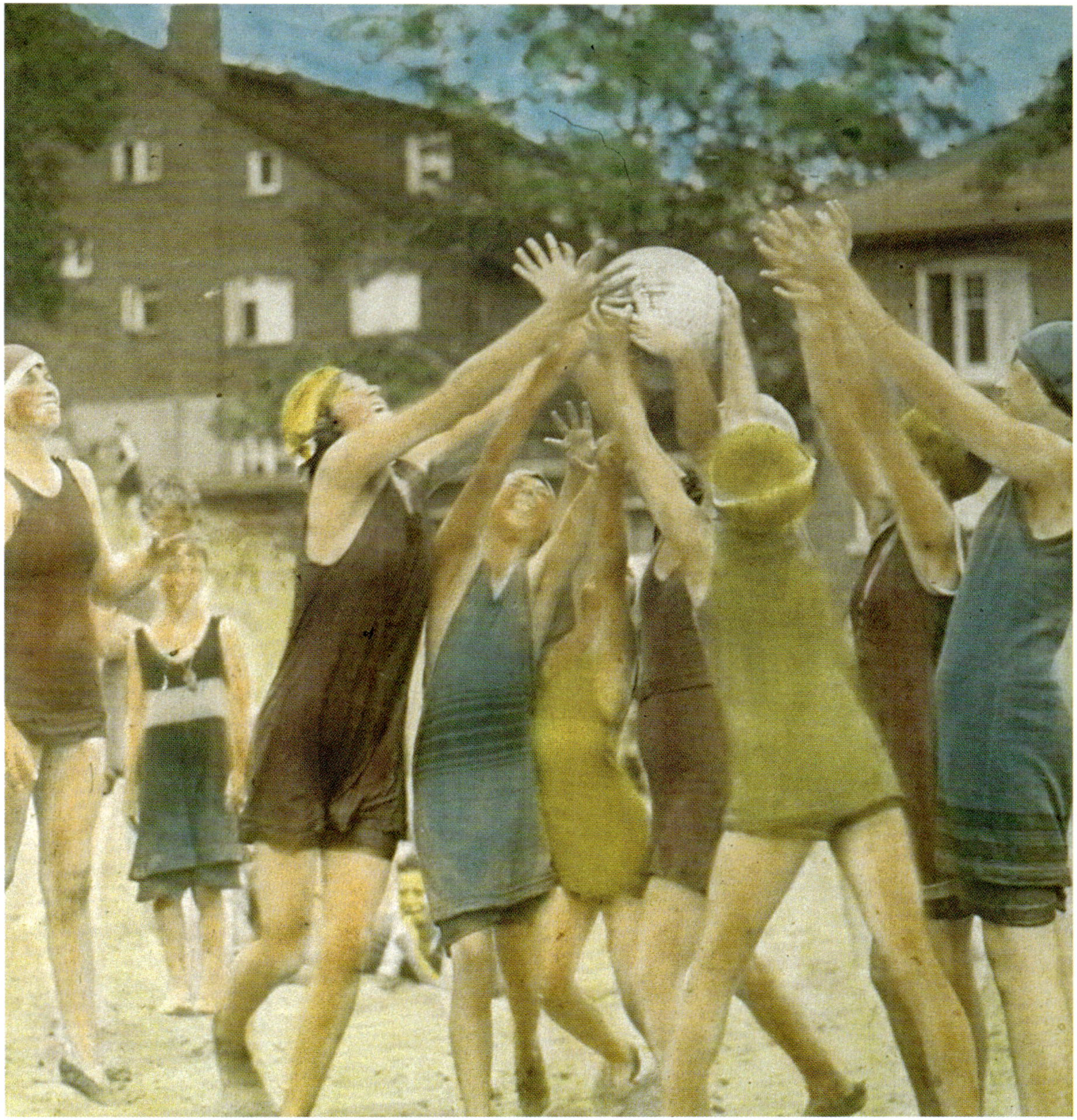

Far Left: *Bathers in a river, 1920s.* Left: *Girls playing on the beach, 1920s.*

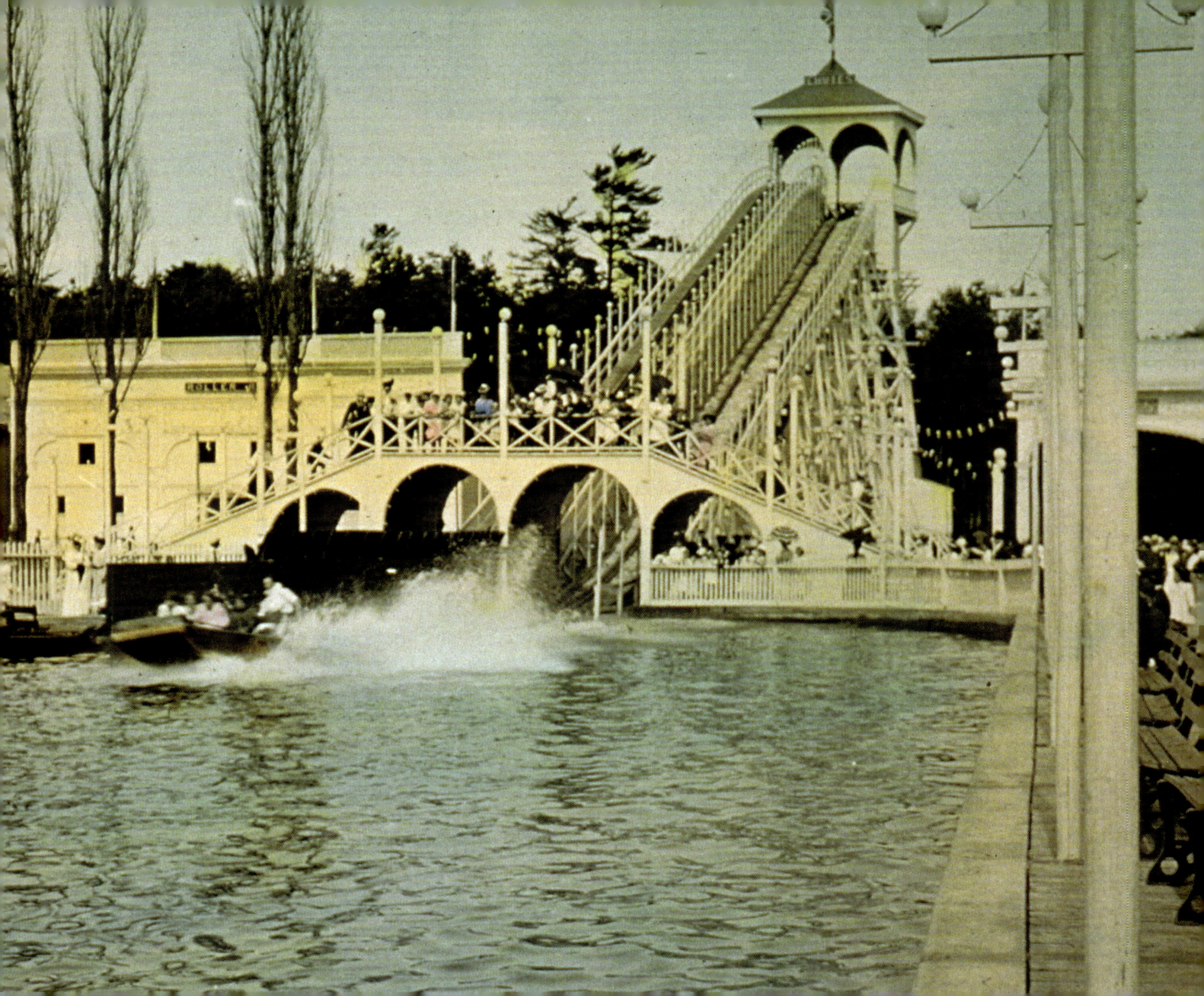

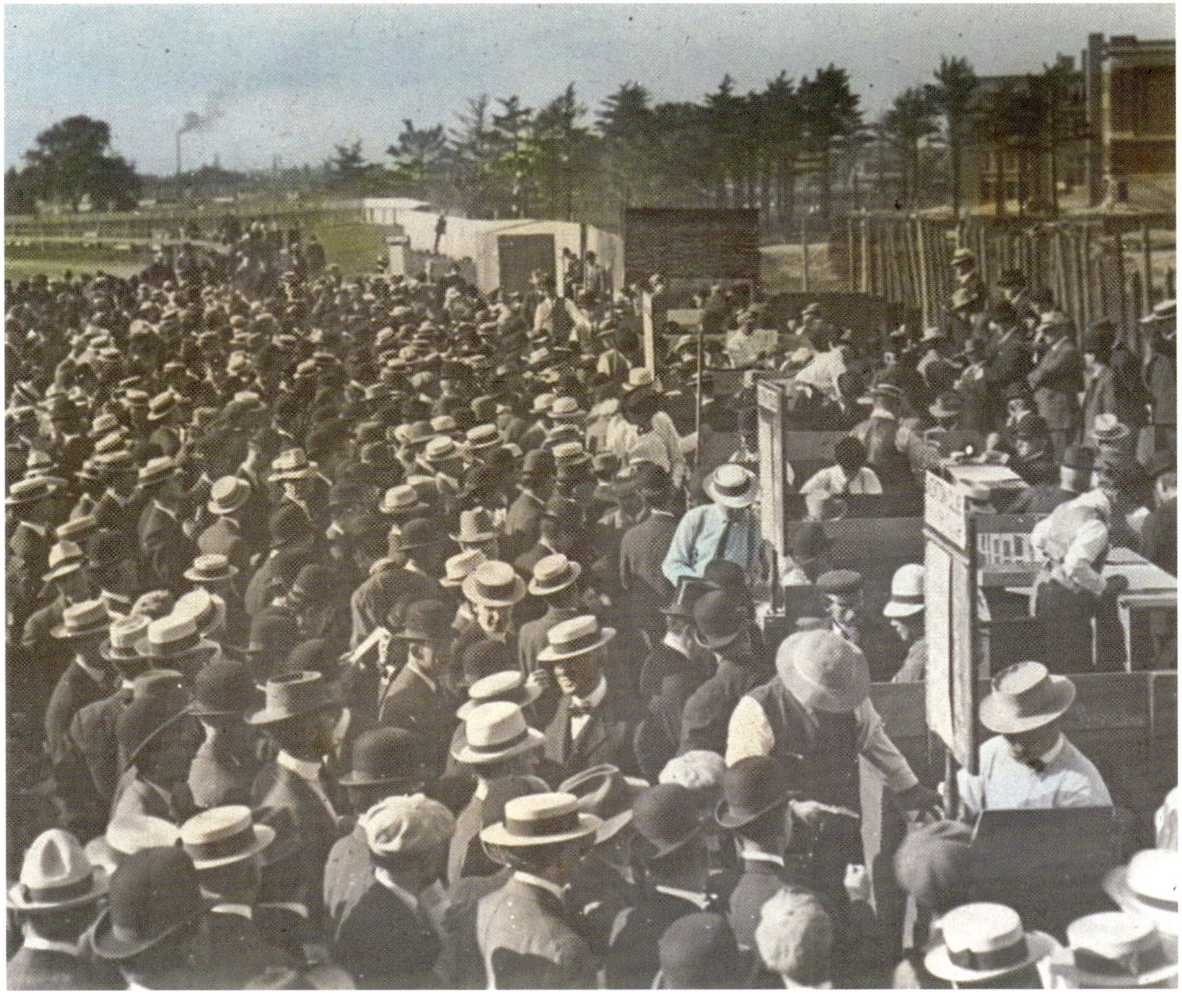

Left: *Water slide, Scarboro' Beach Amusement Park, 1910. This ride was called "Shoot the Chutes" and was the most popular of many that opened in June of 1907. Scarboro' Beach was inspired by Coney Island and cost the Toronto Railway Company $600,000 to construct.* Right: *Dufferin Street betting, 1910. This racetrack, located between College and Bloor Streets, was torn down in the 1950s.*

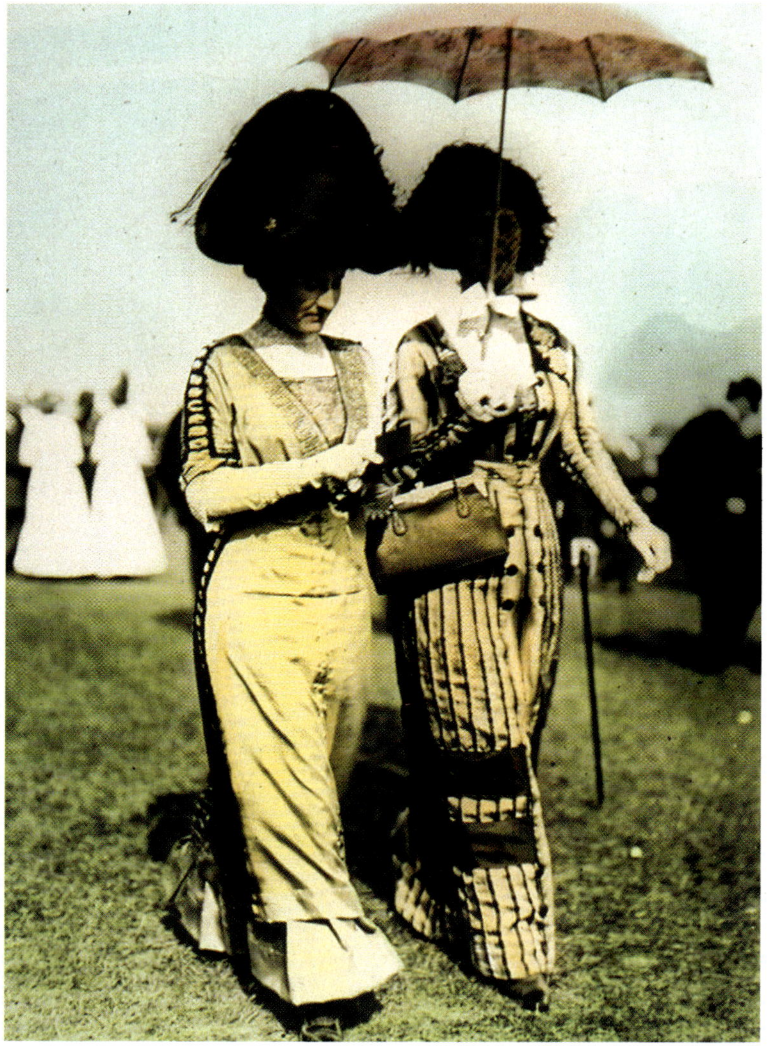

Left: *Fashions at Woodbine, 1910. The prestigious Queen's Plate ran at Woodbine starting in 1883.* Far right: *A fashionable group at Sunnyside, 1923. Strollers such as these would have made ample use of Sunnyside's promenade, or boardwalk, which was twenty-four feet wide for most of its length.*

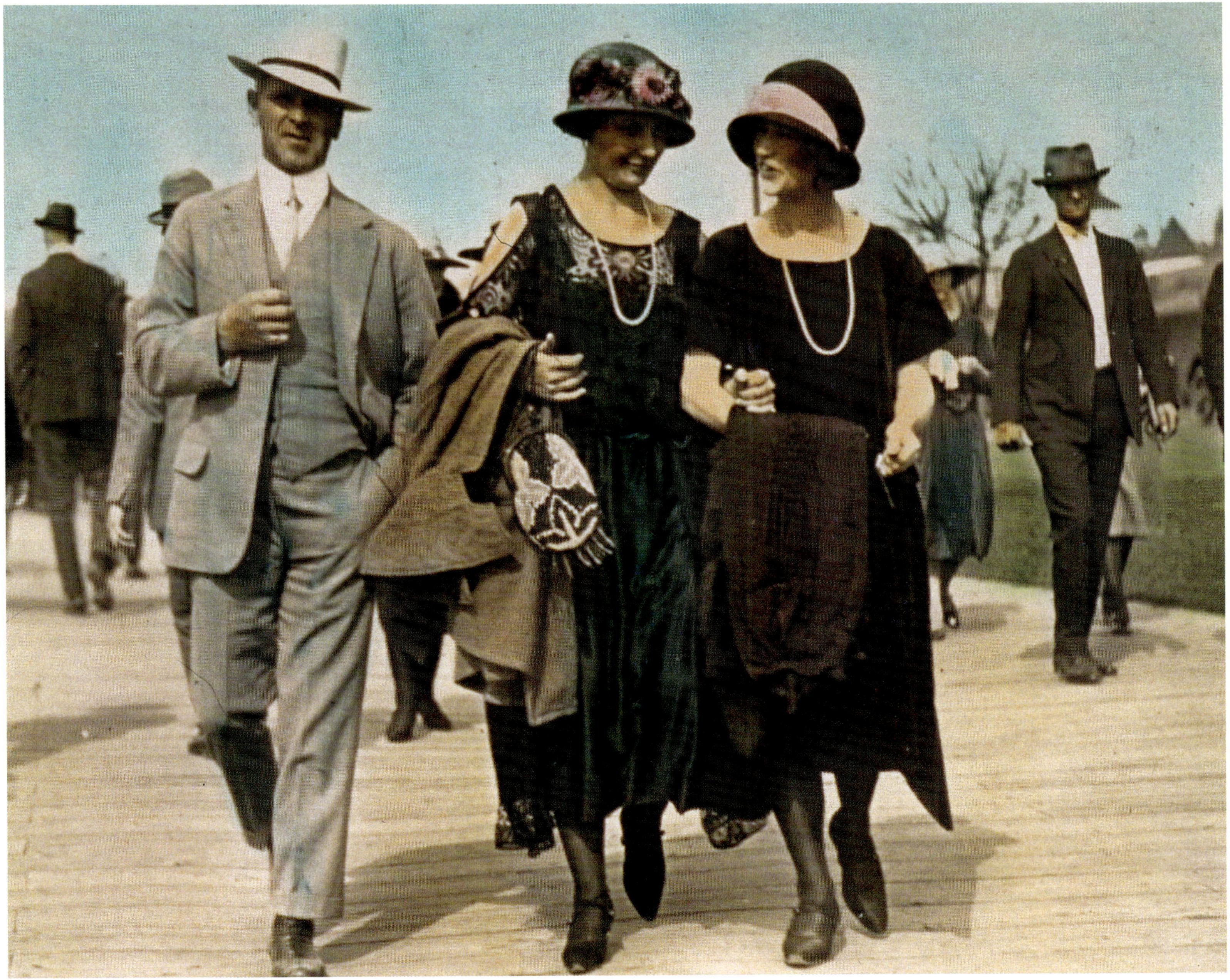

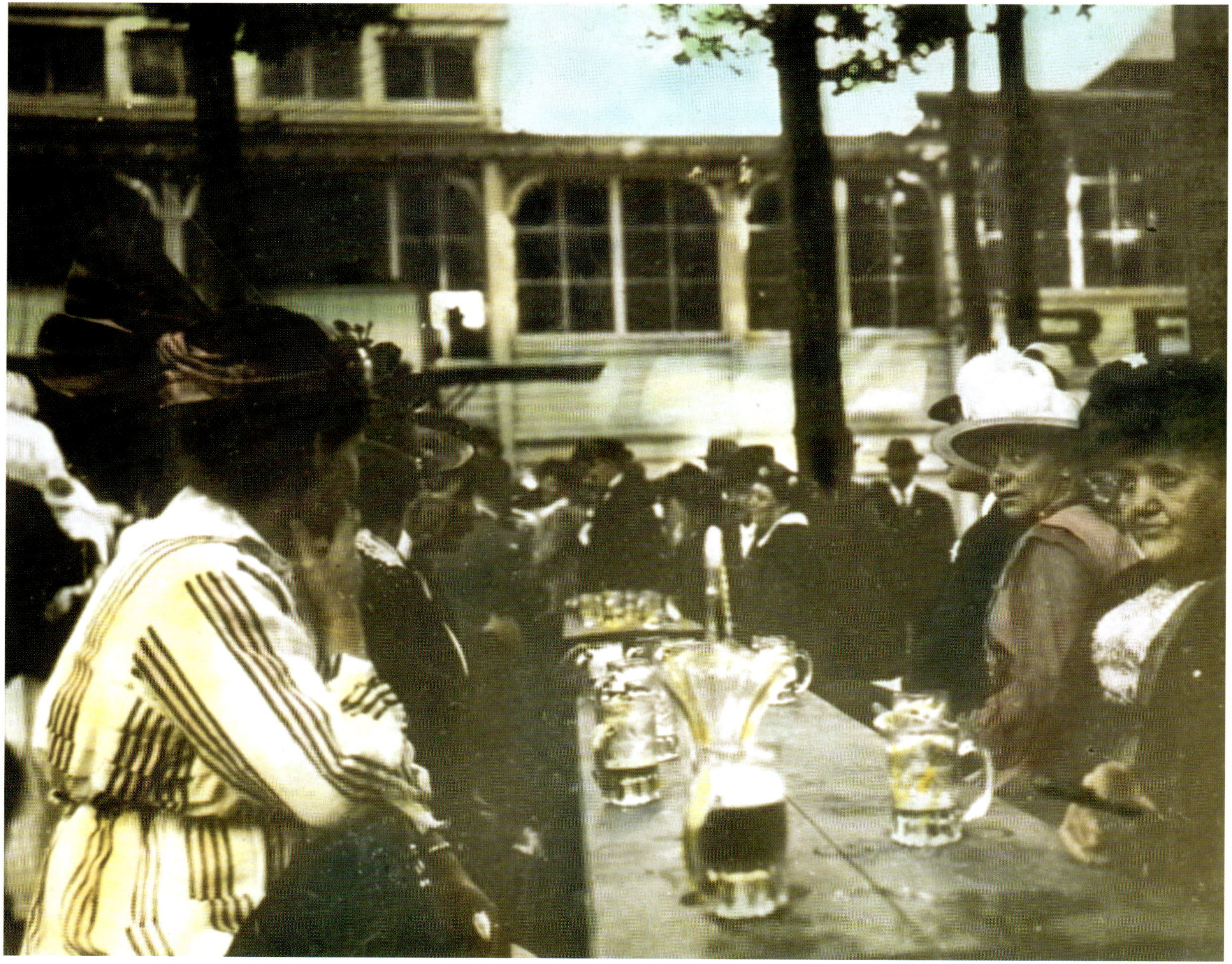

Left: *A Methodist picnic, circa 1910. There were over 60,000 Methodists in Toronto at this time, equal to the Presbyterians in power. The Church of England (Anglican) still had the largest number of aherents (over 100,000). Temperance may well have been the topic for this table.* Right: *Munro Park, a popular destination in Toronto's east end, 1907.*

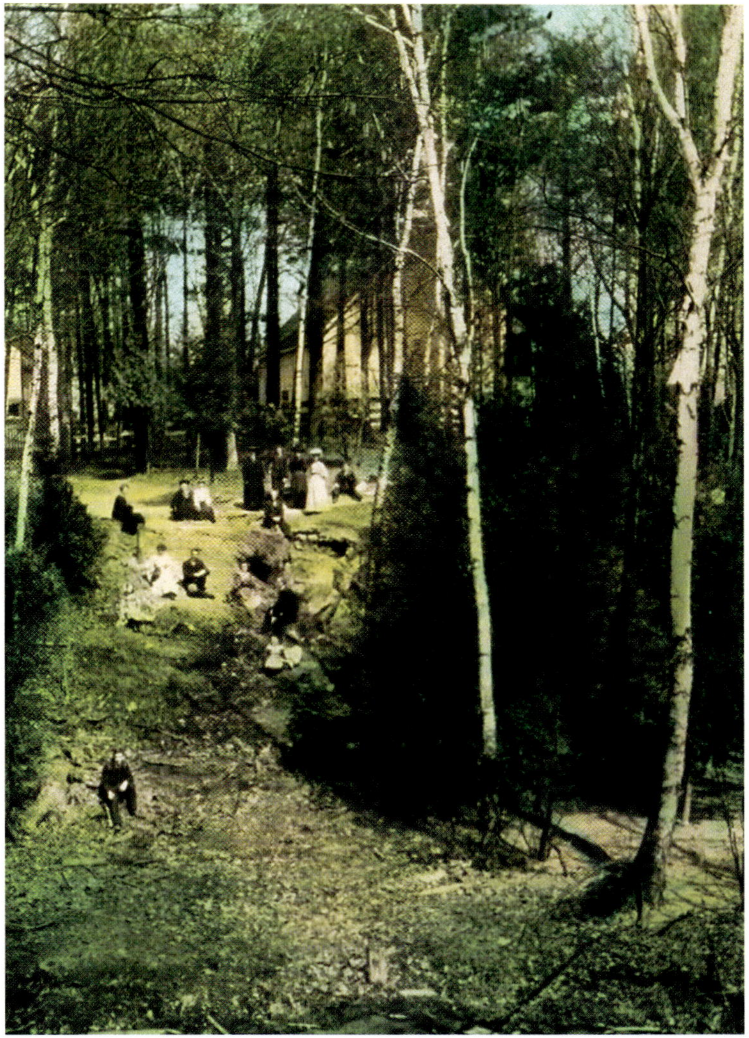

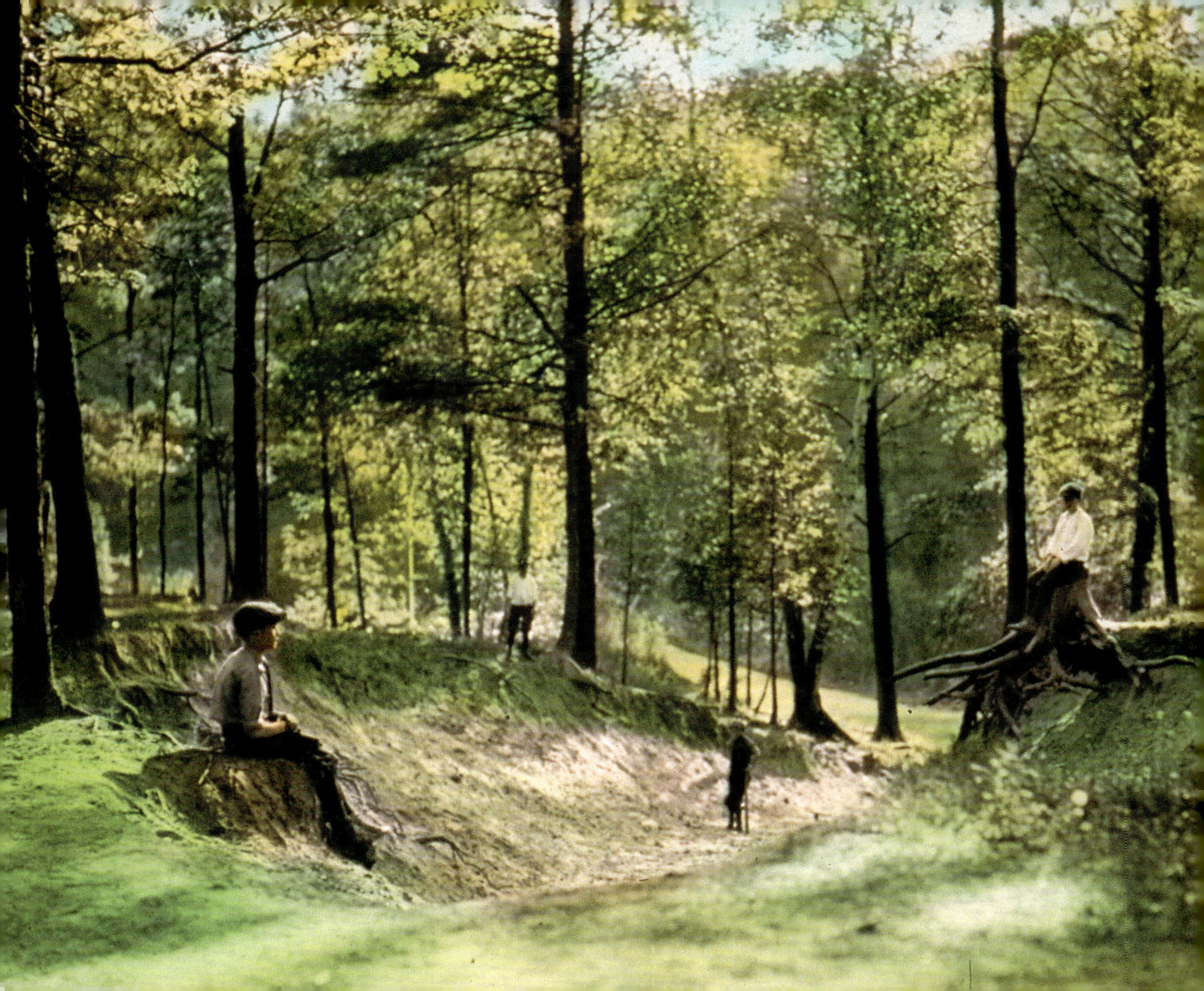

Left: *High Park, 1922. The park, originally the estate of architect John Howard, was donated by him to the city in 1873.* Right: *William Lyon Mackenzie King and his parents, 1921. This was to be the election year in which King and his Liberals would win a bare majority, and he would begin the first of many years as prime minister.*

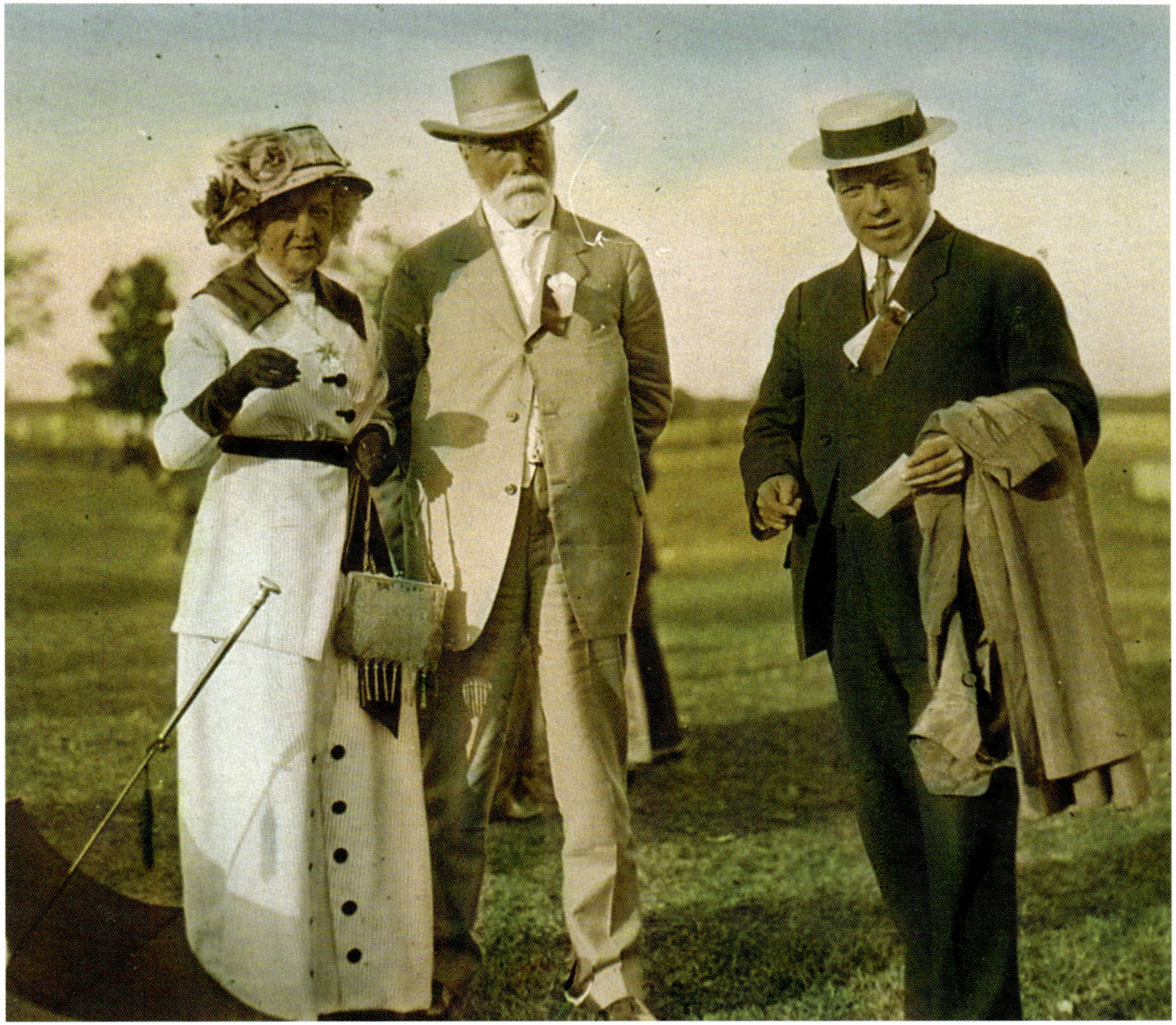

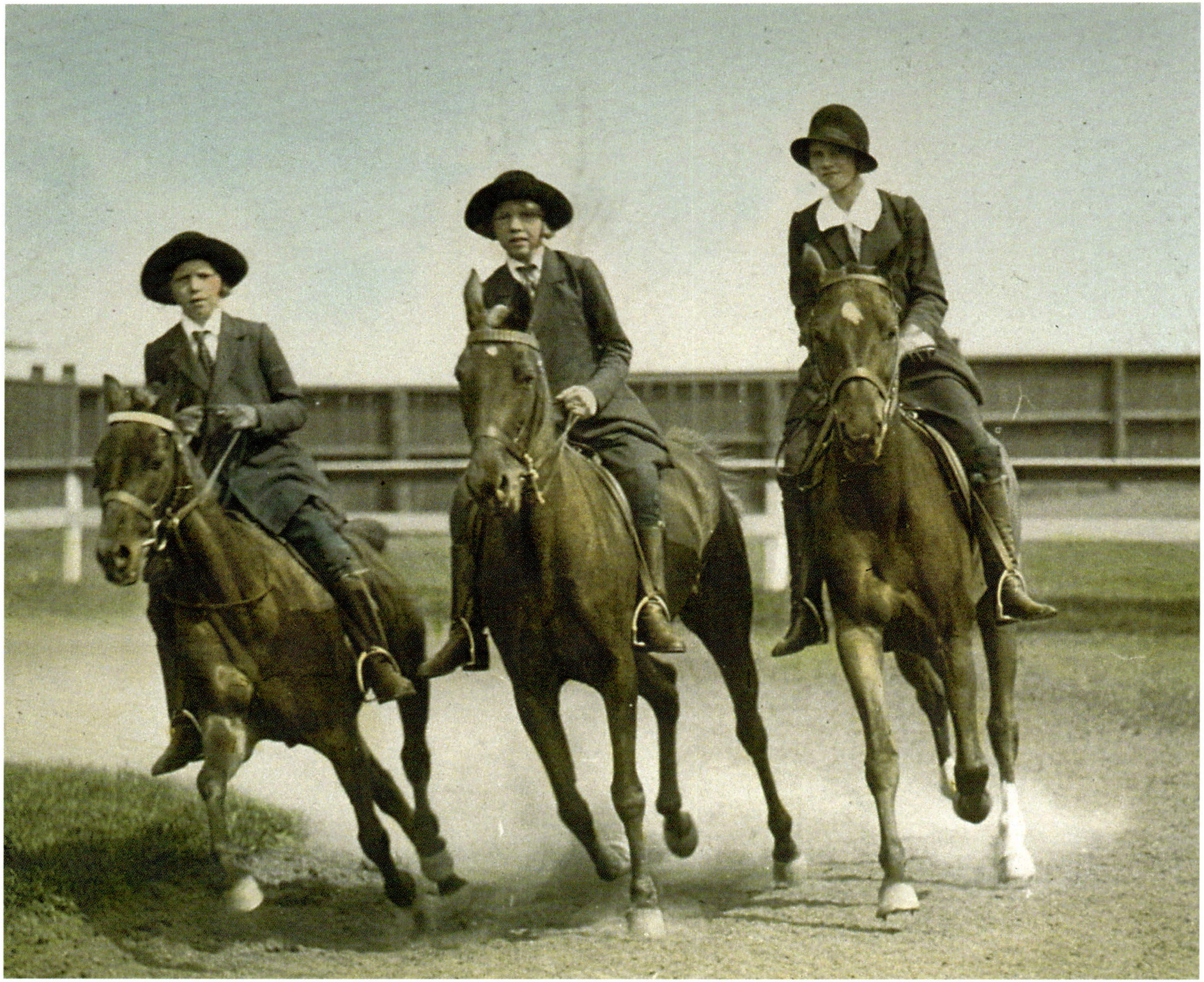

Left: *Children riding, probably Eatons, at the Eglinton Hunt Club, circa 1929.* Right: *Ethel Catherwood, circa 1928. Catherwood, the "Saskatoon Lily" won the gold medal for women's high jumping at the Olympics in 1928 with a record-breaking height of 5'11". She also won Canadian and Ontario championships.*

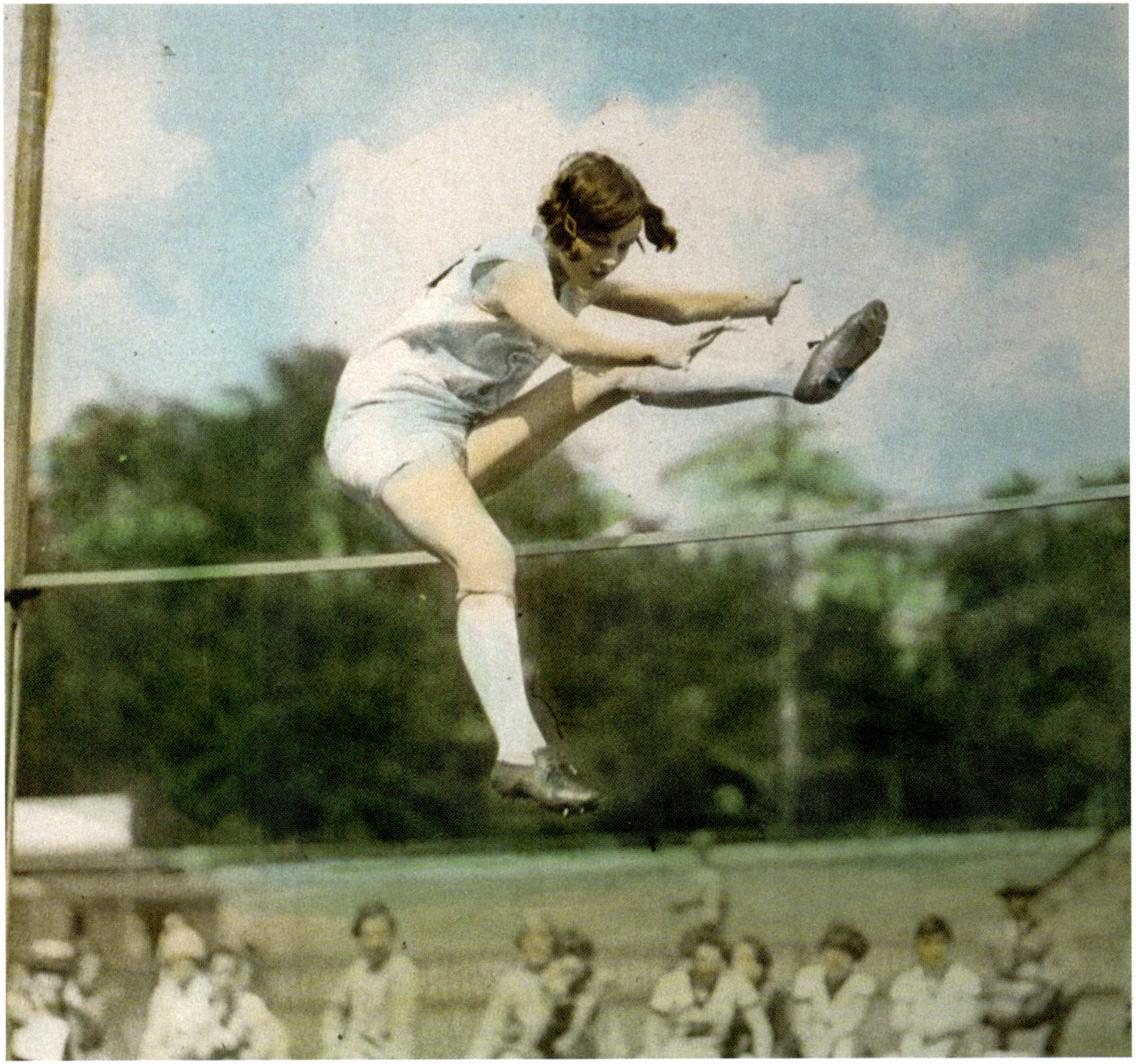

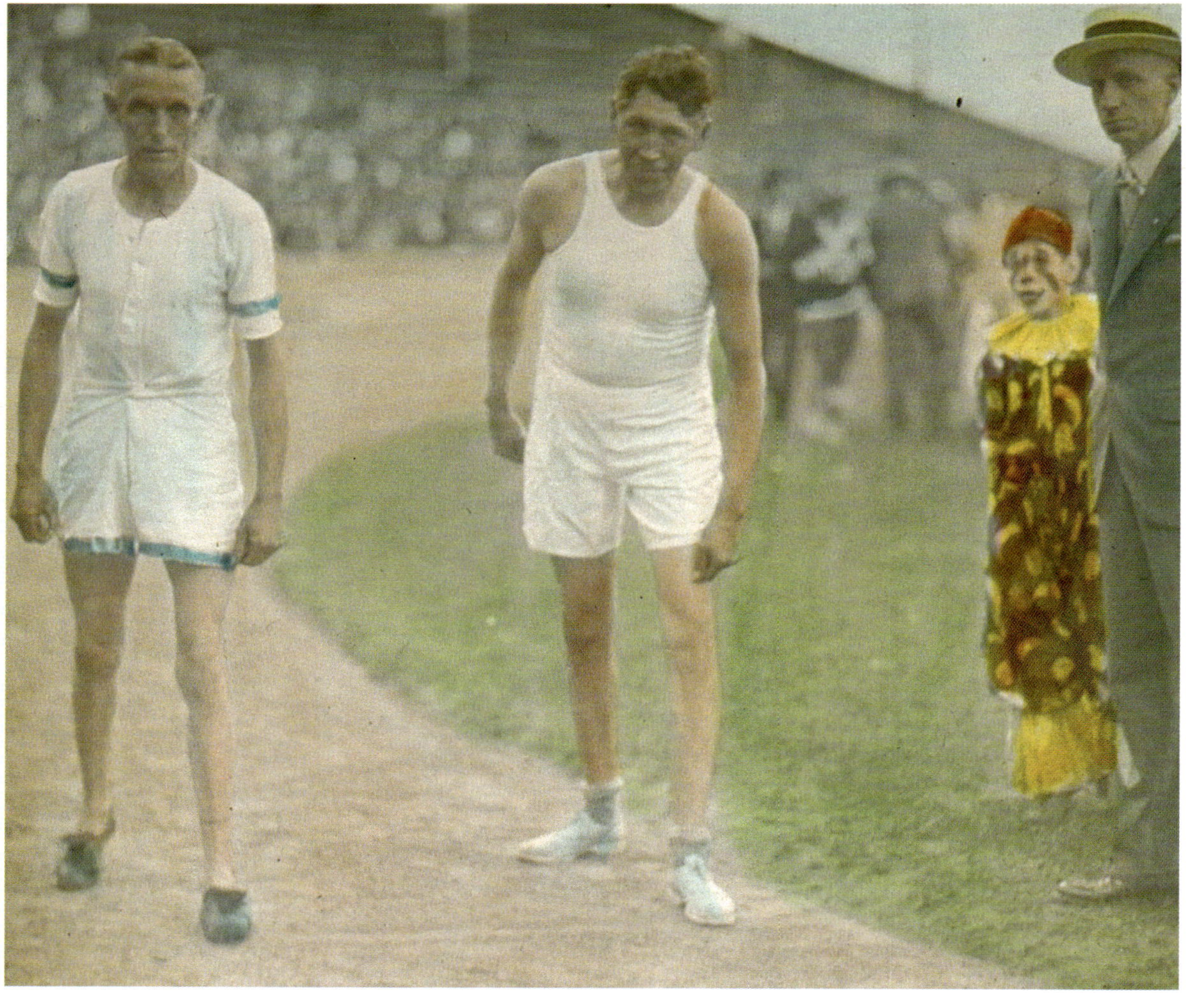

Left: *Alfie Shrub and Tom Longboat, 1931. Tom Longboat, the famous Six Nations runner, lived in Toronto until 1944.*
Right: *Toronto Golf Club, 1926. This golf club, Toronto's first, was established in 1876 by James Lamond Smith at his summer home east of downtown Toronto. By 1912 a new course had been set up in Etobicoke.*

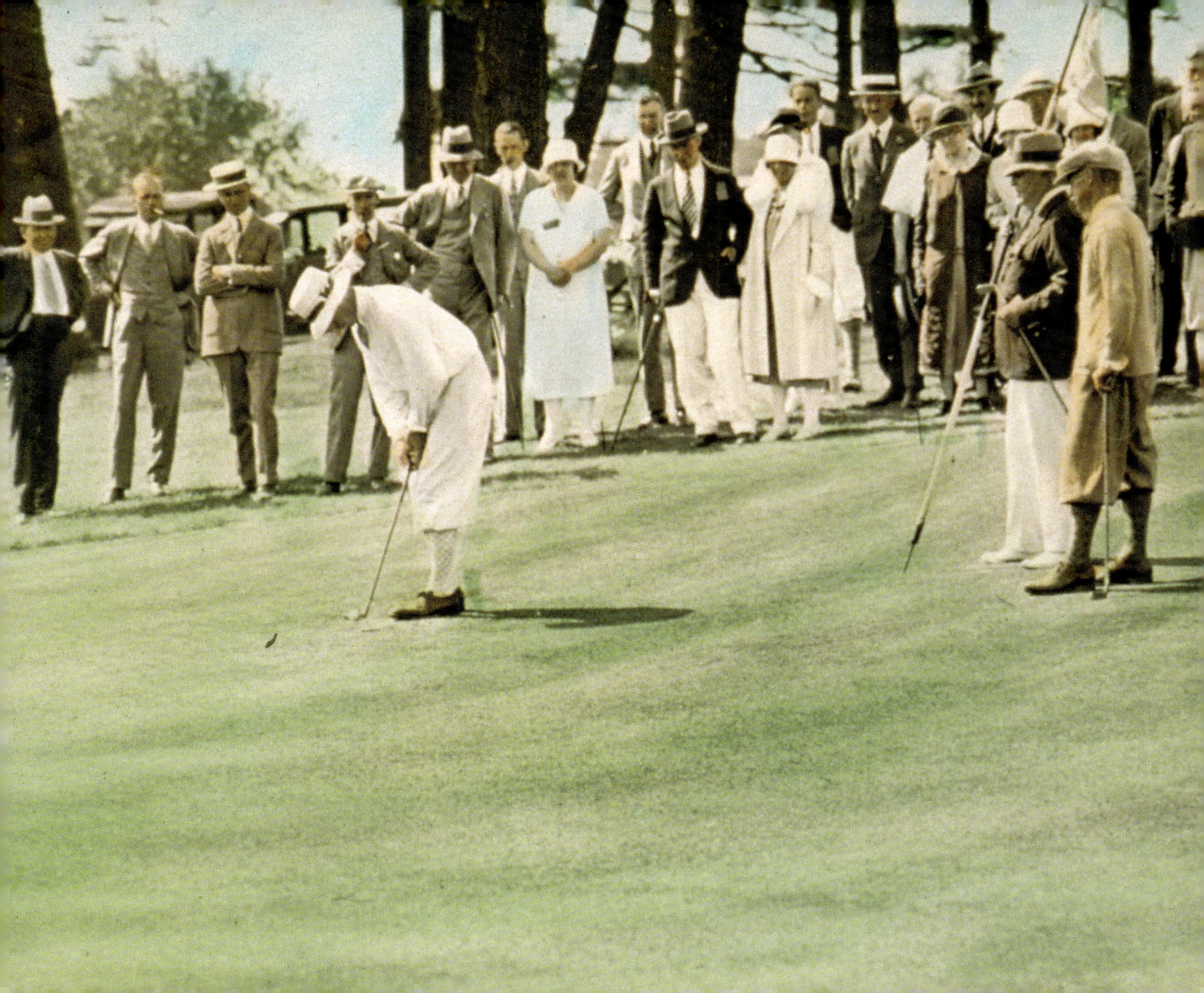

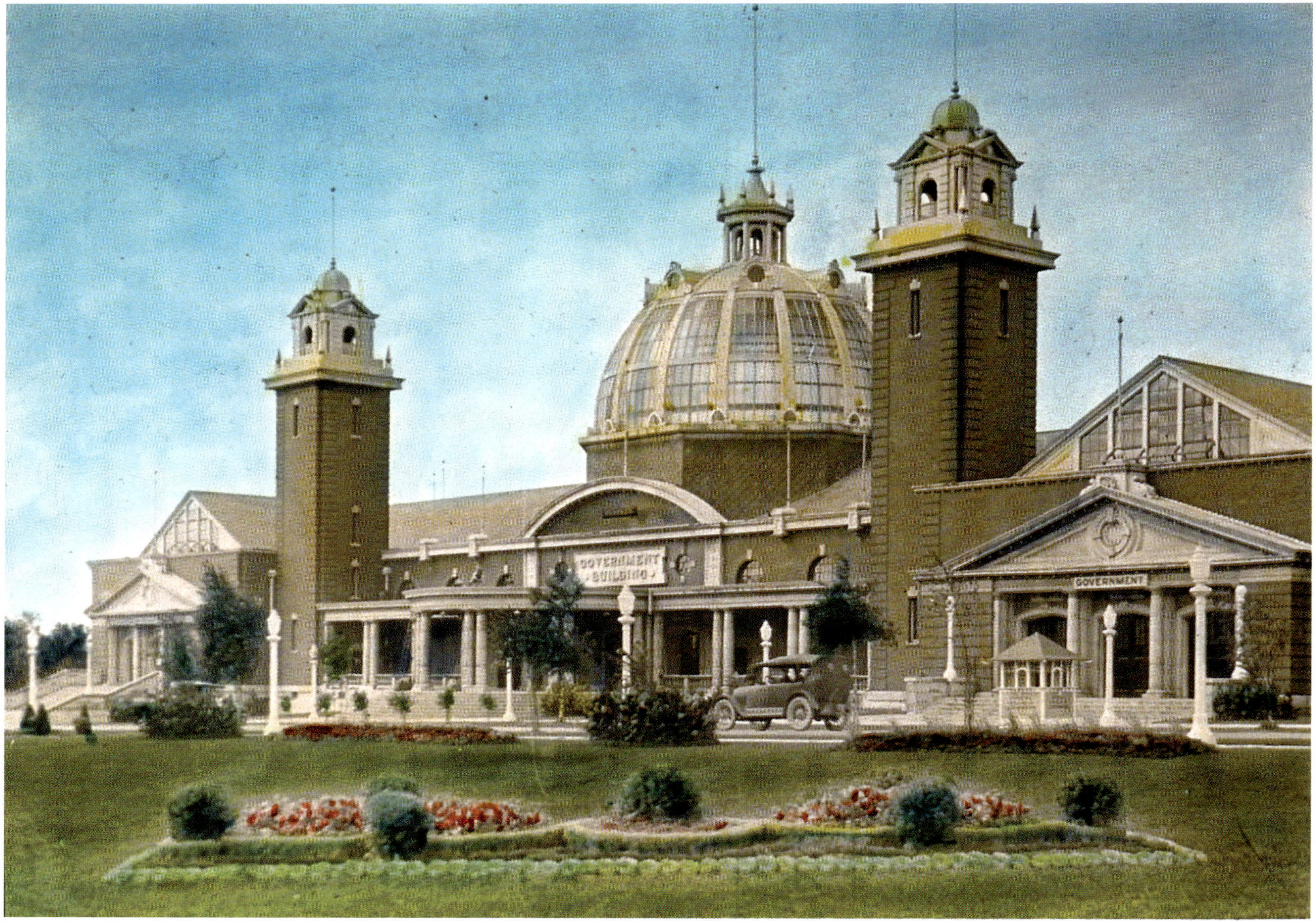
GOVERNMENT
BUILDING
GOVERNMENT

Left: *Government Building, 1923. The Canadian National Exhibition is oldest annual fair in the world. Its roots reach back to the provincial agricultural fairs of the 1840s, but it began in earnest with the founding of the Industrial Exhibition Association of Toronto in 1879.* Right: *Premier George Howard Ferguson and prize twins, 1925. Ferguson was the Conservative premier of Ontario for most of the twenties, setting a tone of industrial development and private investment. The CNE, established as an industrial fair, was the perfect venue for him.*

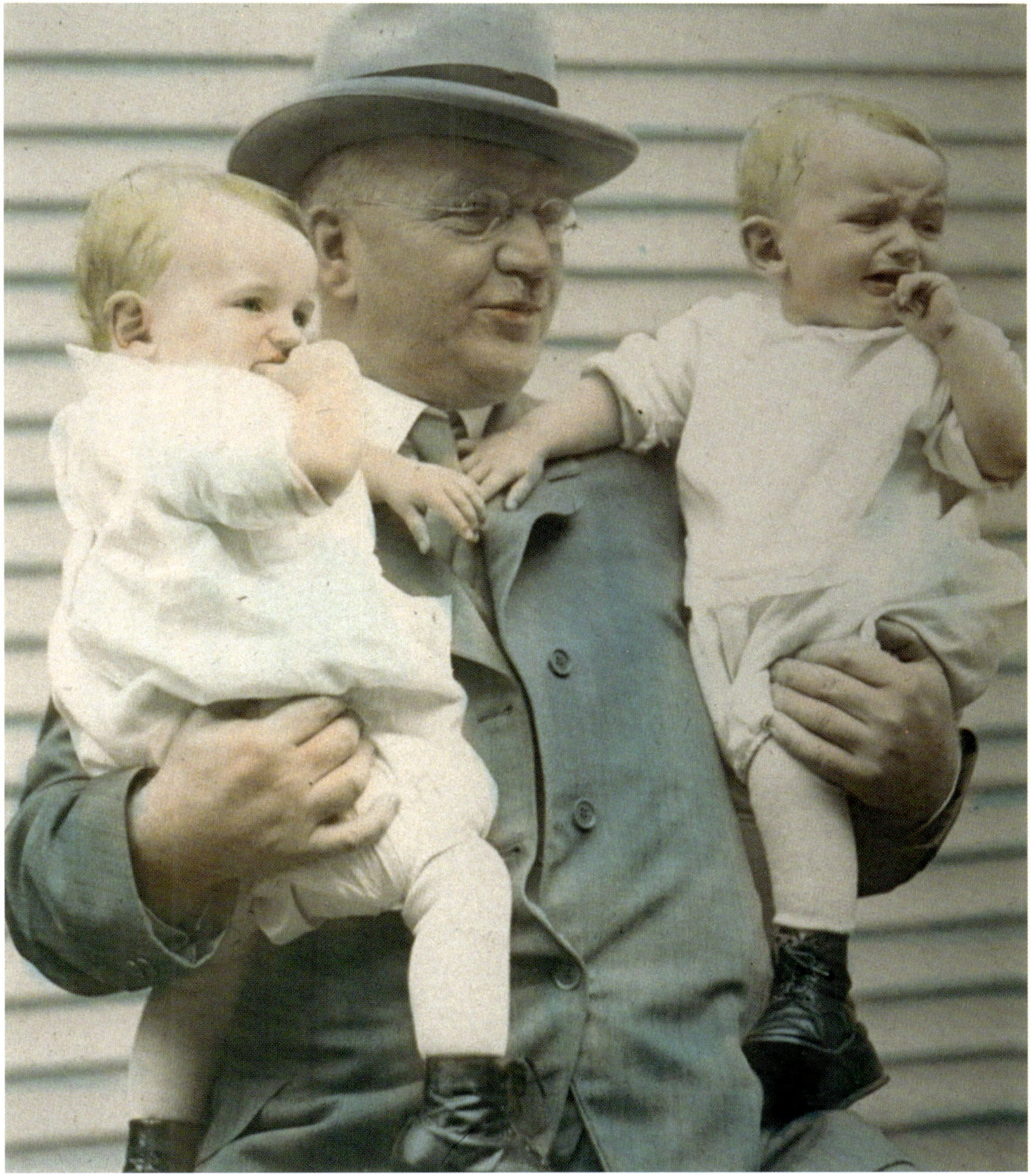

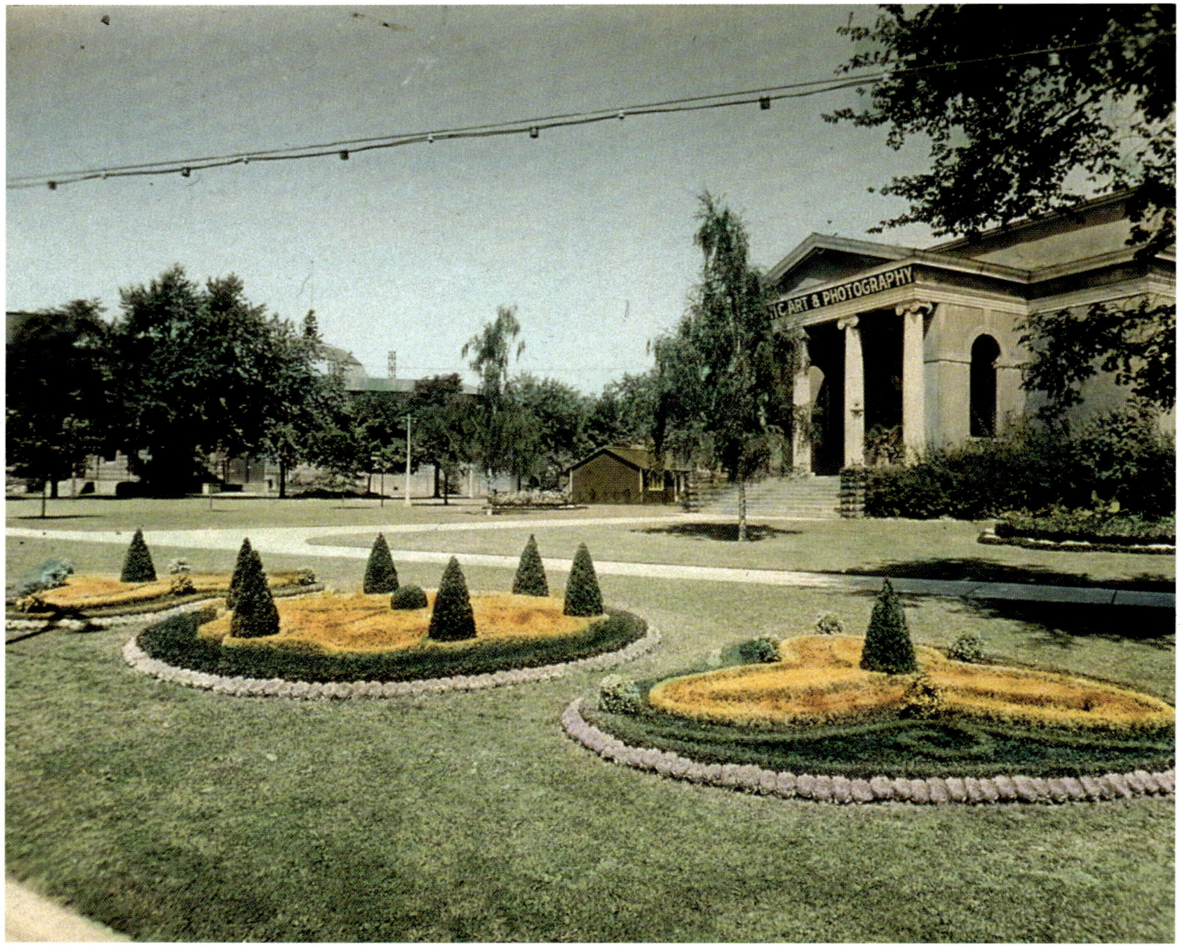

Left: *The Graphic Art & Photography Building, 1921. This building, of particular interest to James, fell prey to a snowstorm during the Second World War.* Right: *Palmistry, or fortune-telling, circa 1910. Entertainments like this were common on the midway and exhibition grounds.*

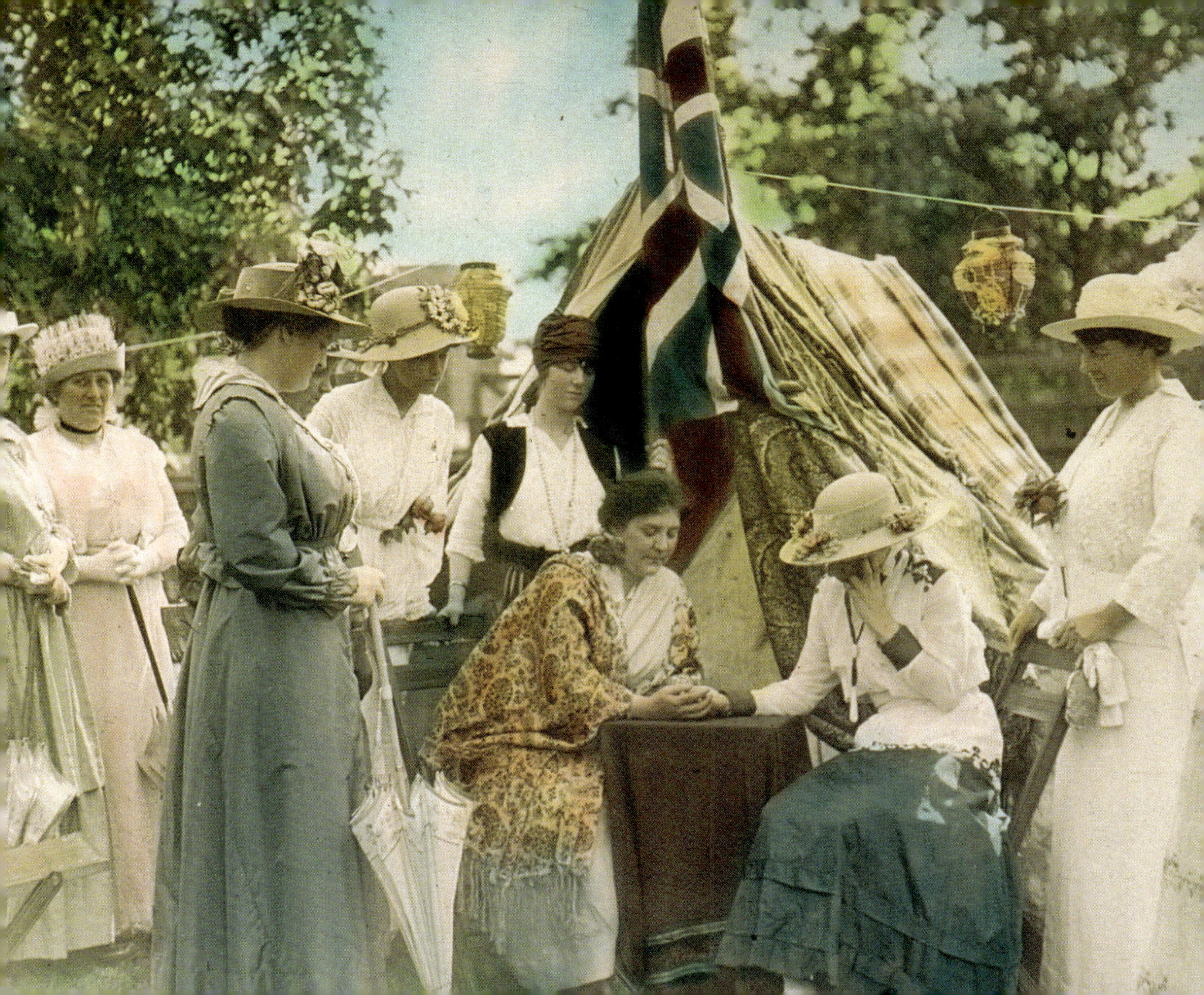

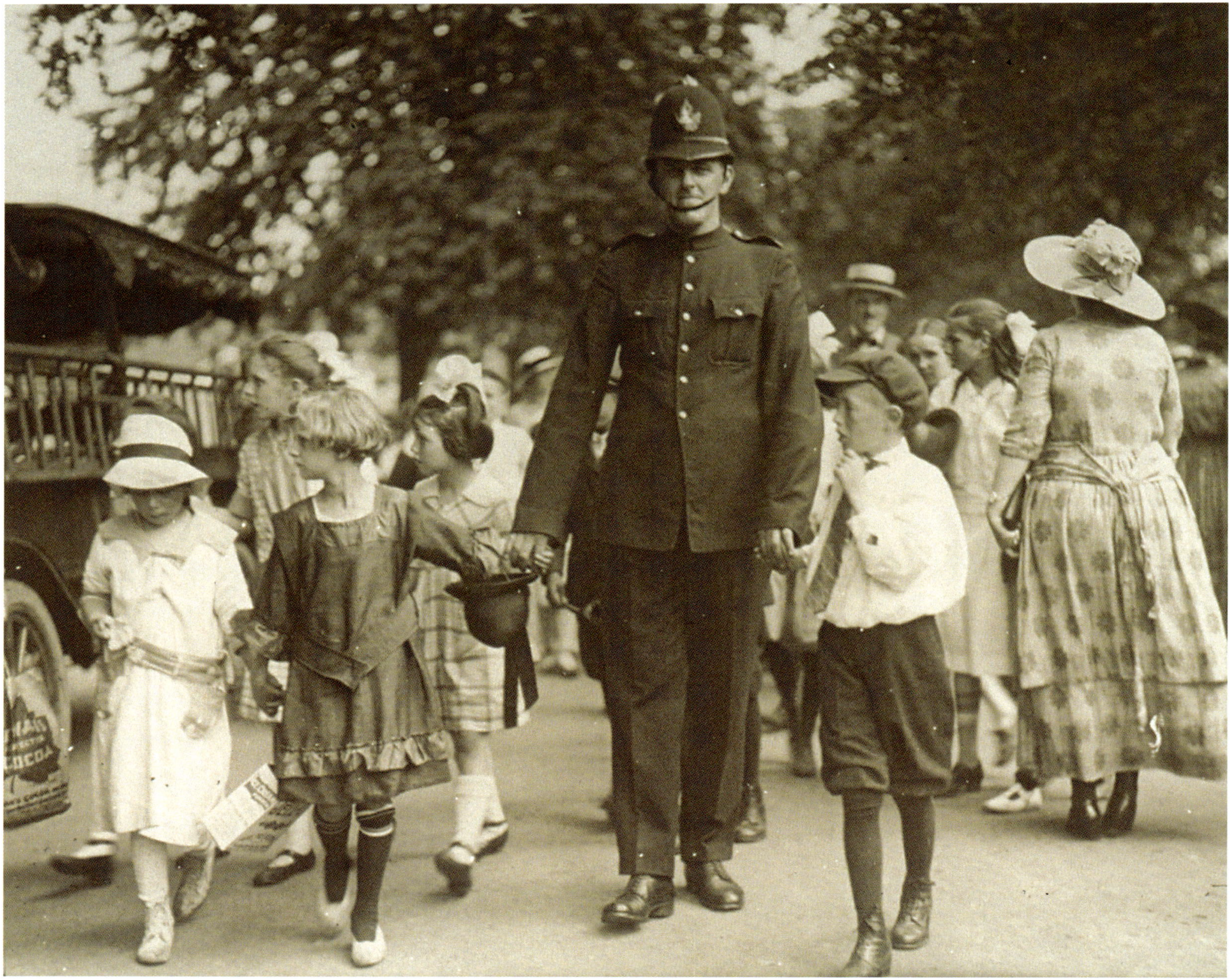

Left: *Lost children at the CNE, 1921.* Right: *Boats for swimmers, 1928. In 1927 George Young won the Catalina Marathon in California and returned to Toronto, a hero. Young agreed to compete that summer at the CNE as a special feature, and the CNE Wrigley Marathon Swims were born. Contestants in these races had to supply their own boats, which carried their manager, an oarsman, and a CNE observer. These boats are lined up at the foot of the Princes' Gates.*

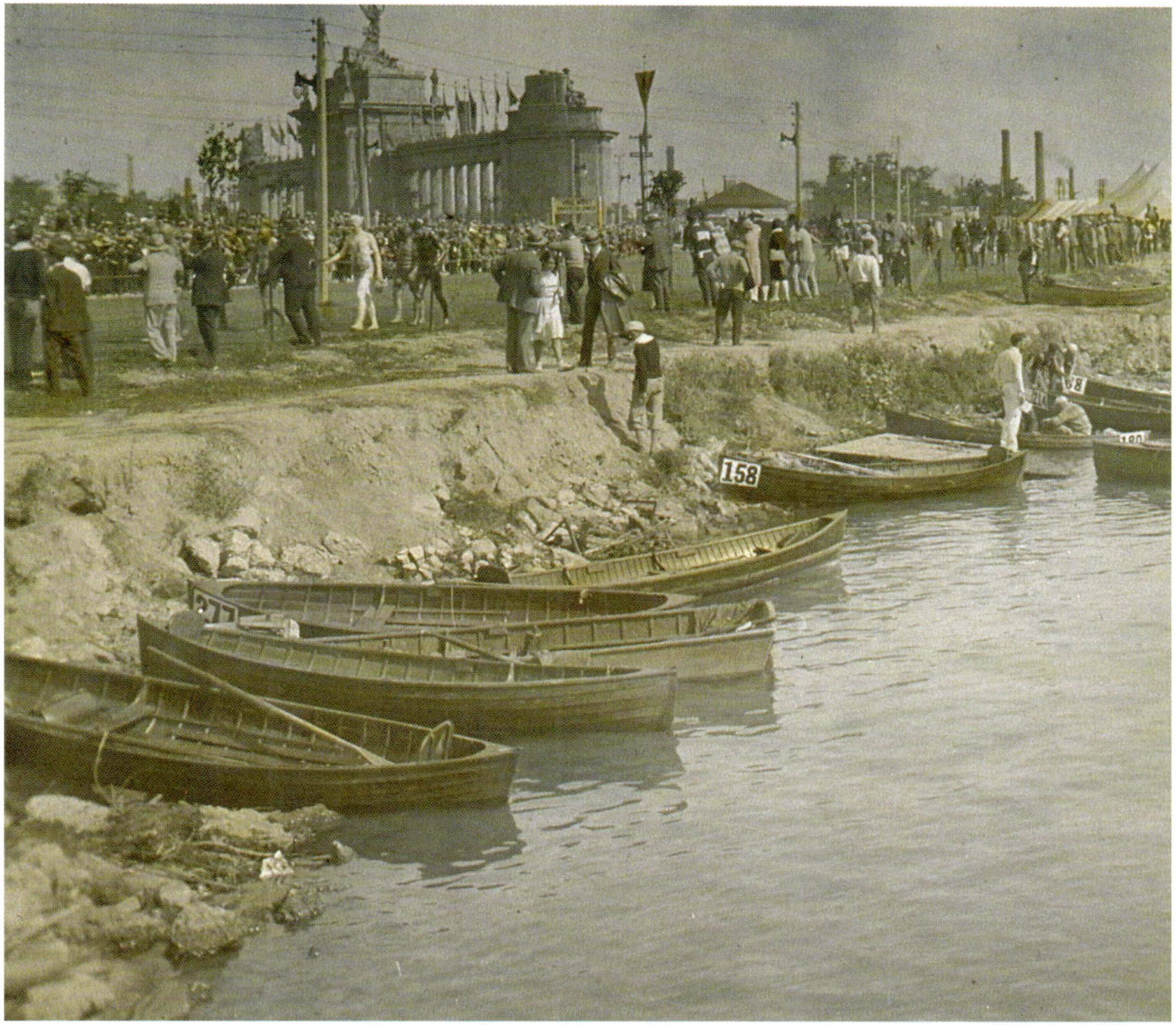

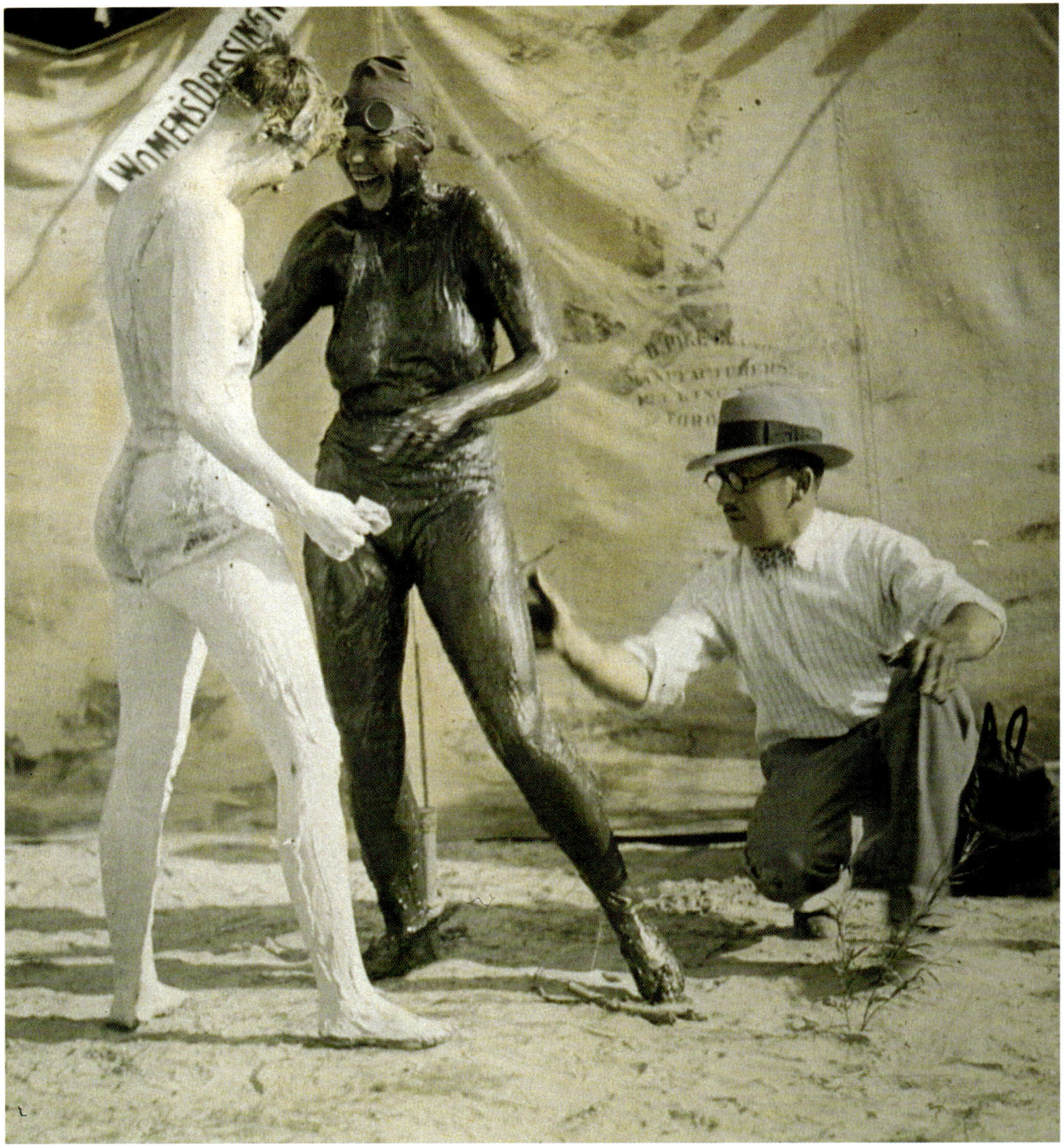

Right: *Swimmers, 1928. The first women's marathon swim was held in this year, and was won by Ethel Hertle, from the Bronx. The women greased themselves for speed as did the men.* Far right: *Exhausted marathon swimmer, 1928. The waters in front of the Exhibition were extremely cold and the races were often more an endurance test than a show of speed. In the year this woman was carried from the water, not a single man was able to complete the men's marathon.*

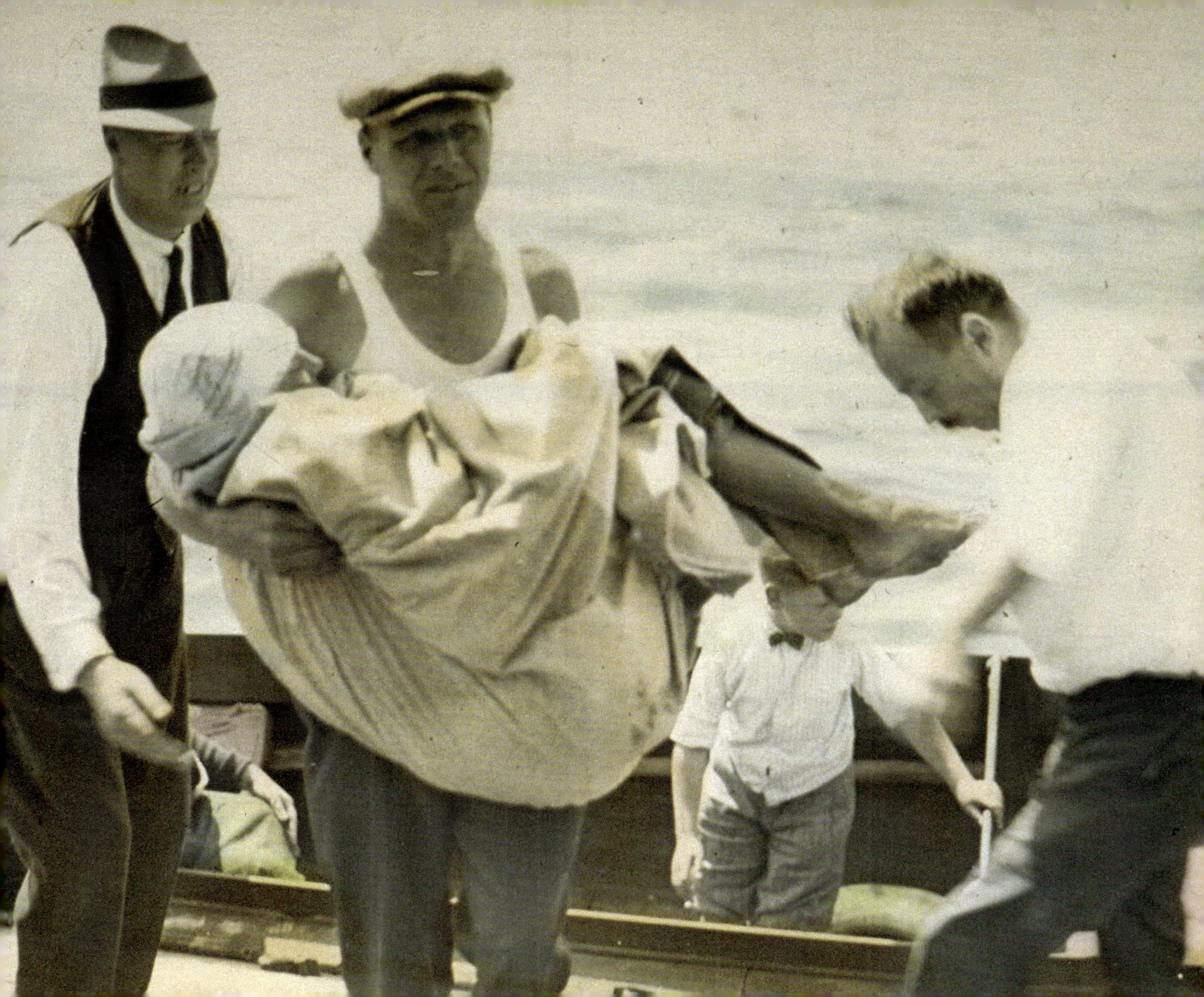

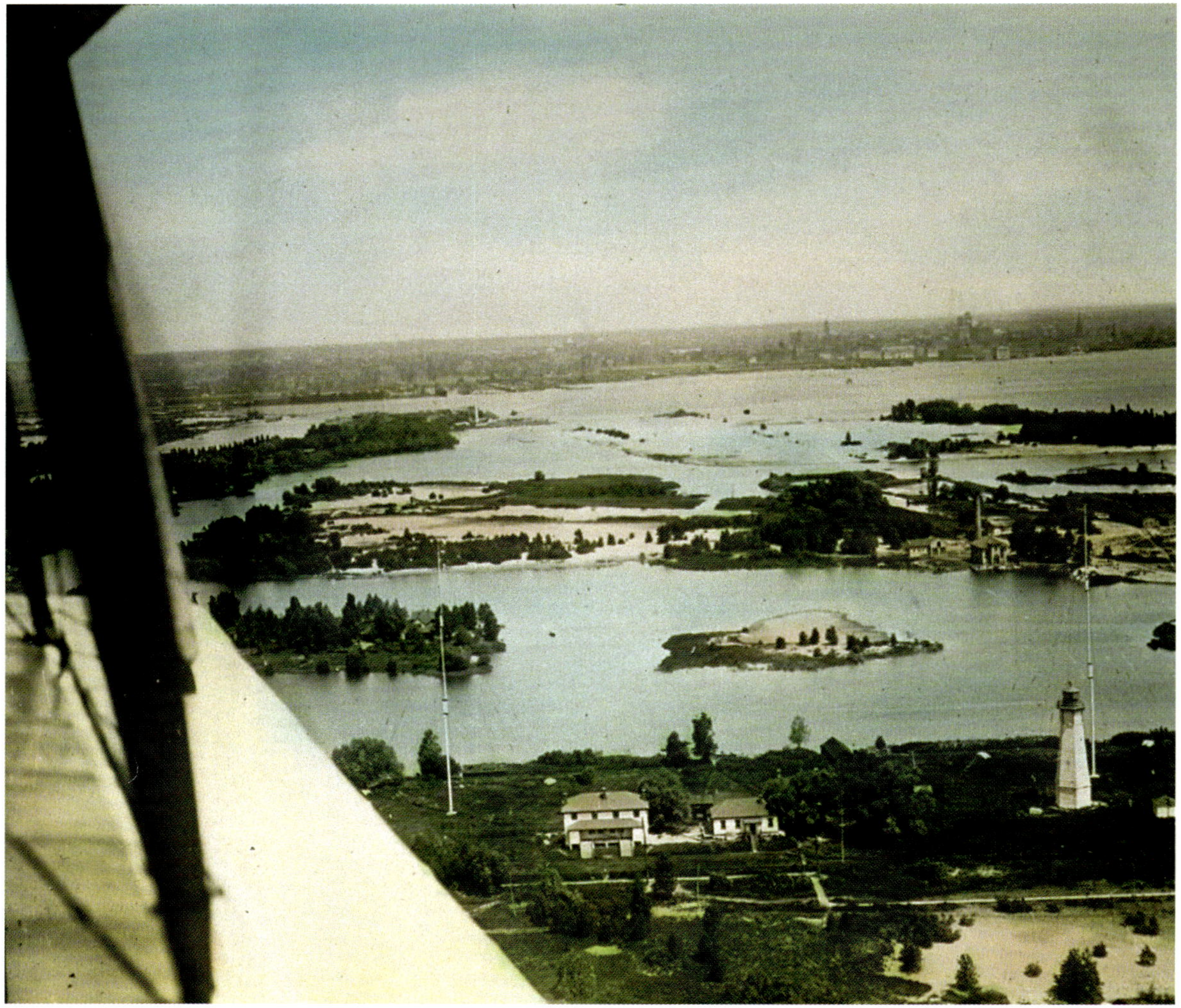

Right: *Aerial view of Hanlan's Point, circa 1916. James took both pictures and moving pictures of Toronto from the air. Visible below is the Gibraltar Point lighthouse, the oldest structure in the city.* Far right: *Bay Street crossing, circa 1910. Torontonians had to cross up to sixteen pairs of tracks to reach the island ferry-boats. Protests as to the danger of this began in 1907, but it was not until the twenties that bridge work would begin.*

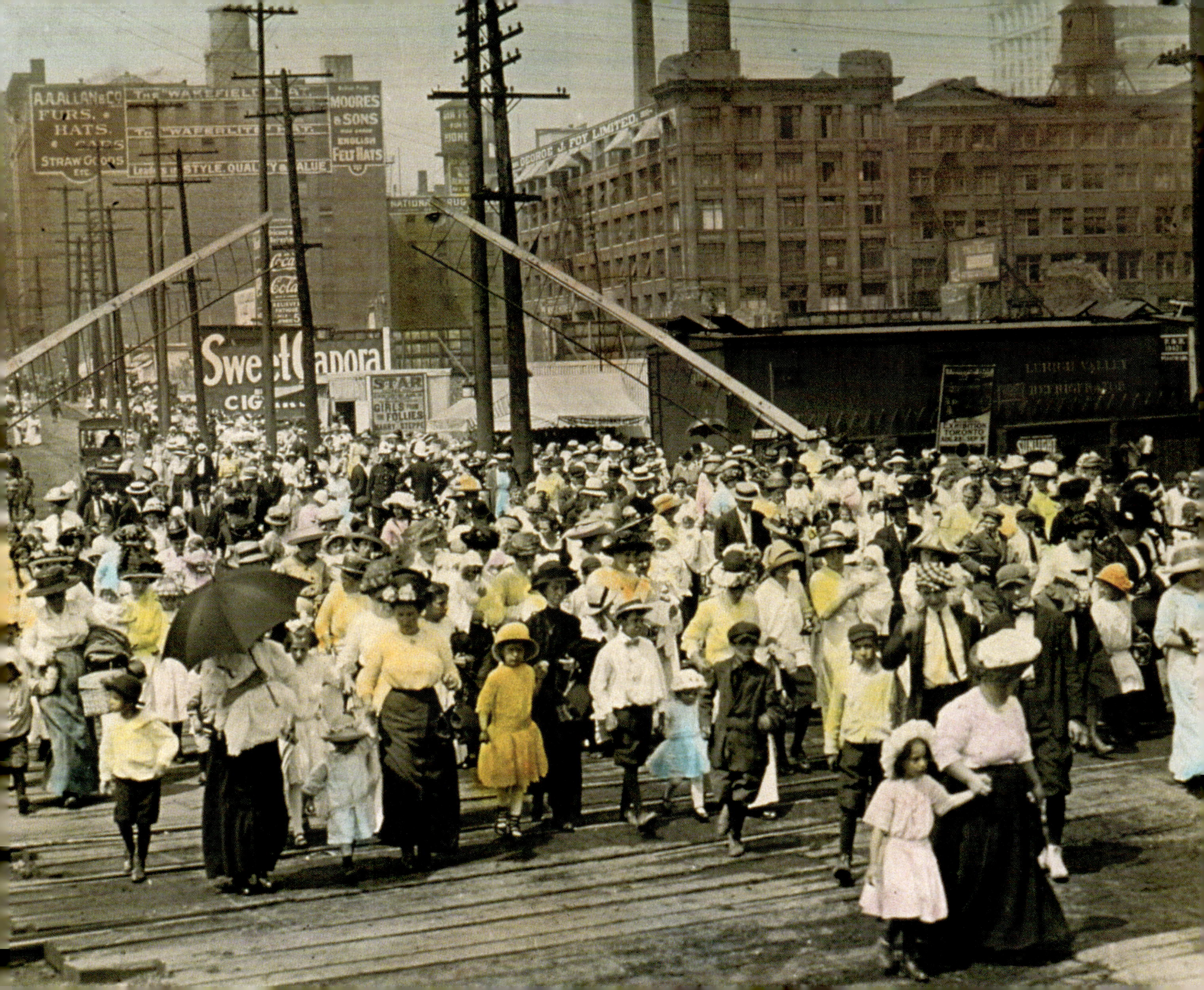

A.A. ALLAN & CO
FURS,
HATS,
CAPS
STRAW GOODS
ETC.
THE WAKEFIELD HAT
MOORES & SONS
ENGLISH
FELT HATS
GEORGE J. FOY LIMITED
Coca-Cola
Sweet Caporal
STAR
GIRLS FROM FOLLIES
EXHIBITION
TORONTO

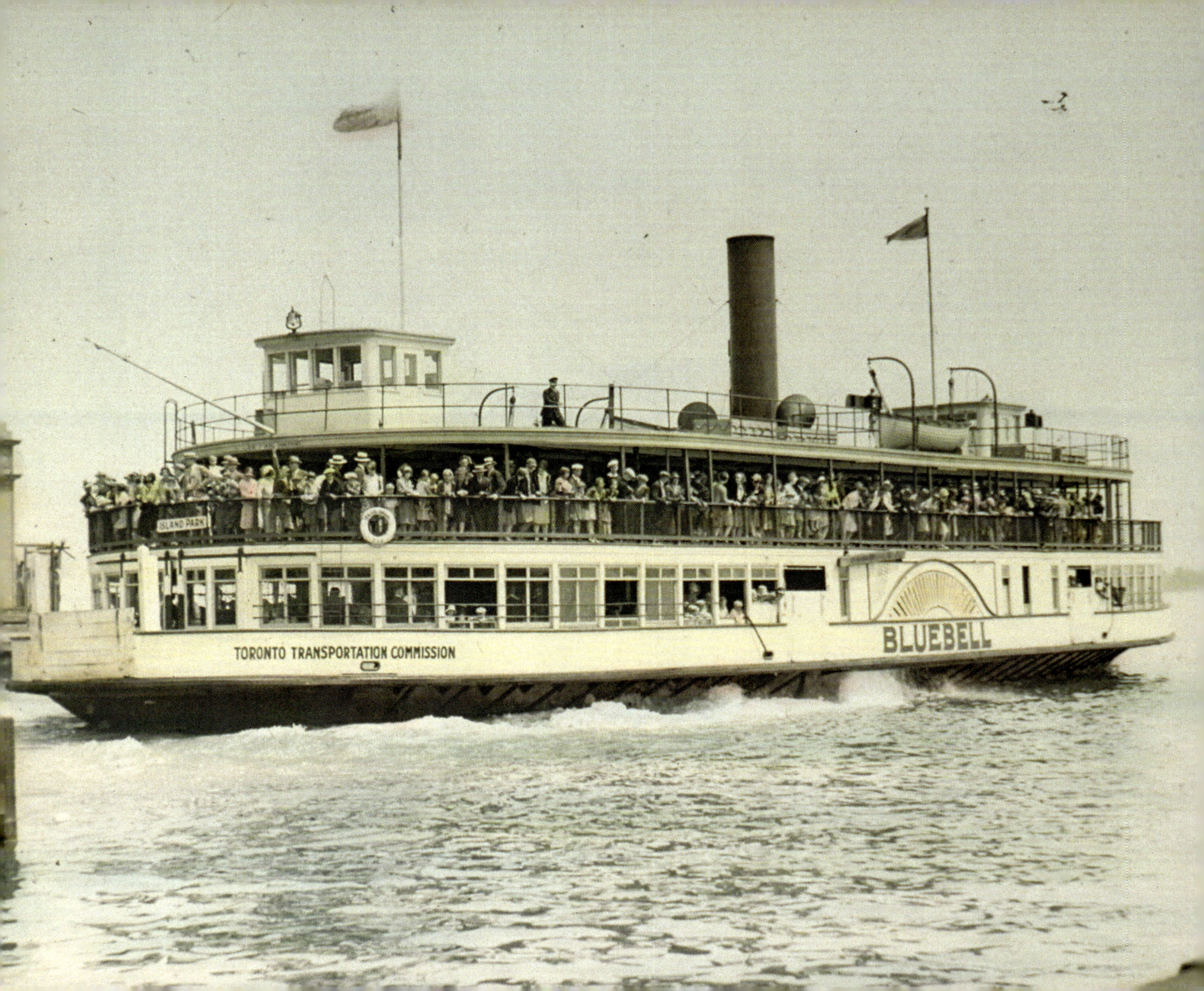
ISLAND PARK
BLUEBELL
TORONTO TRANSPORTATION COMMISSION

Left: *Toronto Harbour, 1928. The Toronto Islands ferry, the* Bluebell, *was launched by the Polson Iron Works in 1906. She could carry 1,300 passengers. She was converted to a garbage scow in 1956, but her sister ship, the* Trillium, *has been restored and still plys the waters of the bay.* Right: *Hanlan's Point Hotel, circa 1907. In 1880 Ned Hanlan leased the point from the city and erected this hotel. An amusement park grew up around it a few years later.*

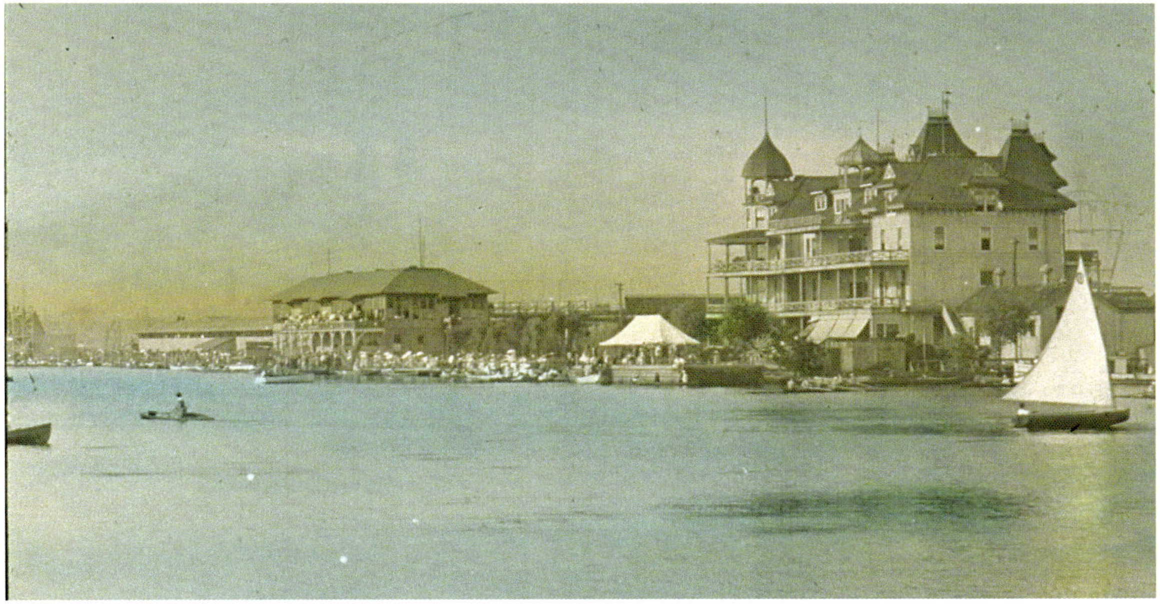

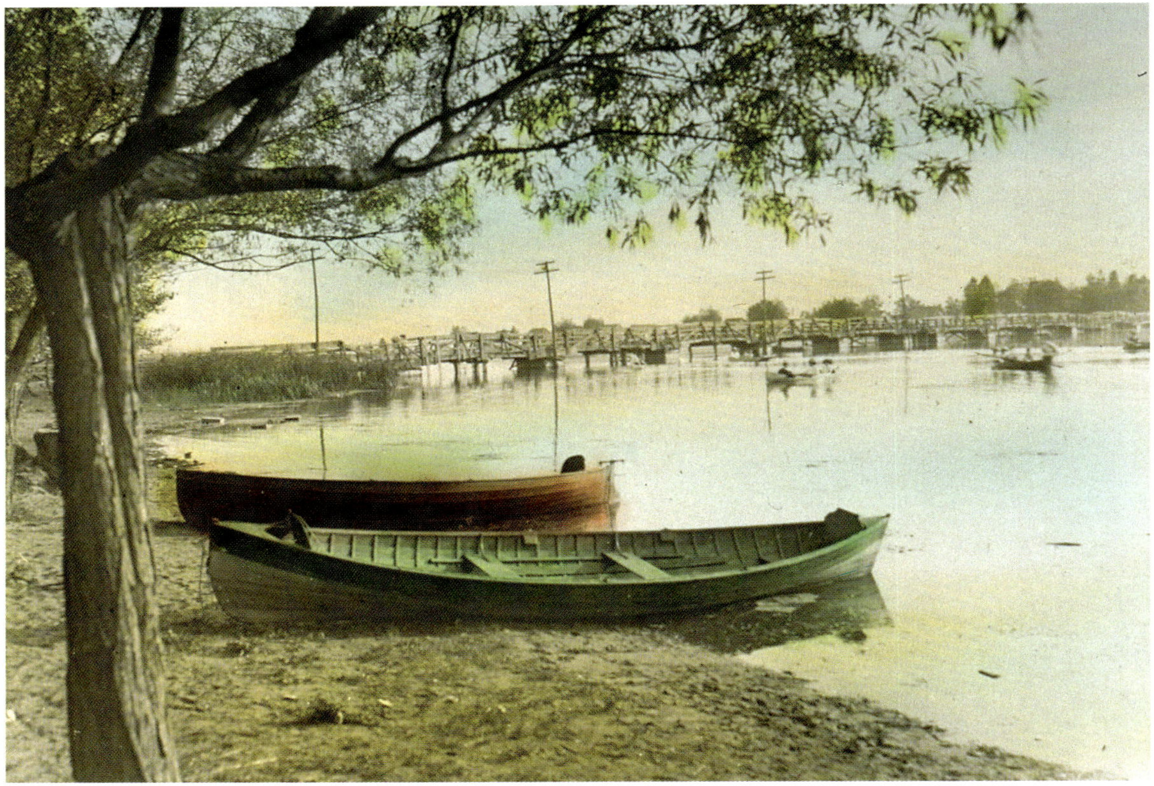

Left: *Hanlan's Point, 1910. The footbridge in the distance connected Hanlan's Point to Turner's Baths.* Right: *Hanlan's Point and Hotel, 1907. Hanlan's Point included a stadium and midway attractions that made it "Canada's Coney Island." In 1909, a fire destroyed most of the buildings. The amusement park was rebuilt but not the hotel.*

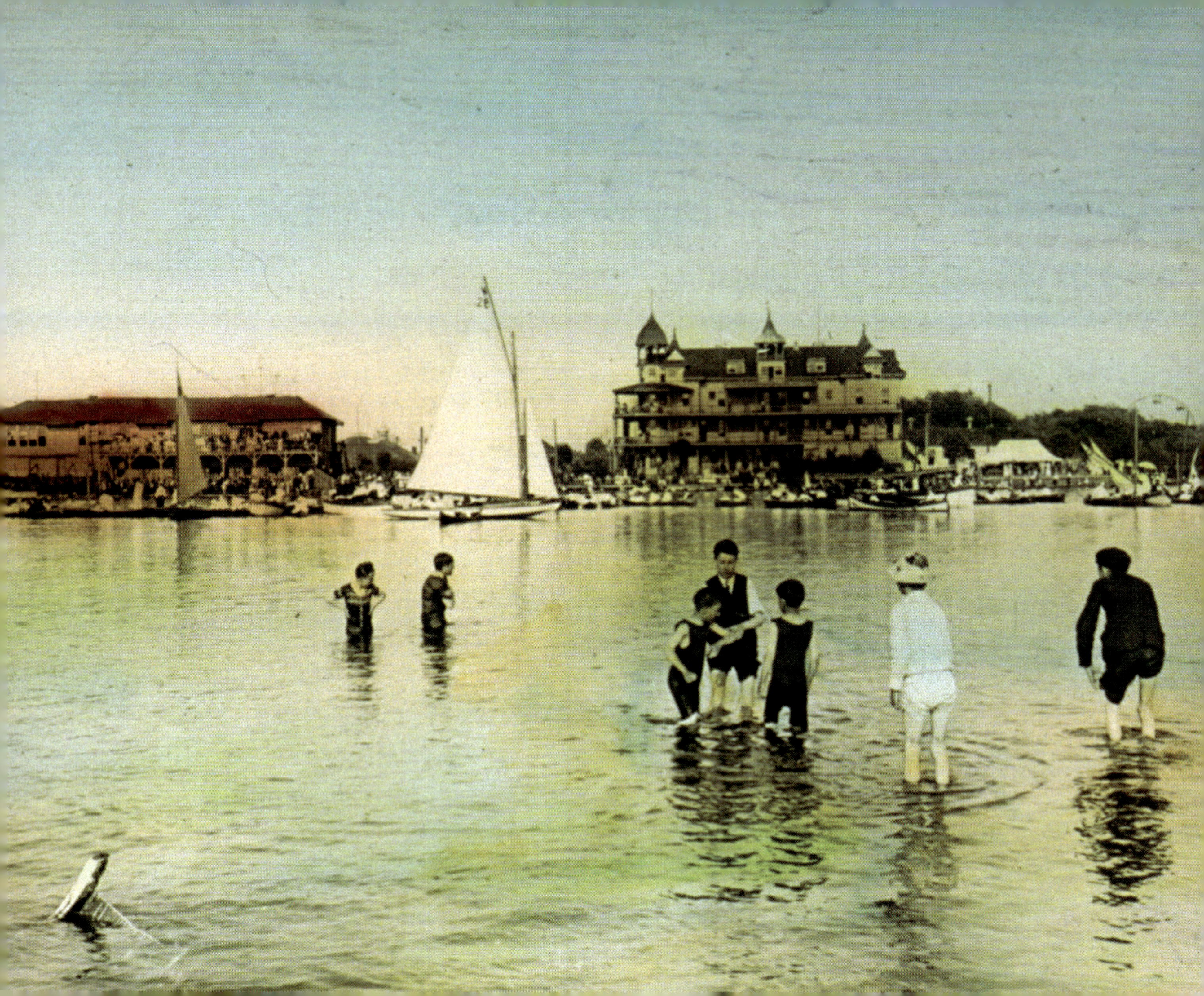

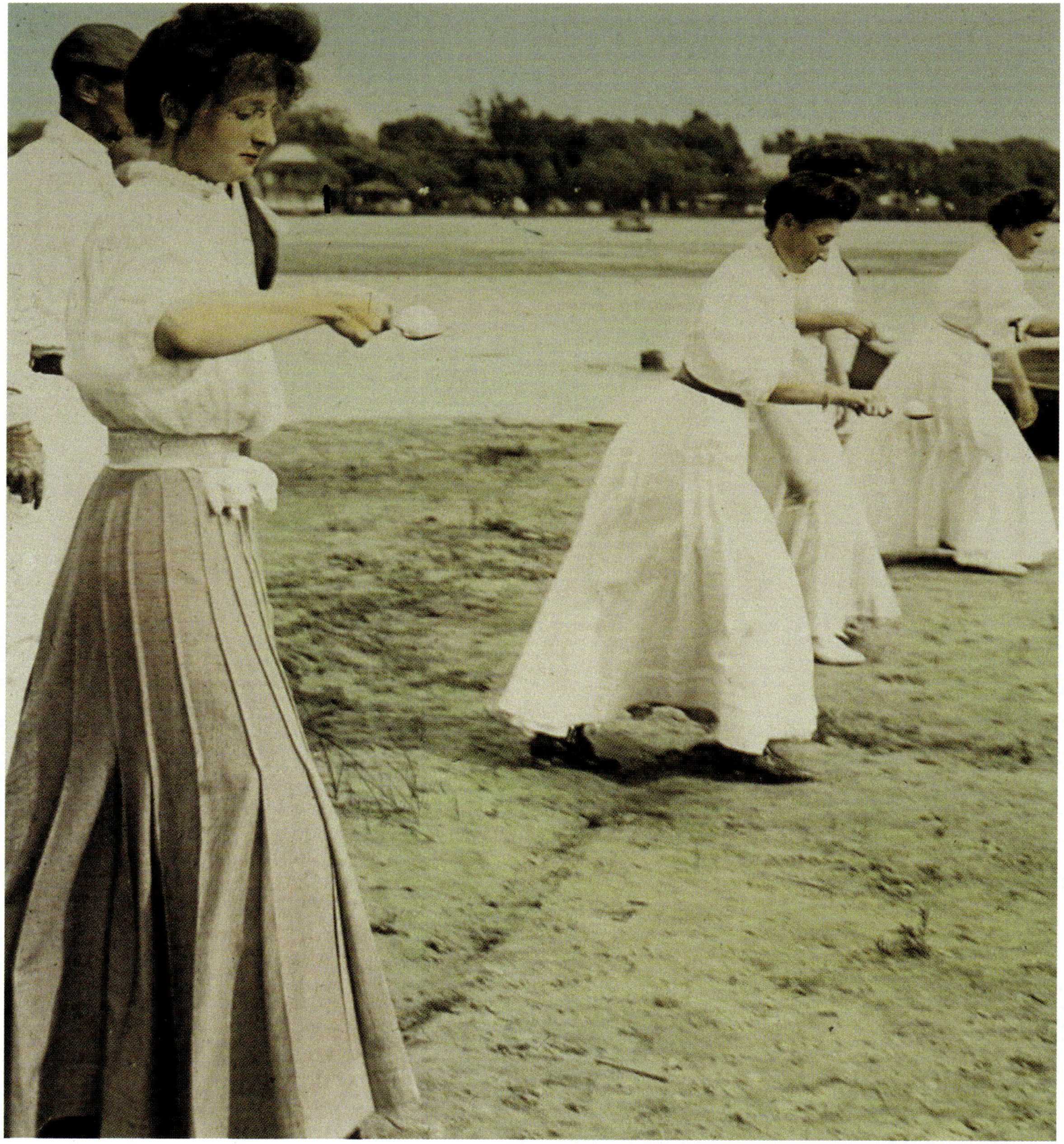

Right: *Egg and spoon races on Hanlan's Point in 1907. By this time, Hanlan's point was a popular tenting, cottage, and picnic area.* Far right: *Family group, circa 1910.*

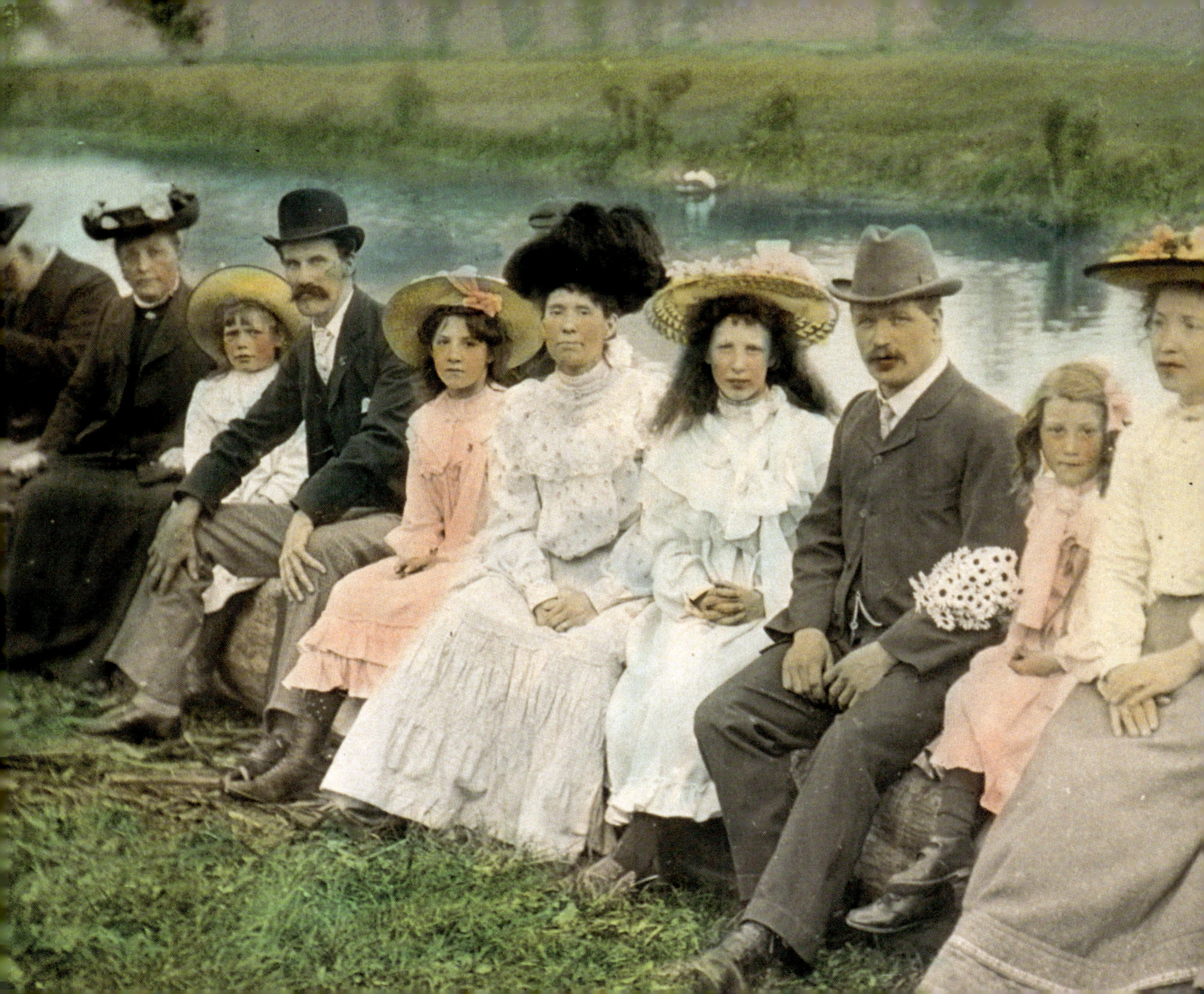

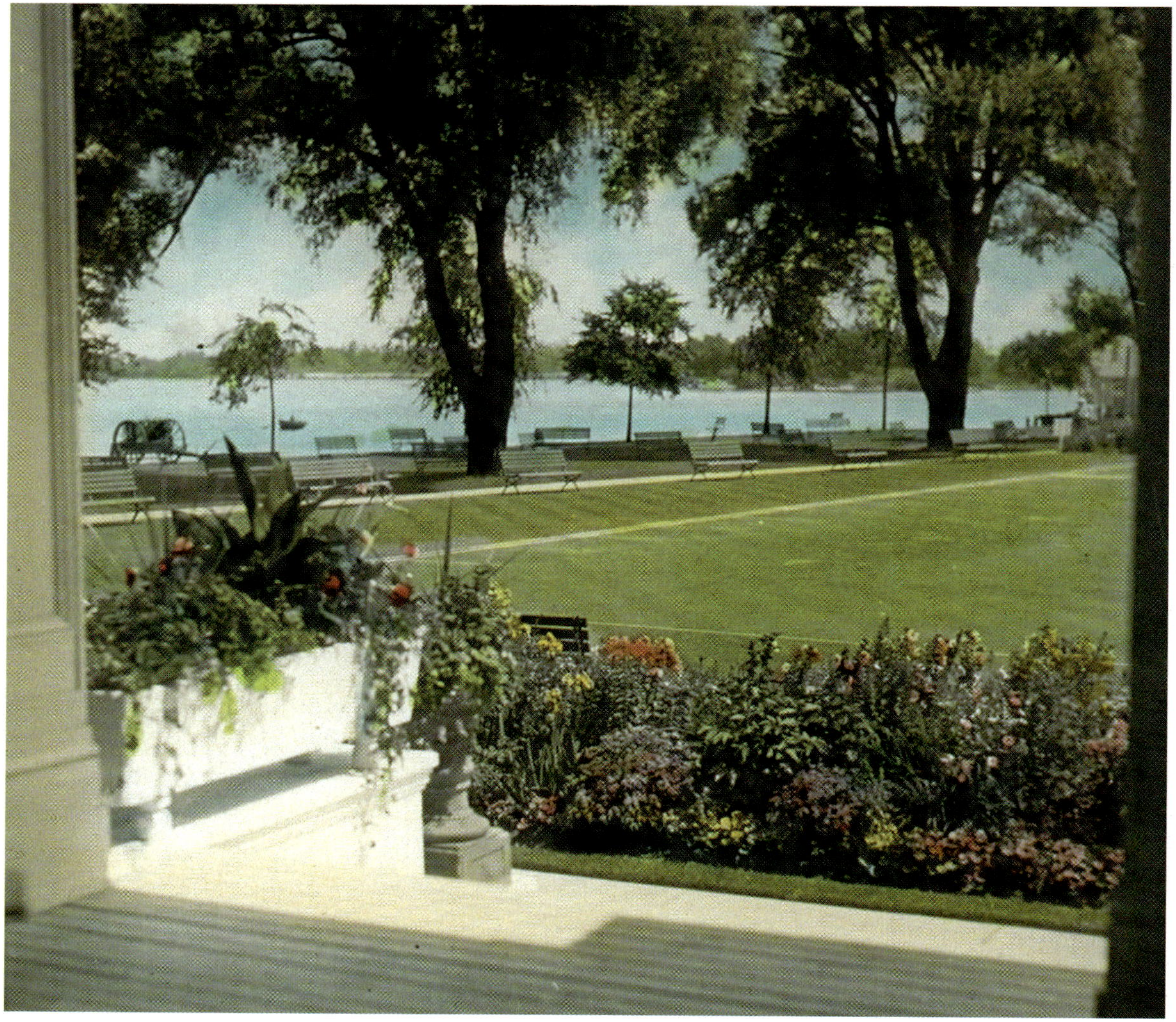

Left: *A view from the Royal Canadian Yacht Club, 1923. The RCYC had its origins in the Toronto Boat Club of the 1850s. This new clubhouse, the third to be built on the Islands, opened in 1922 and is still standing.* Right: *Women at the Royal Canadian Yacht Club, 1923. Visitors to the RCYC were always impressed by its gardens.*

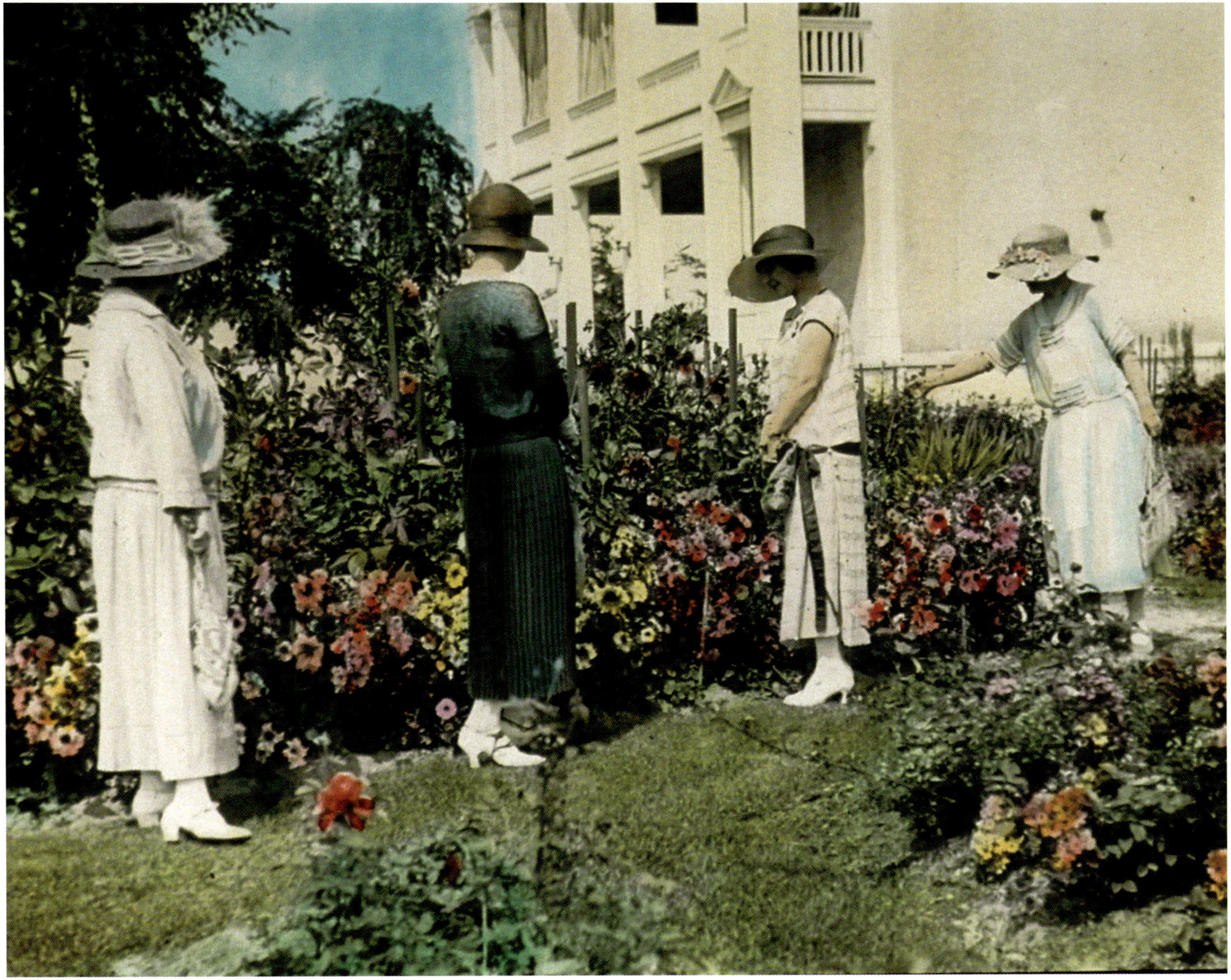

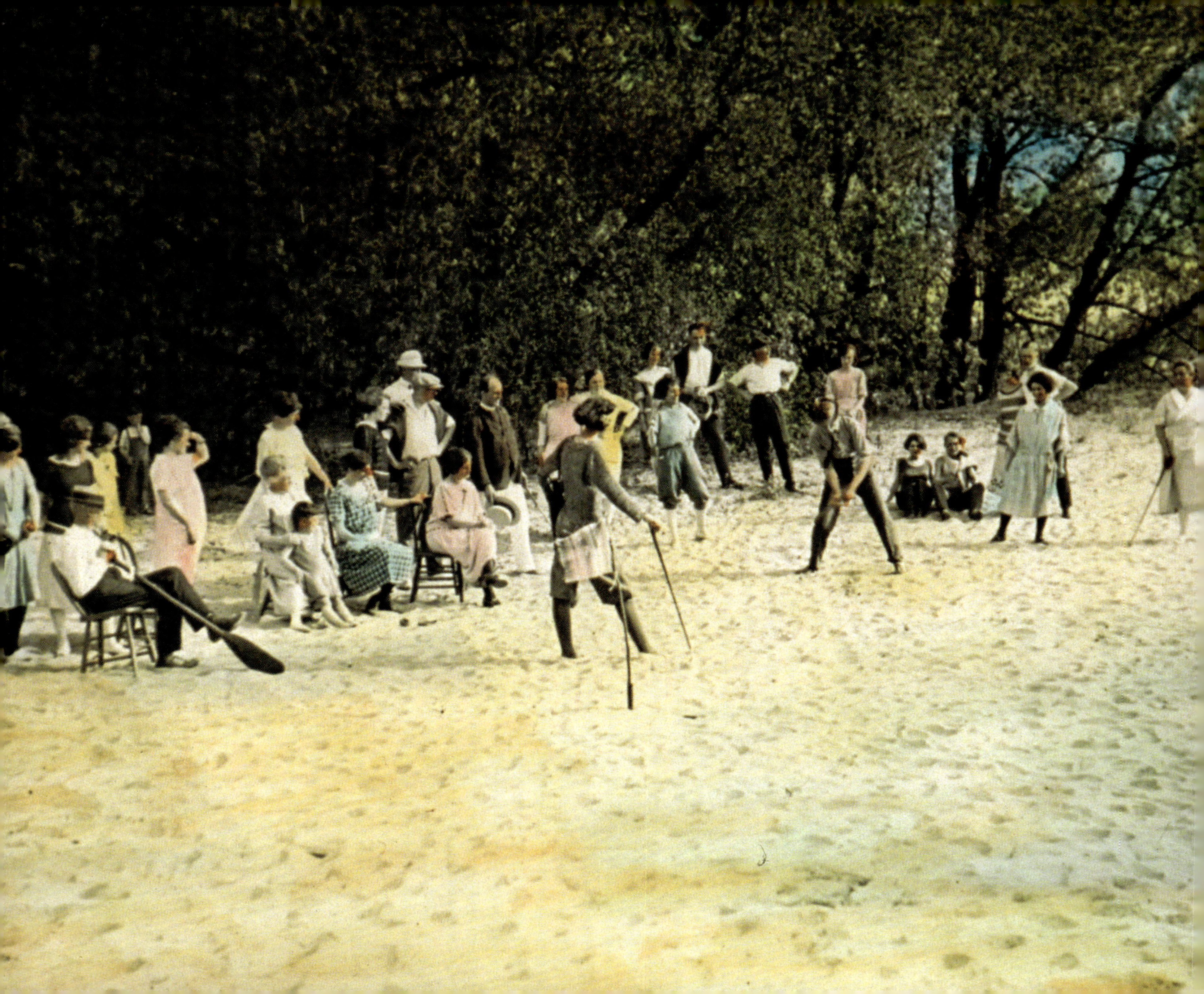

Left: *Putting, Mugg's Island, 1923. Mugg's Island, between Centre Island and Hanlan's Point, remained undeveloped until it became the home of the Island Yacht Club in the 1950s.* Right: *Island Boardwalk, circa 1920. This is how the lakeside of the Islands appeared before the current breakwater was constructed in 1937.*

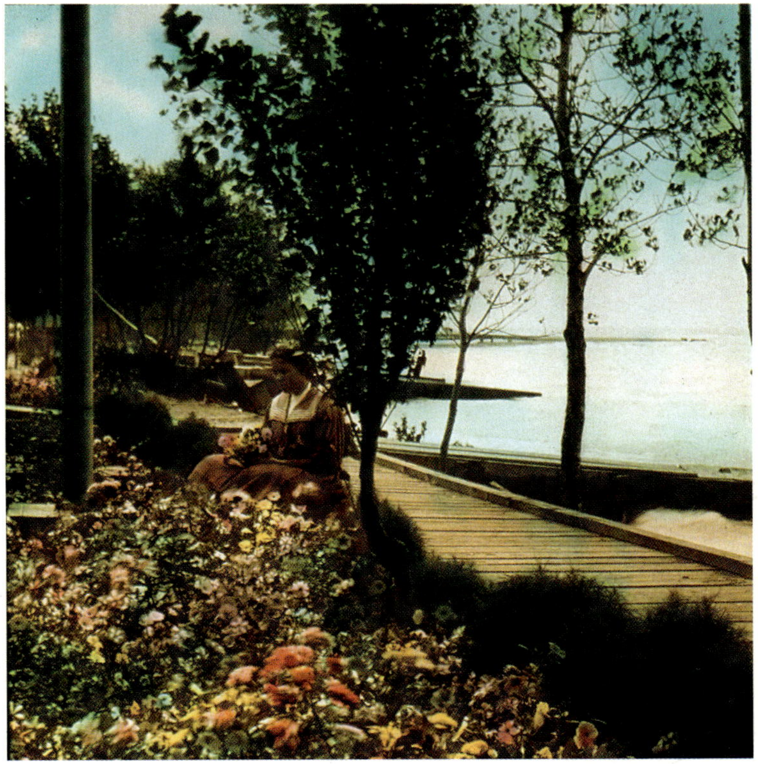

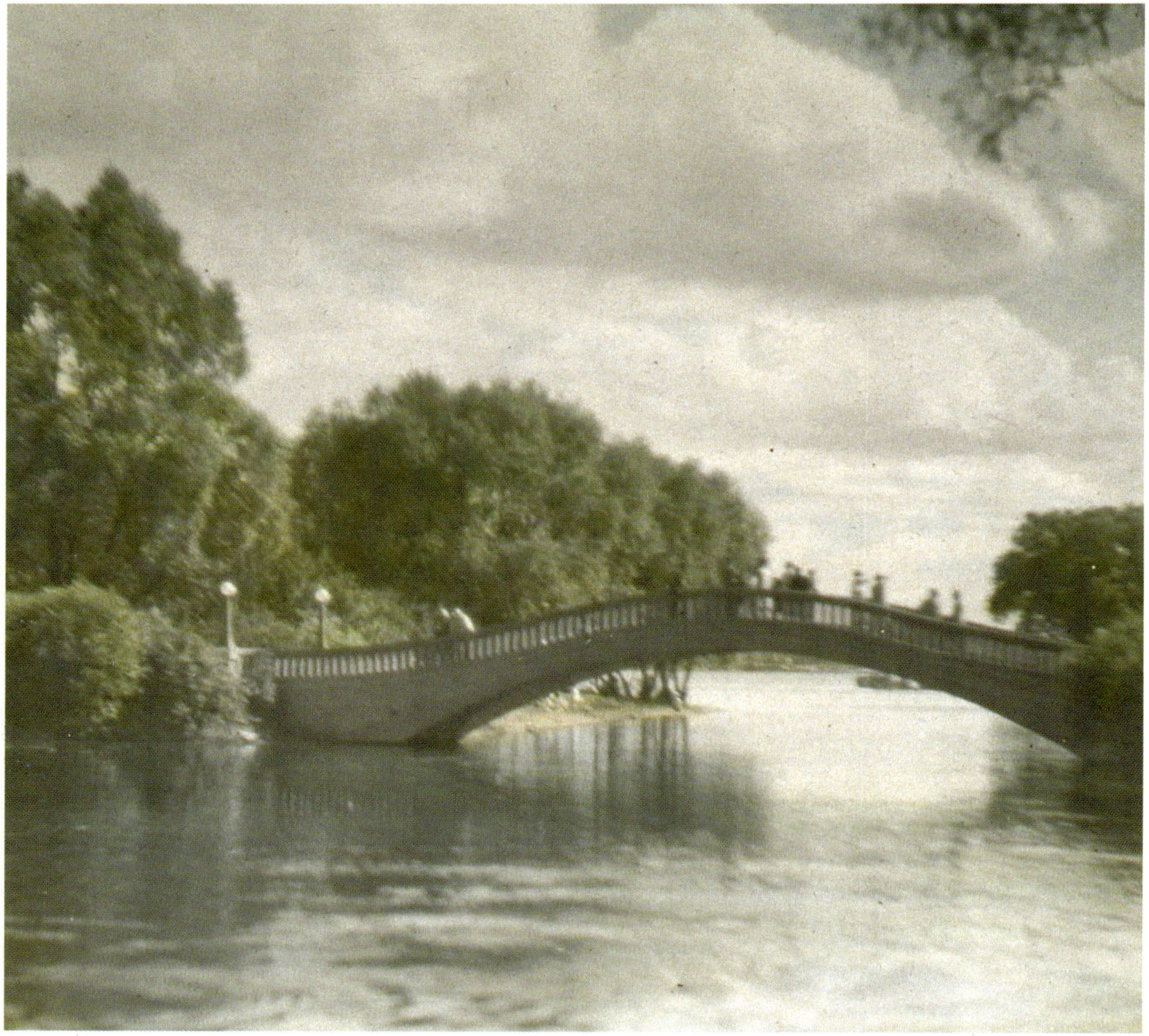

Left: *Bridge, Centre Island, 1928.*